PIEDMONT PLANTATION

Copyright © 1985 The Historic Preservation Society of Durham

All rights reserved. No part of this book may be reproduced in any form or by any means without permission from Preservation Durham, formerly the Historic Preservation Society of Durham. For more information visit www.preservationdurham.org.

This book was originally published in 1985 in cooperation with the Stagville Center, the Federation of North Carolina Historical Societies, and the North Carolina Department of Cultural Resources, Division of Archives and History. Reprinted in a paperback edition in 2001 with the support of the Federation of North Carolina Historical Societies.

Front cover: Cabins at Horton Grove. The main plantation house, photo by George McDaniel.
Back cover: Plantation barn, photo by George McDaniel. Photos courtesy of the Historic Stagville State Historic Site.

Library of Congress Catalog Card No. 85-81002

ISBN 978-0-9615-5772-0 (paperback)
ISBN 978-1-4696-8480-2 (ebook)

Distributed by the University of North Carolina Press
www.uncpress.org

PIEDMONT PLANTATION

• • • • • • •

The Bennehan-Cameron Family and Lands in North Carolina

By Jean Bradley Anderson

PRESERVATION DURHAM

The American Descendants of the Camerons of Ferintosh, Scotland — Chart I

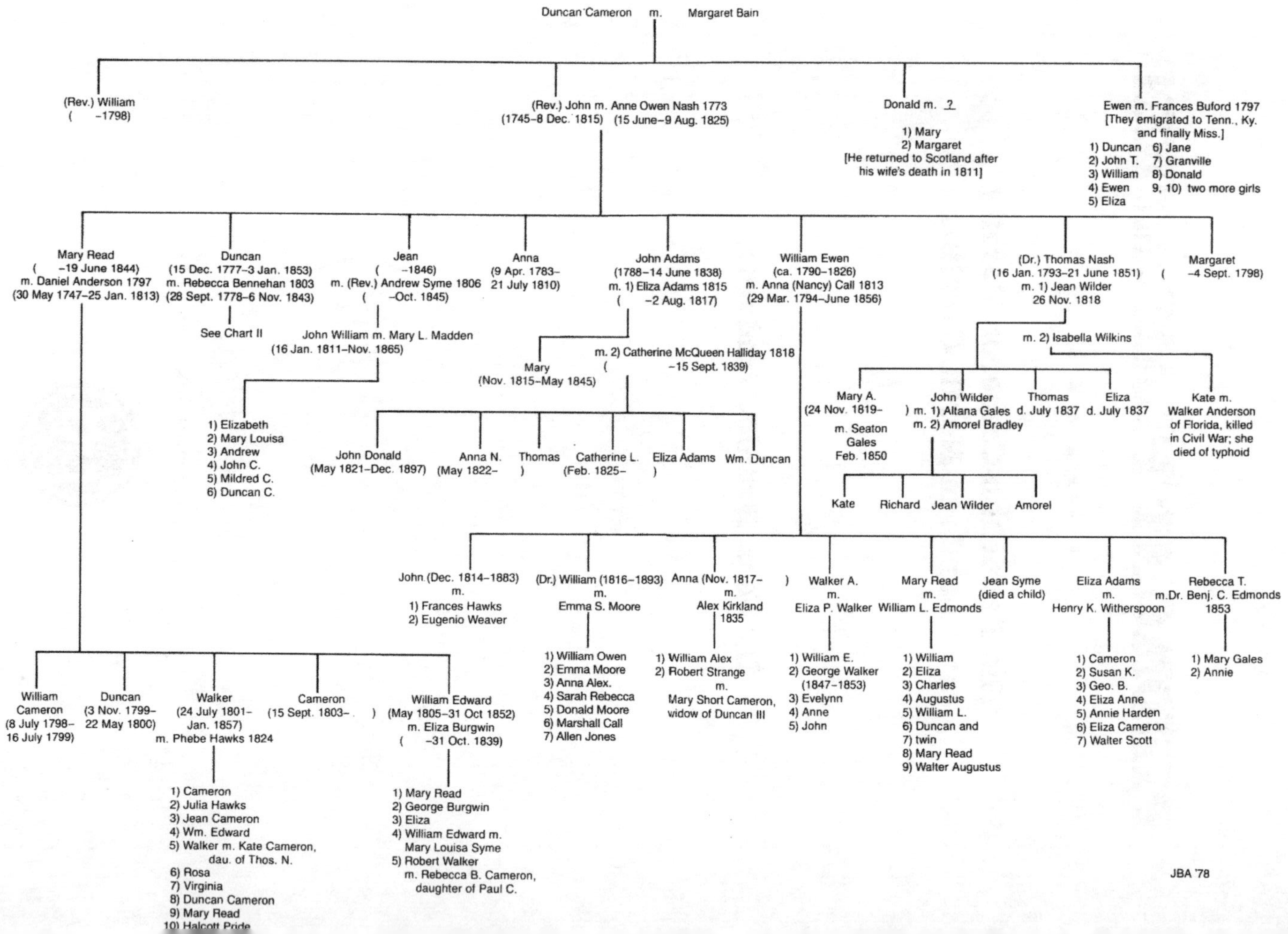

Duncan Cameron m. **Margaret Bain**

Children:

(Rev.) John m. Anne Owen Nash 1773
(1745–8 Dec. 1815) (15 June–9 Aug. 1825)

Donald m. 2
1) Mary
2) Margaret
[He returned to Scotland after his wife's death in 1811]

Ewen m. Frances Buford 1797
[They emigrated to Tenn., Ky. and finally Miss.]
1) Duncan   6) Jane
2) John T. 7) Granville
3) William 8) Donald
4) Ewen   9, 10) two more girls
5) Eliza

Descendants of (Rev.) John and Anne Owen Nash:

Mary Read
–19 June 1844
m. Daniel Anderson 1797
(30 May 1747–25 Jan. 1813)

William Cameron
(8 July 1798–16 July 1799)

Duncan
(3 Nov. 1799–22 May 1800)

Walker Cameron
(24 July 1801–15 Sept. 1803– Jan. 1857)
m. Phebe Hawks 1824
1) Cameron
2) Julia Hawks
3) Jean Cameron
4) Wm. Edward
5) Walker m. Kate Cameron, dau. of Thos. N.
6) Rosa
7) Virginia
8) Duncan Cameron
9) Mary Read
10) Halcott Pride

Duncan
(15 Dec. 1777–3 Jan. 1853)
m. Rebecca Bennehan 1803
(28 Sept. 1778–6 Nov. 1843)
See Chart II

Jean
(–1846)
m. (Rev.) Andrew Syme 1806
(–Oct. 1845)

John William m. Mary L. Madden
(16 Jan. 1811–Nov. 1865)

Anna
(9 Apr. 1783–21 July 1810)

John Adams
(1788–14 June 1838)
m. 1) Eliza Adams 1815 (–2 Aug. 1817)
m. 2) Catherine McQueen Halliday 1818 (–15 Sept. 1839)

Children:
1) Elizabeth
2) Mary Louisa
3) Andrew
4) John C.
5) Mildred C.
6) Duncan C.

John Donald (May 1821–Dec. 1897)

Anna N. (May 1822–)

Mary (Nov. 1815–May 1845)

Thomas

Catherine L. (Feb. 1825–)

Eliza Adams m. **Wm. Duncan**

William Ewen
(ca. 1790–1826)
m. Anna (Nancy) Call 1813
(29 Mar. 1794–June 1856)

John (Dec. 1814–1883) m. 1) Frances Hawks 2) Eugenio Weaver

William Edward (May 1805–31 Oct. 1852)
m. Eliza Burgwin (–31 Oct. 1839)
1) Mary Read
2) George Burgwin
3) Eliza
4) William Edward m. Mary Louisa Syme
5) Robert Walker
m. Rebecca B. Cameron, daughter of Paul C.

Anna (Nov. 1817–) m. Alex Kirkland 1835
1) William Alex
2) Robert Strange
m. Mary Short Cameron, widow of Duncan III

William Owen, Emma Moore, Anna Alex., Sarah Rebecca, Donald Moore, Marshall Call, Allen Jones

(Dr.) Thomas Nash
(16 Jan. 1793–21 June 1851)
m. 1) Jean Wilder 26 Nov. 1818
m. 2) Isabella Wilkins

Mary A. (24 Nov. 1819–) m. Seaton Gales Feb. 1850
- Kate
- Richard
- Jean Wilder
- Amorel

John Wilder m. 1) Altana Gales 2) Amorel Bradley

Thomas d. July 1837

Eliza d. 1837
Kate m. Walker Anderson of Florida, killed in Civil War; she died of typhoid

Walker A. m. Eliza P. Walker
1) William E.
2) George Walker (1847–1853)
3) Evelynn
4) Anne
5) John

Mary Read m. William L. Edmonds
1) William
2) Eliza
3) Charles
4) Augustus
5) William L.
6) Duncan and twin
8) Mary Read
9) Walter Augustus

Jean Syme (died a child)

Eliza Adams m. Henry K. Witherspoon
1) Cameron
2) Susan K.
3) Geo. B.
4) Annie Harden
5) Eliza Cameron
6) Eliza Anne
7) Walter Scott

Rebecca T. m. Dr. Benj. C. Edmonds 1853
1) Mary Gales
2) Annie

Margaret (–4 Sept. 1798)

JBA 78

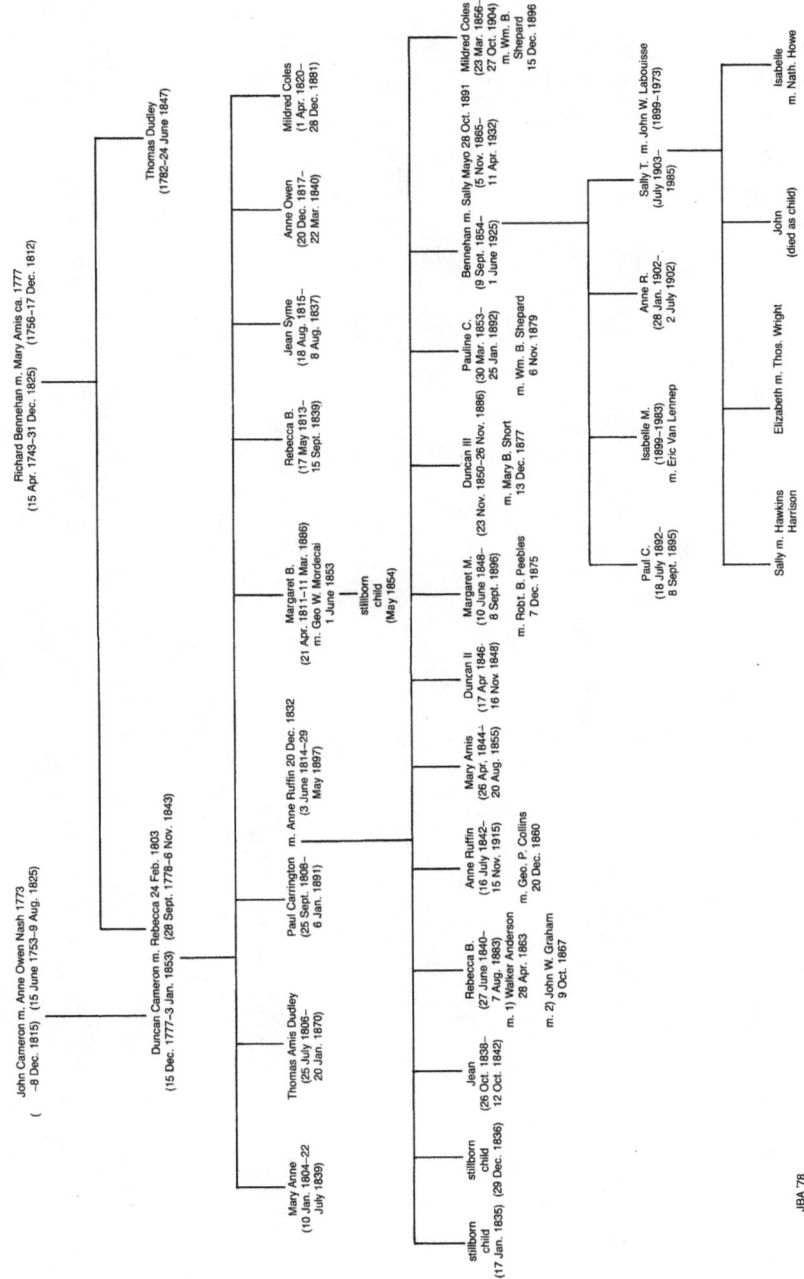

To view a full size version of these charts, please visit
https://www.opendurham.org/people/cameron-duncan

Table of Contents

Acknowledgments	v
Introduction	vii
1. New Terrain	1
2. The Building of Stagville	9
3. The Cameron Connection	17
4. The Building of Fairntosh	27
5. Duncan Cameron at Fairntosh	35
6. Paul Cameron at Fairntosh	49
7. Working the Land	65
8. Overseeing the Work	77
9. Mills, Stills, and Shops	85
10. Masters of Slaves	93
11. "When All Went Down in Night"	115
12. "One Long Dark Night"	125
13. Bennehan Cameron at Stagville and Fairntosh	133
Appendix A: Land Transactions Concerning the Plantations	146
Appendix B: Bennehan and Cameron Slaves Acquired by Purchase or Gift	160
Appendix C: Overseers of the Plantations	167
Appendix D: Cemeteries on the Plantations	171
Appendix E: Census Information Concerning Agriculture	177
Appendix F: Lists of Plantation Tools and Livestock	181
Appendix G: Census Information Concerning Mills	184
Chapter Notes	187
Bibliography	213
Index	217

Acknowledgments

This history is an expansion and reworking of two reports written for the Division of Archives and History of the North Carolina Department of Cultural Resources. Additional information, corrected errors, and modified conclusions resulting from my third perusal of the manuscript sources have made this version, I hope, a more precise portrayal of the subject. In 1974 Charles Richard Sanders wrote and published a short treatment of the family and estates; he is due gratitude for making widely known the existence and importance of the surviving plantation houses. His interest and that of others, notably the Historic Preservation Society of Durham, led to the gift by the Liggett Group of a portion of the grounds and buildings at Stagville to the State of North Carolina. In 1977 this portion of Stagville became a state historic site.

I should like to acknowledge again the assistance that I received during all three phases of my research. Besides the daily courtesies and aid of Carolyn Wallace, Curator of the Southern Historical Collection, University of North Carolina at Chapel Hill, and her staff — Richard Shrader, Michael Martin, Walter West, Karen Jackson, and Brenda Marks — I have been helped by many persons: Elizabeth Collins, great granddaughter of Paul Cameron; N. E. Gilchrist, last manager of Fairntosh; Allen Needham, present manager of Stagville Farm; John Flowers, Betsy Buford, Jimmy Renfrew, Brian Hovey, Steven Cruse, Kenneth McFarland, Terry Erlandson, and Kathleen Needham, past or present members of the Stagville Center staff; Florence Tilley Clark, Essie Ladd Nutt, Goldie Bragan, Paul T. Hall, Willis and Minnie Hart, Arthur Revis, and Thaddeus Johnson, former residents or workers on the plantations; Catherine Bishir, Sydney Nathans, and Mildred Mangum Harris, variously concerned with aspects of the same history — all assisted me with their friendly favors, knowledge, or guidance.

Generous help has been given me by others who either facilitated the gathering of illustrations or supplied the photographs themselves: Walter E. Shackelford, Duncan Heron, David Lathum, James McPherson, Jesse R. Lankford, Jr., William E. King, and again Kenneth McFarland. Stephen Cruse made the adaptation of D. G. McDuffie's map of the Cameron lands. To all of them I give sincere thanks.

Finally, I am especially grateful to my husband, Carl Anderson, for his encouragement, careful criticism, and good counsel through every phase of the work. For errors that I have undoubtedly but unwittingly committed — of fact or judgment — I take full responsibility and beg forbearance of those better informed.

Introduction

Piedmont Plantation traces the evolution of a vast plantation complex in North Carolina and the family connected with its history. It begins with the founder, Richard Bennehan (1743–1825), at the time of his coming to North Carolina (1768) as part owner and manager of a country store in the backcountry, and follows the establishment and growth of what became a uniquely successful agricultural enterprise through the marriage of Bennehan's daughter, Rebecca, to Duncan Cameron (1777–1853), like Bennehan, a Virginia entrepreneur seeking his fortune in Carolina.

The minutiae of their lives and of those descended from them, particularly in relation to the plantation world they inhabited, are contained in several large collections of manuscripts in the Southern Historical Collection of the Louis R. Wilson Library of the University of North Carolina at Chapel Hill. The central and most important collection is the Cameron Family Papers that fills forty linear feet of shelf space and includes over one hundred and seventy-three volumes spanning the years 1768 to 1981. The Bennehan Cameron Papers (thirty-six feet and sixty-eight volumes) overlap the earlier collection by about twenty-five years and continue up through the first quarter of this century. At the time this research was undertaken, the Bennehan Cameron Papers were for the most part still under seal. The materials now available would supply additional details of the agricultural history of Stagville and Fairntosh and of Bennehan Cameron's life during the final years of the last century and the first twenty-five of this. Two other collections of related family papers, the Thomas Ruffin Papers and the Mordecai Family Papers, reveal some of the same events from different angles and supply missing or additional facts.

In all these collections it is the family letters that illuminate most clearly the past to which these papers belonged. Besides biographical information, they disclose the attitudes and motivations crucial to a meaningful reconstruction of the long chronicle of events. Up until 1800 these letters are scattered only sparsely through other correspondence and records, but from the turn of the century on to the death in 1925 of Bennehan Cameron, Richard Bennehan's great grandson, they occur in profusion. A particularly rewarding group of letters, both for the information they contain and their readability, are those written by Paul Carrington Cameron (1808–1891),

Duncan Cameron's son, from the time of his college days in Connecticut in the 1820s, through his planter days on the Bennehan and Cameron lands (1836–1859), and to the long decline of his life in Hillsborough, the county seat of Orange County, North Carolina.

The scores of volumes mostly of accounts hold a storehouse of information on merchandising from 1768 to the 1880s, primarily concentrated in the eighteenth century and the antebellum period. In addition to these volumes, reams of loose accounts kept by the masters or the plantation overseers give seasonal reckonings of production and sales of the plantation staples and provide an economic history to parallel the human.

There are also annual tax lists of land and slaves and one or two of house furnishings. Many comprehensive listings of the slaves by name, family group, and sometimes by age supply data that have already proved their usefulness to historians. Such records were vital to the efficient management of the family's wealth and lands, for the slaves owned by the four children of Duncan Cameron totaled roughly 1,000 persons in 1860. Figures for the state as a whole in that year show only four other slaveholders with 300 slaves or more. Only two percent of slave owners had as many as fifty slaves.

In addition there are many legal papers from Duncan Cameron's thirty years at the bar or on the bench, company rosters for the War of 1812 in which Duncan Cameron held an administrative post and the rank of general, overseers' letters primarily from the plantations in Alabama and Mississippi, wide correspondence from important men all over the state throughout the collection, and quantities of receipted bills for the purchase of everything from gloves to gravestones. There are accounts, too, for services rendered by doctors, skilled artisans, teachers, overseers, and builders.

Selected data from some of these groups have been utilized in the text not only for their importance to the history told here but also for their value to local historians and to general historians searching out hitherto neglected aspects of the past. Many details are included, for example, concerning the building, furnishing, repairing, and refurbishing of the plantation houses and the construction of various ancillary buildings, particularly slave quarters. Besides the names of the craftsmen engaged in the carpenter's trade, these data supply a variety of information about materials, their sources and costs, the division of tasks, working practices, wages, and skills, all important to the history of North Carolina's material culture.

Also included here is an analysis of the slave force. Those slaves who were acquired by purchase or inheritance are listed with the names of their former owners, dates of acquisition, and, when possible, their ages. It is from this group of individuals that all the other Bennehan and Cameron slaves were descended.

Agricultural information makes up a chapter: the size and variety of crops grown and the receipts from their staples, fluctuations in kind and number of livestock, and inventories of farm equipment. Another chapter examines the plantation overseers, their origins, interrelationships, competence, training, terms of service, and wages. In sum, here are the materials to reconstruct a plantation world and its people.

The geographical location of Stagville, the home of the Bennehans, her sister plantation, Fairntosh, the home of the Camerons, and their satellite farms is part of their uniqueness. Now in Durham County, Stagville and Fairntosh lie on the eastern edge of the Piedmont, the middle section of North Carolina, in the northern third of the state adjoining the Virginia border. The Piedmont of North Carolina, traditionally thought of as the stronghold of the yeoman farmer, is not a likely place in which to find what was one of the largest plantations in the state. Yet that is where it lay — the Bennehan-Cameron plantation complex — some twenty to thirty thousand acres on the Eno, Little, and Flat rivers, the headwaters of the Neuse River. In 1860 only 311 farms in the state were larger than 1,000 acres, and only two percent of landowners had more than 500 acres. In the same year statistics for Orange County, the county that then contained the home plantations, showed that only about one percent of landowners had as many as 1,000 acres.

When Richard Bennehan left his native Virginia to come to Snow Hill Plantation on the Little River where the store he was to manage was located, he could not have foreseen how propitious the location was to be to his fortunes. He could only have known that it was in a fast developing area on a main travelled road through the backcountry. At that time, 1768, the nearest town, Hillsborough, was only just beginning to acquire the mix of Scottish merchants, summer gentry from the long settled eastern towns and plantations, and ambitious professional men that very soon were to give that small village a luster out of all proportion to its size. Even a few years later when Bennehan made his first purchases of land, its attraction for him could only have been the rich river bottomland it comprised and the abundant crops it promised. Yet, within a decade this area of the state would receive the new capital of Raleigh, a hub of political power twenty-five miles southeast of Stagville, and the university at Chapel Hill with its cultural magnetism twenty-five miles southwest — both factors in the growth of population, roads, business, and wealth and stimulants for change and improvements. Richard Bennehan played a part in the establishment of both.

Land on Flat River had been entirely taken up by earlier settlers or land speculators when Bennehan moved to the neighborhood. Only by gradual accumulation over half a century, therefore, did the family lands grow to their enormous extent, covering parts of four counties: Granville, Orange, Person, and Wake. Use of this land by five generations of the same family and for one purpose — agriculture — gave it a uniform quality reflecting conscientious management and unstinting care while preventing radical topographical change. To be sure, within the last century roads and power and rail lines have somewhat disturbed the terrain and dispelled the isolation; and the sale and development of the outlying farms have materially reduced the area left for study in the field. Still there is much evidence to be found both above and below ground, including the plantation houses and their outbuildings.

The general neighborhood of the headwaters of the Neuse possesses interest quite apart from its Bennehan and Cameron association. William Johnston, Bennehan's partner and neighbor, represented Hillsborough in the crucial Provincial Congresses of 1776 and on the committee of safety for Hillsborough District. At his plantation Snow Hill, Daniel Boone allegedly spent a month equipping for his western exploration for the Transylvania Company, that immense and illegal land speculation and development venture of which Richard Henderson was chief and Johnston treasurer. Henderson, too, was no stranger to the area, having lived in Hillsborough before being hounded from the judicial bench and forced to flee from the wrath of the Regulators in 1770. Flat River was the home of Willie P. Mangum, member of Congress for thirty years and president pro tempore of the Senate for three. He studied law with Duncan Cameron and tutored Cameron's sons before embarking on his own career of law and public service. It was the home, too, of Governor William B. Umstead and of many of the early and influential families in the development of the city of Durham: the Mangums, Parrishes, Blacknalls, and Dukes.

With Raleigh to the southeast, Hillsborough to the west, and Chapel Hill to the southwest, the Bennehan-Cameron plantation complex became a nexus for the state's leading men. Over the long years any day of the week might have brought to the door men like governors Thomas Burke or David Swain, General William Davie and Judge Archibald Murphey, Justice James Iredell and Chief Justice Thomas Ruffin, doctors James Webb and Edmund Strudwick, bishops John Ravenscroft and William Green, college presidents Joseph Caldwell and Kemp Battle — all friends of either the Bennehans or the Camerons. Three generations of Camerons served in the state legislature and severally contributed their efforts to banking, the law, railroads, business, agriculture, and industry. Underpinning their participation and success in the larger world was the fundamental relationship of the family with their lands. It was a symbiotic relationship. The family enriched as well as exploited the land while the land in turn sustained them, enriched them, and made possible their engagement in events beyond its borders.

Because the family letters that survive are primarily those of the men, it is their characters and relationships that seem most interesting. The relationship of Duncan Cameron and his son Paul and in turn that of Paul and his sons Duncan and Bennehan play a conspicuous role in this history. The number of Paul's letters and the length of time they cover (almost seventy years), his stewardship of the plantations during the antebellum period, and his safe guidance of the family and fortune through the perils of the Civil War and its aftermath make him by any measure the central figure in this drama. No understanding of Paul Cameron is possible, however, without knowledge of the character of his father.

Duncan Cameron's public career is amply documented. He was a politician and a statesman, a lawyer, judge, and banker. He was a strong supporter of education and religion and philanthropy, public and private. A firm Federalist at the start, he became a champion of the progressive reform movement in the state after the War of 1812, and after constitutional reform in the 1830s set the state on a progressive course, he was an active member of the Whigs. He had great political power based on his many years in the legislature, where he had gained political savvy and important contacts, and on his private wealth and professional success. The private man emerges in his own and others' letters as proud, pious, perspicacious, reserved, deeply revered, and strictly obeyed. He had acquired from his father, John Cameron, an Anglican minister and scion of the ruling branch of the clan Cameron, learning and ability and an uncompromising authoritarianism. As a young lawyer Duncan Cameron was shrewd and fearlessly ambitious; he took on political enemies and professional competition with confidence. When animosity or personal affront led to a duel, he showed his mettle on the field of honor and emerged there, too, victorious.

Thomas Ruffin, the maternal grandfather of Cameron's grandchildren, praised him as a benefactor of a very large family and of society in general. These claims are fully supported by the family papers and other documentary sources. What the Cameron Papers also show, however, is that he was a benevolent despot. The right to control as a husband, father, and master was grounded in the culture, the law, the church, and in his case in awareness of his own superiority. A realistic recognition of his own capacity probably gave him early a mandate for leadership. Wealth and professional achievement gave outward proof of that right. He lived out his life in total mastery of all around him.

It was a cause for concern as well as surprise to Paul Cameron, therefore, that his control in his own family was so uncertain, that his own children seemed often unmanageable and wilful, disrespectful and destined for failure. To be sure, he held the purse strings and kept his sons on tight rein just as his father had kept him, but although he could limit their actions he could not inspire them with enterprise. Paul's surprise is understandable, for he was ever a dutiful and respectful son to his father. Despite desires and plans contrary to his father's, Paul never risked open defiance but knuckled under, venting his frustration only in words. Their most serious contention was over the choice of Paul's career, Duncan expecting Paul to follow in his footsteps as a lawyer and professional man, Paul determined to strike out on his own as a cotton planter in the Deep South.

Paul's desire reflected the larger economic and agricultural situation in the state. Worn-out soils and outmoded farming practices were producing poorer and poorer crops each year, and economic and social stagnation had overtaken the state. As a consequence, the early decades of the nineteenth century had seen a flood of emigration to the newly opened land in the Deep South or west to the states of Tennessee, Kentucky, Indiana, and Illinois. Like his contemporaries, Paul wanted to join this exodus, feeling that opportunity lay elsewhere. One estimate in 1815 put the number of native North Carolinians in other states at 200,000; the 1850 census revealed that 300,000 native white North Carolinians had gone to other states. While Paul's predilection for agriculture was genuine and his reason for wanting to go to the Deep South sound, there was also probably an unwillingness to test himself in the same arenas as his father; he recognized that his own talents were of a different order. But he stayed.

While not exactly putty in his father's hands, Paul was nevertheless malleable. A generous and affectionate nature made him an obedient child. He spent his boyhood trying to win his father's approval and his manhood proving his worthiness to retain it. Hard-working, conscientious, and receptive to new ideas, he absorbed from both his father and father-in-law, Thomas Ruffin, progressive ideas on agriculture and economics; from them, too, he probably took his socially and politically conservative attitudes. When his father's death brought him financial and psychological independence at last (he was forty-five years old), he was only temporarily helpless. He quickly matured into the expansive planter that later generations admired. He proved more than able to husband and increase the large fortune he inherited, to manage the plantation complex profitably, and by anticipating the drift of the times to invest wisely for an unknown future. He could work like a Trojan and orate like an Athenian. He played the bountiful patrician with panache while the plantation world lasted.

If he had any failures in a long lifetime it was in the field of human relations, for he was impetuous, hot-tempered, and sensitive to the quick. A sentimental view of life and unrealistic expectations added to his disappointments and pain. Within his father's household his place as a son and brother was unchallenged: he had six sisters and a mentally retarded brother; but as a schoolboy and college student uncontrollable flare-ups of anger threatened him with legal action and in one instance resulted in expulsion from the state university his grandfather and father had always supported. Throughout his life rash words or injudicious actions would occasionally lead to a quarrel or worse. As a father and husband in his large family he showed himself devoted and loving, but it is reasonable to suppose that there, too, emotional storms now and then ruffled the waters.

Although Paul Cameron continued his father's support of education and religion, he was not a religious man. Resignation to God's will, characteristic of his father's acceptance of misfortune, was not in his character. He resisted and raged, ever the fighter. Besides a felicity with words, with which he exorcised his demons, he had the saving grace of a keen sense of humor. His letters are informative, packed with details and the shadings of mood and conviction, couched in a style of no mean literary skill. Ability to observe closely and describe with humor gives his letters substance and the charm of his personality. It is not easy, therefore, to account for his failure or sense of failure in his relations with his sons.

The heartbreak Paul felt at the death of his three-year-old first son probably contributed to the difficulties he had with the younger two. They would have sensed early the indulgence and overattachment their father showed them and in consequence the power it gave them. Paul, too, would have recognized his partiality at times and reacted by tightening the reins. Never far from his consciousness was the grief he suffered which motivated his relations with them, releasing floods of affection or the fury of helpless anger. On their part so unstable a parent must have seemed both lovable and maddening. In addition they lacked their father's and grandfather's singlemindedness of purpose; as inheritors rather than creators of wealth, Paul's sons were naturally drawn to the pleasures that life offered. They were products of a radically changed social and economic climate brought about by the Civil War, and the clay Paul was trying to mold was very different from his own. Somehow either by inheritance or training or the spirit of the times, the old Cameron strain of conscientiousness was lost. Perhaps they were not the lazy ingrates he thought them, but they lacked Paul's strict dutifulness, energetic application, and desire to please that had characterized Paul's conduct as a son.

Duncan, the elder son, would stick at nothing very long; after running away from a series of schools, he ran away from a series of jobs. Paul could make nothing of his behavior. Only after Duncan's early death was Paul Cameron able to idealize his son's character in the light that sentiment threw around him; but even in Duncan's lifetime Paul's wry humor found amusement in Duncan's antics.

Bennehan, the younger son, was like his father in many ways. He did well in school because it was expected of him, completed his training in law though he never practiced, and was drawn powerfully to the land. Although he was outwardly his father's double and possessed in like degree his strength of body and passion, a wayward spirit guided the spending of his energies. Good-natured, high-spirited, and fun-loving, he delighted in horse racing and fashionable society. Despite good intentions and repeated commitments to new efforts on their part and old lessons and further loans and indulgence on his, nothing altered the way Paul's sons led their lives. In the Cameron letters may be traced the many factors on which hinged the making and unmaking of a dynasty.

Conspicuously absent so far from this review of the family are its women. The comparative sparseness of their letters, particularly in the first three generations, partly accounts for the apparent insignificance of their roles, but other causes, too, contributed to it. Their lives were led in the shadows of their male relations and in the seclusion of their homes. Their position as women, combined with the twin evils of plantation life, isolation and illness, limited their independence and scope for action and their development as forceful individuals.

Isolation as an inherent drawback of plantation life was recognized by all who endured it; its other name was loneliness. From the earliest days during the Revolutionary War right down to the Civil War planter families suffered and complained of its effects. During the Revolution when Samuel Johnston promised the newly married Mrs. Bennehan a visit from his wife, she was moved to tears of gratitude. Mary Amis Bennehan had been brought up in the longer settled and more cultivated society of Halifax and Northampton counties and had found the backcountry wilderness particularly lonely. In 1848 when Thomas Bennehan's death left Paul Cameron the only man in the family on the vast plantation lands, he lamented his loneliness in a letter to his parents. And in the late 1850s, at the plantation's height, when Paul found it impossible to secure a teacher for his children, he well understood the reason and decided to endure it no longer. His solution was to move to town — to Hillsborough — in 1859. He had visited his parents in Raleigh often enough to see what urban living offered. Any mid-century town was likely to possess besides a church, a school or two, a bank, and a bevy of lawyers and doctors, an array of stores that supplied easily and quickly whatever merchandise was needed. Most important, it provided the society of one's own kind, a basic necessity of the human condition. The rise of towns was beginning to doom plantation life for the planter even before the loss of his slaves.

The social and psychological effects of isolation bore hardest on the gentlewomen in the big house and probably harder still on the Bennehan and Cameron women because of the extent of their own lands and the timidity of their natures. Except for the overseers' houses and the accompanying quarters widely scattered over the huge expanse, the plantation house was an island in a sea of corn and wheat fields, pasture, and forest. Stiuated many miles from the nearest town (Hillsborough was eighteen miles away) and even the nearest neighbor, the women of the family developed a way of life unhealthily dependent on one another for companionship. The occasional visitor made little change in the unvarying routine of caring for the children, tending the sick, and overseeing the servants. They lacked the leavening distraction of different people and different places. If occasional shopping could have taken them to town, or regular church services have supplied a weekly outing, if a tea party with friends or a stroll in a busy street had varied the flatness of their lives and focused their thoughts beyond the walls of their home, they might have surmounted the isolation. Not even suitors breached the seclusion of Duncan Cameron's daughters. It was to the men instead that fell the errands to the country store, the visits to town, the diversions of musters, tax listings, and the myriad of duties of plantation management that brought them into touch with life beyond the plantations.

Isolation helped make these women unnaturally shy, uncomfortable with strangers, and prone to decline even the rare invitation to a party or wedding in town. As young women Duncan Cameron's daughters had only one friend, their old governess. When their father's position of bank president resulted in the family's temporary move to Raleigh in 1829, their relations saw it as the salvation of his daughters, their chance for more sociable, happy lives of unaccustomed novelty and cheering company. It might have helped them but it came too late.

The other evil, illness, was of course not confined to plantations, but plantations, because of their geographical location, were especially vulnerable to malaria. Though the anopheles mosquito was not recognized as the carrier of the disease, the millponds and swampy river edges where they bred were sensed as factors in its cause. Year after year chills and fevers laid the inhabitants low, resulting in weakened constitutions and susceptibility to other diseases. The large population of slaves housed in close, often unclean quarters, fed ample but unwholesome diets, and tired from long, hard labor were easy victims of infectious and contagious diseases which would run like wildfire from farm to farm. House servants would carry these additional plagues to the white family in the big house. The reports of headaches, bouts of nausea, fevers, chills, and aching joints that fill the letters bear witness to their suffering. Medical treatment consisting largely of bleeding, salivating, and purging along with depressive and addictive medicines added another dimension to their distress. As illness beset them, it was the women's lot to shoulder the nursing and endure the anxiety and exhaustion it entailed. In Duncan Cameron's family illness led to pervasive melancholy and depression of spirits, and with cause. Five of his daughters languished for years with tuberculosis; four of them died of it. The fifth and youngest daughter fell prey to what can only have been a psychosomatic illness that made her an invalid all her life. Only a sixth daughter survived unscathed.

Their letters say something about the position of these women as women. In Mary Amis Bennehan's cramped writing is seen a scanty education even though the affluence of her family might have afforded the best. When she needed to write a letter that required unusual tact and diplomatic phrasing, her husband wrote it for her and had her copy it. In her daughter Rebecca Cameron's letters the outstanding characteristic of her easier style is devotion to husband and family. Innocent sweetness and concern for all the family typify the letters of Rebecca's daughters, in addition to a painful desire to please their adored father, Duncan Cameron. Accustomed to suppress unbecoming opinions or disturbing thoughts, these women were by custom, training, and clothing allowed only the most limited manifestations of self. Perhaps the latitude illness gave for expressions of mental and physical distress explains its prominence in their letters and lives.

Another escape hatch for these women, as for thousands like them, was religion. The Revolution had all but extinguished the Episcopal church in North Carolina, and in the backcountry of Orange County no formal reorganization took place until almost the 1820s. Then only rarely did a church service within reach provide the chance to share with understanding co-religionists the pleasures or perplexities that life brought. And after the building of the plantation chapel at Fairntosh in 1825 even that resource was denied them. But religion could bring the spiritual comfort of promise of a better world to come in which would be redressed all the ills they suffered in this one. To be reunited with loved family members, to be cured of mental anguish and bodily pain, to be delivered from the special personal and physical restrictions their position as women imposed — these were promises any woman might cling to with every fiber of her being.

Although represented by only a handful of their own letters, the huge slave population of the Bennehan-Cameron plantations cannot be overlooked. Their presence made possible the plantation world itself. Their names, personalities, problems, and illnesses invade every letter of the white family. Yet these same letters provide no answer to a question this history raises — what were the attitudes of the Bennehans and the Camerons to slavery and their slaves?

In the Bennehan correspondence, that of Richard and his son, Thomas, are found only polite messages to specific slaves or comments about a slave's capability or performance of duty. They tell of no runaway slaves, no beatings, no plots to harm the white masters such as are found in the Cameron correspondence. Their actions tell more than their words. Richard Bennehan took an ailing slave with him to a spa to enjoy the same treatment he himself received; Thomas Bennehan freed in his will a family of faithful servants. Easygoing masters with conscientious overseers, they seem to have been untroubled by the daily realities of chattel slavery. A simple acceptance of the institution along with genuine feelings of attachment and sympathy for those slaves they knew best, uncomplicated by feelings of compunction or guilt, seems to have characterized the Bennehans' position on slavery.

The Camerons' views are harder to describe. Nothing in Duncan Cameron's own writings bears on the subject. From the company he kept, however, and his own actions, certain assumptions may be made. He matured at a time when ringing liberalism of new leaders was showing slaveholders the inconsistency of their holding both slaves and impassioned beliefs in liberty and individual rights. Early in his career as a lawyer he was called on to free the slaves of a man whose conscience had been touched by the spirit of the times. As the principal agent in carrying out this request he had accomplished the task. Another client and friend was an outspoken antagonist of slavery and wrote Cameron about the death of a favorite slave whom he had honored with an expensive coffin and burial "alongside of some white christians, where she lies as soft & sleeps as sound as they. . . . being persuaded that in the next world the freemen of America will not be permitted to domineer over the inhabitants of Africa whom they treat with human barbarity in this." Such sentiments must have found some echo in Duncan Cameron's opinions even if unexpressed, for he was secretary of the North Carolina Manumission Society and involved with its work for some years. As the nineteenth century unfolded, the change in the philosophical and social climate and the change in Cameron's economic position undoubtedly tempered his youthful views; otherwise he could hardly have justified to himself his extraordinary wealth based largely on slaves and their labor. The repressive laws against blacks enacted in the 1830s armed the planters against the slave uprisings that they feared. The inflammatory abolitionist movement in the North made the planter dig in his heels to maintain his stance. The concept of paternalism that legitimized for him the institution of slavery armed him to withstand anti-slavery sentiments from without and his own conscience within. The church, too, provided him with heavenly sanction.

Duncan Cameron seems to have accepted unquestioningly the laws of the land, and nothing in his letters hints at any private qualms concerning the codes and institutions under which he lived. He fulfilled the obligation laid on him by his brother-in-law's will to free a family of slaves in 1848, but a few years later, when his own will was executed, he freed not one of the many hundred slaves he owned.

Paul Cameron, although a very different person from his father, seems to have viewed slavery and his slaves much as his forefathers had. The only statement on the black race from Paul's pen came long after the Civil War when events had much soured his sentiments but probably had not changed a lifelong conviction. He saw blacks as members of an inferior race who, like children, were in need of supervision, care, and control. This view of the slave-master relationship, paternalism, aptly describes what many slave-owners undoubtedly felt. Evidence suggests that even many slaves, particularly those long associated with whites and those in positions of responsibility, saw themselves in just such a relationship with their masters. It was, moreover, an obviously convenient cover for those masters who recognized in the arrangement only the economic value to themselves. For the large majority of slaves, however, even the pretense of such a relationship was missing.

If events on the larger stage had not conspired against Paul Cameron's world, he would unquestionably have lived out his life in the belief that he was both a just and tender master served by loyal and affectionate slaves. A man of strong emotions and overreactions, he evaluated everything in personal terms; he responded to faithful service with affection and to indifference with dislike. He could be callous, stubborn, and unmoved if judgment so dictated, but by nature he was affectionate, sympathetic, and responsive; the conflict exacted an emotional toll. Thus when at the end of the Civil War most of his hundreds of slaves abruptly left the plantations or refused to work — a natural reaction to years of enslavement whether harsh or benign — Paul took this action as betrayal of himself and family. The pain he felt he transformed into anger and then into acute distrust and dislike justified on the grounds that they had deserted him. The kind and strength of his reaction show that at least on his side an emotional content had informed his relationship with his slaves. The genuineness of his paternalism meant that he was never able to accept blacks as free men any more than he could accept his children as equals. Unable to be party to a new relationship, he rejected them completely, wishing to be rid of a presence that could only remind him that on their side at least the relationship had been a sham.

These individuals and their relationships and the institutions and beliefs by which they lived form the dynamics of the microcosm recreated here. But in it are also glimpsed the larger world and its drama of which this is a small part. On this small stage is reflected the transformation of a backcountry wilderness into a recognizably modern civilization with all its intermediate stages. The family's history mirrors the flowering and demise of antebellum culture, an agricultural way of life felled by a national event of first magnitude. Paul Cameron's interests, investments, and manner of living reflect the first stirrings of industrialization in the South and its accompanying urbanization. The Stagville store's rise and fall chart a general pattern. At first a commercial and financial power in a rural society, it was a supplier of goods and services, a broker of land and commodities, and a lender of cash and credit; but it was doomed to decline with the rise of urban institutions that performed the same functions. The Reconstruction era is most evident in Paul's children who had to adapt to changed economic and social patterns and adopt the attitudes that legitimized them. The history that follows can thus be viewed as a miniature of the larger scene; it can also be understood on its own terms and within its own context. It is a chronicle of everyday life which, as Hope Chamberlain said in *This is Home,* is the material of which history is rightly constructed.

1. New Terrain

In December 1768, Richard Bennehan, an ambitious young man twenty-five years old, left his native Virginia to seek his fortune in piedmont North Carolina.[1] He was leaving the apprentice stage of his life and entering one of independence and responsibility. His destination was William Johnston's Little River store at Snow Hill Plantation in which he had just bought a one-third interest.[2] The terrain he traversed and the landscape he saw must have looked very promising. Well drained by three rivers, the Eno, Little, and Flat, which together formed the Neuse River just a few miles to the southeast of Johnston's plantation, the area straddled the western edge of the Durham Triassic Basin and included broad, low valleys covered by rich alluvial soils in the southeastern reaches, while to the northwest it encompassed gently rolling uplands and a few steep cliffs, rarely rising more than 500 feet above sea level, underlain by the volcanic and sedimentary rocks of the North Carolina Slate Belt. The ridges were covered by well-drained, sandy loam or firm red clays.[3] All these soils were very productive in those early days before overuse and erosion exhausted their nutriments: the bottomlands for corn and pasture, the uplands for grain, tobacco, and later, cotton. Forest covered most of the land and was interrupted only by widely scattered clearings here and there for a lone farmstead or cultivated field. It was quite literally a frontier.

The road Bennehan travelled, the main intercolony route of the backcountry, followed the earlier Old Indian Trading Path which led from Petersburg, Virginia, to the Catawba Indian settlement on the border of South Carolina and on to the Cherokee lands in Georgia. One of the few main established routes in the backcountry, it carried local traffic as well, and as it ran directly through Johnston's plantation, it brought to his store whatever traffic there was.

The store drew its local customers from a wide radius, for its nearest competitor was fifteen miles away in Hillsborough, the county seat of Orange County, then an extensive territory that had been formed in 1752 to accommodate the fast-developing settlements around the headwaters of the Cape Fear and Neuse river systems. A reporter writing the year before Bennehan's arrival marvelled at the growth: "Twenty years ago there were not twenty taxable persons within the limits of the . . . County of Orange, in which there are now four thousand taxables."[4]

This section of North Carolina had fallen within the Granville District when Lord Granville's claim was finally delimited in 1744 and his land office opened, fifteen years after the other lords proprietors had sold back their claims in Carolina to the crown. Because portions of this area had fallen, too, within the crown grant to Henry McCulloh, conflicting claims arose between McCulloh and Granville. Granville did not welcome the competitive land speculation within his own boundaries and was slow in working out an agreement with McCulloh. As a consequence, settlers on McCulloh's lands waited for titles to the farms they had long settled.[5]

In 1763 William Johnston had obtained from McCulloh 400 acres which became the heart of Snow Hill Plantation; there he built a dwelling house, a store, a blacksmith shop, and a mill.[6] Johnston had come directly from Scotland, like his fellow merchants in the Hillsborough area.[7] Most of his farmer-neighbors, however, both earlier and later arrivals, were descendants of Scotch-Irish and English immigrants and had come into the neighborhood from southside Virginia, immediately or ultimately (the Harrises, Carringtons, Dukes, and Mangums, for example), or from colonies farther north (the Hopkinses, Umsteads, and Cains), or from older settlements to the east in North Carolina (the Alstons). For all of them the newly available, relatively cheap virgin land, no longer frequented by remnants of the Sioux Indian tribes — Eno, Adshusheer, Shocco, and Occaneechee — who had inhabited the area as late as the beginning of the eighteenth century, was irresistible.

Only little more than twenty years had passed since the coming of the first settlers when Richard Bennehan arrived on the scene. Any picture of the society into which he moved in 1768, therefore, must be starkly plain. Made up primarily of yeoman farmers, accustomed to hard work and marginal living conditions, the first settlers brought with them few material comforts, if they had more than a few to bring, and depended largely on their own labor and ingenuity to supply their needs. Inventories of their estates itemized the slender sum of their possessions within the one- and two-room log houses with small unglazed windows and low doors in which almost every family began life on a frontier. As a bare minimum they required a bed, table, chest, a few chairs, pots, dishes, tools, a gun, a Bible, and sometimes a loom. Rarely, an estate included a few silver spoons and books and even more rarely, a musical instrument, a rug, or pictures. Except for a few huge holdings like the McCulloh, Gabriel Johnston, or Edmund Strudwick tracts, Orange County land was being taken up in small grants, and plenty of cheap tracts were available for ambitious young men who wanted to rise in the world.

The society from which Richard Bennehan came, long settled in Richmond County in the northern neck of Virginia, where the land was held in large tracts by a few old established families, was a static one, and a man of modest fortune or none, like Bennehan, had little chance to acquire land or better his condition.[8] Although the Bennehans had been land- and slaveholders, the early deaths of Richard Bennehan's grandfather and father accelerated the partitioning of the inheritance and precluded any increments that time might normally have made to their portions. Both Dominick Bennehan, who died in 1716, and his son Dudly, who died in 1750, left wills by which they devised property and slaves.[9] Dudly's will, however, provided only for the two oldest children, who were bequeathed his land, and his widow Rachel, who was to have the use of his personal estate until her death. Richard, as the fifth in a family of six sons and one daughter, could expect nothing. He must nonetheless have received the fundamentals of an education, for he always wrote excellent letters in a clear, firm, confident hand. Probably in his middle teens he was apprenticed to a local merchant with whom he remained until about eighteen years of age. At that time three men of Richmond County, John Woodbridge, William Glascock, Jr., and Leroy Hammond, one of whom was his employer, gave him a letter of recommendation for honesty and industry when he wished to venture into an area with more scope for advancement.[10]

Petersburg, to which Bennehan went probably in 1762, was already a village of some age. A seventeenth-century fort and a subsequent trading post had left a nest of settlers who continued to prosper. The licensing there in 1730 of a tobacco warehouse foreshadowed what was to become Petersburg's main livelihood. Because of its situation at the falls of the Appomattox River, natural forces favored its growth. By river it had access to the Chesapeake Bay and soon became an important port for both coastal and transatlantic trade. The falls were harnessed by mills to create its second industry, flour-milling. Through its situation at the head of the Old Indian Trading Path, it served as a gateway to the whole southwest backcountry from which it drew tobacco and wheat; as the locus of converging trade routes from the regions to the south and west, and from eastern North Carolina, it became the collection point for produce from those areas as well.[11]

Scottish merchants quickly saw the potential in the location of Petersburg and began to establish factors there for their import-export firms. These Scots and their families made up a large part of the town's population. They were not country people but urbanites accustomed to the best that the British empire and Europe could provide in both cultural and material surroundings. They also had money to spend and could attract and support growing numbers of artisans and artists. Horse racing provided amusement at least as early as 1751. A theatrical company visited the town the next year, and Petersburg had its own theater by 1763. A Masonic lodge, the third oldest on the American continent, was chartered there in 1755. Taverns and inns of good quality were a natural outgrowth of the considerable volume of trade which brought farmers and merchants streaming into town, often after many days on the road.[12]

In Petersburg Bennehan must have acquired not only maturity, experience, and judgment with which to undergird a mercantile career of his own, but also general know-how through rubbing elbows with all manner of men. More to the purpose, he probably gained from them awareness of where future growth was likely to occur and sound investments were to be made, and proven advice that for those who got there first, the frontier offered the main chance.

Through Edward Stabler, his employer, Bennehan unquestionably met William Johnston, who would have visited Petersburg periodically to settle accounts, order new merchandise, and enjoy the society of his fellow Scots. When Johnston offered Bennehan a one-third partnership and management of his Snow Hill store in 1768, Bennehan tried to up the offer to one-half interest; but failing in that, he no doubt gladly accepted Johnston's terms as a sterling opportunity. Many years later, after he had proved his worth and become a man of property, Bennehan succeeded in obtaining the one-half share.[13]

General stores in the backcountry were not necessarily to be found in towns; they were quite as likely to be located at important crossroads on main-travelled roads. They stocked everything a farmer might want for his farm, house, and family — from tools, hardware, harness, and lumber, to molasses, medicine, cloth goods, and coffins. The customers could pay up their accounts in cash if they had any, but were more likely to pay in raw materials — tobacco, wheat, corn, feathers, tallow, or beeswax — products which the merchant could in turn sell at his store or transport to his factor as payment on his account. Careful records show how Bennehan managed the Snow Hill store; it was clearly a profitable business from the start.[14] Bennehan's initial capital investment of £250 soon multiplied, and in just over ten years he listed his wealth on a local tax list as over £31,000 and paid a tax in that year of much inflated currency, 1779, of £429/5/9.[15] He was already one of the five richest men in Orange County. On the same list Johnston's wealth is given as £65,000.

During his first eight years in North Carolina Bennehan lived at Snow Hill, aided by a clerk in the store, probably James Martin most of that time, and at least one Negro slave, a man named Scrub, whose name is found in the store records as early as 1771 and later on Richard Bennehan's own slave list.[16] From Bennehan's share of the profits was deducted his rent. Coexisting with the carefully calculated business relationship of Bennehan and Johnston was a warm personal friendship.

The Revolutionary War found Bennehan and Johnston on the side for independence, unlike many merchants who were loyalists at heart and fence-sitters by expedience. An event in Bennehan's life and in that of the emerging nation coincided briefly in February 1776. Bennehan's support of the rebel cause at that time was not a choice forced on him by local pressures but seems to have been a genuine response to a political urgency. A letter from him when he was about to set out with a contingent of troops embodied at Hillsborough on the way to Cross Creek, where a confrontation with the loyalists was building, gives James Martin instructions regarding Bennehan's papers and the money in his "little blue trunk" if he should not return.[17] The engagement now known as the Battle of Moore's Creek Bridge was fought on 27 February 1776 and seems to have been Bennehan's only active participation in the war, if he did in fact see action in that battle. No official records show his support of the patriot cause, but the obituary of his grandson refers to Bennehan as having been a colonel in the Revolutionary War.[18]

After Bennehan's return, he apparently became involved in militia musters. John Butler of the Committee of Safety for the Hillsborough District signed a paper in June 1781 which excused Richard Bennehan and Hezekiah Ferrell (Bennehan's overseer) from the next draft as a reward for their having apprehended two deserters from the Maryland line.[19] The reverse of the same paper shows a receipt from John Rhodes dated 17 November 1781 for Bennehan's contribution of sixteen shillings specie for clothing for Ezekiel Kinchey to serve as Bennehan's substitute in the state legion "agreeable to Law Pass'd at Wake Court House."

Very soon after his military exploit in 1776 Richard Bennehan took steps that changed his life forever: he became both a husband and a planter. He bought 1,213 acres of land, and he married Mary Amis of Northampton County, North Carolina. Thomas Amis, Mary's father, had died in 1764 leaving her land and five slaves whose number had increased over the years so that she brought with her a modest fortune when she became Bennehan's bride.[20] The land Bennehan bought consisted of two tracts, both owned by Tyree Harris, former sheriff of Orange County and object of the Regulators' fury. One tract, 893 acres, lay to the east of Johnston's plantation and west of Flat River. The other was Harris's home place, the Brick House Plantation, of 320 acres on the east bank of Flat River at the point of its confluence with the Eno River where they form the Neuse.[21] Into this house the Bennehans moved; Richard Bennehan's grandson Paul Cameron, writing in 1855 to his sisters about cleaning out the well at the Brick House, referred to it as the well "that our grandfather used nearly a 100 years ago."[22]

Although the Brick House stood until the 1970s when its owner demolished it because of its advanced state of deterioration, no photographs have been found of it. A volume of Richard Bennehan's personal accounts, however, contains a list dated May 1776 and titled "Household Furniture" which describes the contents of the Brick House when the young Bennehans went to housekeeping there.[23] Among the most interesting items are the following:

1 carpet	1 white counterpain
11 leather bottom chairs	1 house bell
2 corner chairs	1 black walnut chest
2 black walnut tables 4 feet	1 iron tea kettle
1 black walnut table 3 feet	3 fenders
1 tea table	2 pr pot hooks and 1 hanging spit
1 dressing table	3 pr tongs
1 bedstead with sacking bottom	2 shovels and 2 pokers
1 bedstead for cording with rods	2 pr candle molds
30 pictures	5 iron pots
1 dressing glass	2 chamber pots
1 knife box	1 pr polished dogs [andirons]
1 suit calico curtains	4 pr snuffers
1 wash stand	2 brass locks
2 pr bed blankets	1 tin lantern
4 table cloths	1 spice mortar
1 cheese toaster	Queens china dishes
1 Japan waiter and 1 glass waiter [trays]	

Miscellaneous other small items complete the list. The cost of the whole lot was £200/5. Richard Bennehan gave Mr. Cocke, obviously a silversmith, forty-five silver dollars to make various pieces of flat silver for him: one dozen tablespoons, one dozen teaspoons, four salt spoons, one soup spoon (probably a ladle).

The Brick House is remembered today as L-shaped. It was probably at the time of the Bennehans' occupancy only a large rectangle without the later wing on the back, with one large room downstairs and two small up: the three fire fenders and sets of tongs suggest three fireplaces. A huge fireplace is well remembered in the middle of a long side of the rectangular building opposite the front door. The two upstairs rooms would probably have shared the chimney, each with a small corner fireplace just above the downstairs hearth.

Richard Bennehan had other expenses connected with his house and farm. He bought a horse, a cow and calf, sows, geese, harness, fodder, seed wheat, corn, oats, flaxseed, a cart, a set of hackles, a whip saw, a flax wheel, hand millstones, hooks, hinges, traces and collars, and potato plantings. He also built a milk house and a stable, underpinned a kitchen, whitewashed the house inside, cleaned the yard and pasture, and hired a slave named Peter to make shoes. He was in a fair way to begin his planting.

Bennehan's new land acquisitions and his advantageous marriage gained for him the economic and social status of a planter.[24] In 1780 only 3 percent of the slaveholders in Orange County owned more than twenty slaves;

among them was Bennehan, whose 1778 list of slaves identifies by name and age thirty-one persons.[25] And in 1780 only 5 percent of the landowners in Orange County held more than one thousand acres; Bennehan owned 1,213 acres.[26] Wealth alone, however, was not in itself enough to ensure inclusion among the gentry. Family, education, good manners, and a good name strongly influenced social status.[27] What Bennehan may have lacked in the way of family and education, he seems to have more than made up for in other respects, for he numbered among his close friends not only William Johnston and his powerful relations in the eastern establishment, but also James Iredell, the McCullohs, and William Richardson Davie. Among the local gentry his intimates were Governor Thomas Burke, William Hooper, Francis Nash, Thomas Hart, and Nathaniel Rochester.

His young and gracious wife undoubtedly helped to cement his place in genteel society. Unfortunately only one description of Mary Amis Bennehan is known — in a letter of James Iredell to his wife in 1778 when he was traveling with his brother-in-law to Salisbury where the next circuit court was to meet. Iredell and Samuel Johnston debated about stopping at the newly married Bennehans' so early in the morning, but chancing it they found their hosts were up and had already breakfasted. Iredell thought Mrs. Bennehan's "amiableness of temper . . . extremely engaging."

> Her life must be a dull one. She has not a single woman she can associate with nearer than Hillsborough, which is at the distance of 18 miles. This is a circumstance she must feel very sensibly, and cannot be sufficiently compensated even by the great worthiness of her husband. The next morning, when your brother told her he would endeavor to bring Mrs. Johnston to see her, she could scarcely speak; tears flowed into her eyes, and it was with difficulty she could express the great pleasure it would give her, and ask me if I could not make her happy in your company also.[28]

With Bennehan's emergence as a planter, two stages of his career were over: the young apprentice and hireling had successfully grown into a shrewd businessman and partner in trade. Now he would assume as well the complex duties of a planter. His strategy would be to plow his mercantile profits into the land from which he hoped to reap future prosperity and security.

2. The Building of Stagville

William Johnston's early death at the age of forty-eight in 1785 left Bennehan, then forty-two years old, suddenly forced to plot for himself a new course that he had not anticipated. While continuing to run the Little River store, which he was able to rent temporarily along with Snow Hill Plantation, he began to look around for a new business arrangement. As an executor of Johnston's estate and guardian of his only surviving child, Amelia, Bennehan could have had no hope of buying the store and the land it stood on: Amelia's home stood on the same tract. His solution was to find a new location and to purchase from Judith Stagg, the widow of Thomas Stagg, a parcel of ridge land which adjoined the bottomlands of his own 893-acre tract on the east.[1] The Stagg tract had been part of an original grant in 1749 from Henry McCulloh to William Strayhorn, who in turn had soon after sold it to William Horton; Horton had then sold 160 acres of the tract to Patrick Boggan. Finally, William Boggan (possibly a brother) had sold the same 160 acres to Stagg.[2]

No metes or bounds are given in the deed from Stagg to Bennehan; the deed describes Bennehan's purchase as sixty-six acres known as "Staggs old Raw Ground." The shape and size of this tract have puzzled surveyors ever since. Even the comprehensive effort of D. G. McDuffie in 1890 to map the entire plantation complex of Paul Cameron omits the Stagg tract. Probably the main virtue of this land for Bennehan was its position in relation to the wagon road (Old Indian Trading Path) to Petersburg which bisected it. Thomas Stagg, who "kept tavern" there from 1758, had tested the advantage.[3] The tract provided an excellent location for a new store, equal to that at Snow Hill yet improving on the old location by its position at an intersection of the wagon road with another road leading north into present Person County and only a short distance from still another road leading southeast into Wake County. Bennehan could hope to retain his old custom and gain new.

Bennehan kept an account book detailing his expenses for the new store beginning with the purchase of the land and recording item by item building costs up to the important notation on 15 November 1787: "Richard Bennehan opened Store at Stagville."[4] Martin Palmer, a Hillsborough carpenter, built the "storehouse," and a lumber house adjacent, on a knoll beside the road (a site well remembered on present-day Old Oxford Highway).

The store was a rectangular, frame, one-storey structure, its short side parallel to the road, with a shingle roof, a cellar, and a large chimney in the end away from the road.[5] The structures were enclosed by fences of paling in which were three large gates and two small.[6] In this store was later located the Stagville post office, established in 1807, for which the store manager thereafter often doubled as postmaster.[7] The sum expended by Bennehan on the land and structures amounted to £685.

The source of the Stagville name can only be guessed. It seems unlikely that Bennehan would have coined a name for his own store and plantation from a former owner's name, whereas he might have retained one already in use and well known. Consequently, the best guess is that the location of Stagg's tavern was already known as Stagville.

Exactly when the Bennehans moved to Stagville is likewise uncertain. If they moved as soon as possible, the construction date of the small wing of the Bennehan house would probably be 1788. A letter from the carpenter Martin Palmer answering a request for his services from Bennehan in August 1790 explains that Palmer could not get to Bennehan's work for five or six weeks until he had finished "enclosing" Mr. Cain's house.[8] The requested work was possibly the building of a house for the Bennehans. The carpenter's notes, however, which detail what must have been all the original structures at Stagville and are labeled "Mr. Bennehan's houses," are unfortunately undated, and they are not in Palmer's handwriting.[9]

The first structure named in the carpenter's notes is "dwelling house" with dimensions which tally exactly with those of the present wing of the Bennehan house and with the measurements given by Bennehan himself on a tax list of around 1816: twenty-four feet by sixteen feet.[10] The notes further describe a roof with a ten-foot pitch, two windows with fifteen lights each, the panes measuring eight by ten inches. A shed ten feet wide was to run along one length of the house and to contain two windows of four lights over six. The windows in the present structure are larger than these and were probably enlarged when the larger section of the house was added. Two windows upstairs covered by plank shutters correspond to the small windows flanking the southeast chimney today. Though nothing was specified as to chimneys in the notes, there were probably two, both where they are today. The present chimneys, however, are not original; even the fine, tall one on the addition is a replacement. Two small rooms at the west end of the wing may have been part of the original arrangement of the space but were probably set off later. Thus the house of one of the wealthiest men in the county — four rooms at most, but probably only two, with a loft reached by stairs rising from the shedroom. Compared to the large, two-storey house of six rooms which Palmer built for William Cain in 1790, Stagville was modesty itself.[11] Perhaps the difference reflects a more affluent background of the Cains, perhaps a more conformable attitude of the Bennehans. No one could ever have called them proud.

A pile of rubble and rock foundations behind the Stagville wing are the only traces of the original kitchen, a very large frame structure with three windows each two feet high and twenty inches wide covered by plank shutters. A log smokehouse twelve feet square, a frame milk house slightly smaller, two slave cabins, and another lumber house completed the original plantation buildings. Foundations of the cabins, too, remain where they once stood at the north end of a line of outbuildings on the farm track east of the house. The cabins were log structures with shingle roofs and, probably like all slave cabins of that time, consisted of one small room with or without a loft, with or without a wooden floor, but always with a large fireplace at which to cook. The cabins were poorly insulated from outside heat or cold and poorly ventilated within. The second lumber house was probably used as a storeroom for odds and ends not in daily use. It also doubled for the Bennehans on occasion as an isolation ward for a sick family member or slave.[12]

Into this new compound the Bennehans moved at latest in 1790 or 1791 if Martin Palmer built the house, and possibly as early as 1788. The family then included besides Richard and Mary two children: Rebecca, born in 1778, and Thomas Dudley, about 1781.[13] After 1787 all letters the Bennehans received were addressed to Stagville. All Rebecca's letters to her brother in school in Chapel Hill were written from Stagville. In 1799, however, a date given by Richard Bennehan on the tax list mentioned above, the larger, main section of the Stagville house was built, thereby adding to the earlier wing a large room, hall, and staircase leading to two upstairs bedrooms. No surviving accounts disclose the builder or cost. Conceived on a grander scale than the original dwelling, this part of the house adds height and dignity to the whole, creating a handsome, imposing, but starkly plain appearance.

A list of furnishings required for the United States direct tax of 1815 itemizes the furniture the house contained at that time.[14] Some of the larger pieces were a mahogany secretary and bookcase, a china press, a sideboard, sets of dining tables, chests of drawers, and a walnut desk. Most numerous were thirty-six Windsor chairs and twelve bedsteads. Many of the listed items had probably furnished the wing and possibly the Brick House before that, but many were also ordered for the new addition. Alexander Taylor supplied a number of the new pieces: the secretary with glass bookcase doors ($100 or £30), an inlaid sideboard (£16), the china press (£20), a lady's bureau (£7/10), a set of four-foot tables, a dozen plain "sitting chairs," two corner chairs (£30), and a settee covered in hair cloth (£15) for a total bill of £45/10 or $451.66.[15]

A piece of furniture that probably antedated all of these was described by Richard Bennehan's grandson Paul Cameron many years later in recalling his grandmother's funeral at Stagville in 1812. He remembered that Dr. Caldwell, the president of the university, who conducted the service, "stood by the side of a tall narrow bench like table which . . . stood in the passage and was used as a side board."[16]

In 1799 Bennehan bought from his Petersburg factors, Watson and Ebenezer Stott, import-export dealers with England and Scotland, a crate of stoneware bottles and butter pots and a set of Queensware dishes: serving dishes, soup plates, mugs, bowls, coffee and milk pots, five dozen blue- and green-edged plates, an enormous number of coffee cups and saucers, and a number of yellow chamber pots in two sizes.[17] Perhaps these items were only merchandise for the store, but the date suggests they were for the new house.

In 1799, the year the house was completed, Richard Bennehan listed 3,914 acres of land in Orange and Granville counties, forty-two slaves between the ages of twelve and sixty, and two stud horses. He paid a tax of £32/10, which included a poll tax for five white males between the ages of twenty-one and sixty.[18] Besides Richard, the polls were probably the storekeeper, clerk, overseer, and blacksmith at Stagville.

Although there is no record of their construction, many farm buildings were added at Stagville: barns, granaries, cribs, and stables. The stud horses of the tax list "stood" at the stables near the store, according to Bennehan's advertisements.[19] Bennehan had invested in stud horses as early as 1777 when he owned part interest in a horse named Sterne, who stood at Snow Hill that year.[20] Bennehan continued to invest in stud horses to improve his own stock and to increase his earnings. Though the Bennehans were not racing men, they did attend the races at Newmarket near Petersburg, at Warrenton, and at Hillsborough, for horse racing was a sport of keenest interest to all at that time, and in those years Virginia and North Carolina were preeminent in the field. Mary Bennehan's cousin, William Amis of Northampton County, North Carolina, owned Sir Archie (possibly the most famous American Thoroughbred of all time), but only after Sir Archie's racing years were over.[21] From Sir Archie were descended most of the later Bennehan and Cameron horses.[22]

Life at Stagville is not difficult to imagine. Family letters paint the picture, but because of the paucity of her letters Mary Amis Bennehan remains a figure mostly in outline in the family portrait. An exceptionally close-knit family, their love and concern for one another established ties that remained foremost in their lives. Though work was hard and constant, helping hands were many, hospitality was bounteous (witness the three dozen Windsor chairs), visitors frequent, and pleasures simple.

Besides the store and plantation, there were additional operations like the blacksmith shop maintained for Stagville and the neighborhood, and after 1802 another store ten miles downstream on a new plantation called Fish Dam.[23] There, too, were another blacksmith shop and a distillery.[24] After 1806 Bennehan added to his services a grist mill on Eno River, and in 1807 the federal government opened a post office in Bennehan's store, thereby certifying Stagville as a center of social and economic importance in the area.[25]

Men who were hired for wages or who were sold part interest in the operations came to Stagville to live and remained for years. John Green and John Wilkins worked in various capacities at both Stagville and Fish Dam plantations, but both were trained blacksmiths and were long associated with the Bennehans. Both Green and a later blacksmith, Andrew Williams, had partnerships with Thomas Bennehan to operate the blacksmith shop.[26] William Bennehan, a nephew of Richard, also came to Stagville in the 1790s as an apprentice in the store. He was later entrusted with the management of the Fish Dam store, but unfortunately died a very young man in 1806 much lamented by all the family.[27] His successor, Robert Seay, also died a young man in 1810; after him William Tharpe managed the Fish Dam store and plantation until succeeded by Mark A. Tate in the 1820s. Tate was still there twenty-five years later. Samuel Yarbrough was Thomas Bennehan's partner in the management of the Stagville store after beginning as its manager in the lifetime of Richard Bennehan. Their partnership was dissolved in 1830. Yarbrough had a nice sense of humor. Writing to Thomas who was away in June 1824 he said, "He [Richard Bennehan] has always caution^d me not to mention to you his being not well and I do not do it at this time."[28]

The Bennehan children's early schooling probably took place at home. In 1795, however, when he was about fourteen, Thomas was sent to Chapel Hill where the new university had just opened its doors. He first attended the preparatory school run in conjunction with the university before enrolling in the college. He took his degree with the class of 1801.[29] Rebecca's letters to him minute the happenings at Stagville while his to her mirror the infant town and the small beginnings of the first state university in the nation. His studies and her reading were an important part of their lives in those years.

Richard Bennehan had an even older and closer tie to the university than this. His old friend William R. Davie had introduced the bill in the state legislature to establish a university and had tirelessly guided it through the slow channels to enactment. Davie concerned himself with the university's early struggles and all phases of its government: faculty, course study, buildings, and student body.[30] From the start Bennehan's interest was enlisted, and the university became a particular beneficiary of Bennehan and all his descendants. With gifts of oyster shells for the lime necessary to construct the first building, of thirty-two "well-bound and well-chosen" books for the library, and of an air pump for the laboratory, Bennehan began a family tradition of generosity and service to the university.[31] He served both as trustee and as a member of the Board of Visitors, the committee which oversaw the academic concerns of the institution.[32]

Politics never tempted Richard Bennehan though planters characteristically savored the prestige that public service could add to their standing. He did accept, however, appointment to the commission delegated to oversee the building of the state capitol.[33] As a result, Bennehan was able to buy a city block in Raleigh, thereafter called the Bennehan Square, which included lots 140, 141, 156, and 157, property that was still in the family one hundred years later.[34]

The 1790s and early decades of the nineteenth century were the great days at Stagville, which became as Paul Cameron later described it, "a sort of headquarters for the Bench & Bar."[35] James Iredell, Samuel Johnston, and William Davie were among the visitors at Stagville and kept in touch with their friend through frequent letters. Even after their removal to Maryland, Thomas Hart and Nathaniel Rochester continued to correspond with Bennehan. Thus Bennehan was drawn into the Federalist deliberations and through his friends into the mainstream of the state's history.

Hospitable to all, the illustrious and the obscure, the Bennehans frequently had young or impecunious relations staying with them; Mary Phillips, Temperance Wilbourne, and Frances Goodwin made long visits at Stagville. After William Bennehan's death, the money from his estate was used to benefit another young Bennehan relation, one Dominick Bennehan. The youth exhibited so little promise during a few years of schooling at Bennehan's expense that his father refused to allow him to benefit further and took him home and set him to work.[36]

Thomas Gale Amis, a nephew of Mrs. Bennehan, and a beneficiary with his cousin Rebecca of their uncle Thomas Amis's will, was sent to the university along with Thomas Bennehan and during those years lived with the Bennehans when not at college.[37] Orphaned early in life, he looked on his Bennehan aunt and uncle as parents and on Stagville as home. Unfortunately he did not look on Rebecca as a sister, and after graduation he suddenly quitted the country on unexplained business in Guadaloupe. After a few years, in one of his long and vaguely mystifying letters to Thomas, he confided that a hopeless love for Rebecca had driven him out of the country.³⁸ He continued an expatriate until he mysteriously disappeared and was presumed dead in 1808.³⁹

Another hopeless suitor for Rebecca's hand was Richard Kay, who wrote to Bennehan in 1793 when Rebecca was only fifteen to ask permission to address her. Bennehan sent him packing.⁴⁰

There is a suggestion in the family letters that Thomas, too, suffered disappointment in love. About the time of Rebecca's engagement and marriage to Duncan Cameron in late 1802 and early 1803, he was sent off, because he was depressed and despondent, with his prospective brother-in-law on a round of court towns, and later on a tour of the North to distract and amuse him.⁴¹ Nothing in his own letters reflected his mood or its cause; perhaps it was Rebecca's marriage that disturbed him, for brother and sister had been unusually close.

For years afterwards Thomas Bennehan's friends and relations tried unsuccessfully to marry him off. Duncan Cameron's sisters in their letters teased and flirted, but he seems to have resigned himself to bachelorhood and to have reserved the right to play the gallant, a role which his letters — gentle, slightly facetious, and even playfully amorous — reflected so well. To Rebecca living in Hillsborough when Jean Cameron was visiting her, he wrote, "To Madame Jane present my love, a sleep or awake her image constantly presents itself to me when I contemplate a fine woman."⁴² A letter from Frances Goodwin chides him, "I hope you will not hurry yourself home as we are all so smart. . . . You had better take time and see the girls when you can, for you very well know that you have no time to lose."⁴³ Another female acquaintance in Petersburg wrote him, "Be sure and come in the Phaeton for when you come in your old single chair it looks so like you did not want a back load."⁴⁴ It was all to no avail. Thomas Bennehan never married.

Instead he made himself useful to his father as long as he lived, and after that to Duncan and Rebecca Cameron and their children, supplying to the latter what Duncan did not — a continuous presence, affectionate, indulgent, interested, and always kind. In after years Paul Cameron frequently reminisced nostalgically about his own youth and his uncle's share in it. "I recall up that dear generous uncle and second father who so loved us all that he could never leave us for any one else."⁴⁵

A retiring man, Thomas Bennehan made no attempt to engage with the world at large. A short spell as a justice of the peace had shown him that "there are too many rascals in our neighborhood," and he soon resigned.⁴⁶ He was also commissioned paymaster to the Seventh Regiment of Cavalry in the Hillsborough District by the General Assembly in June 1806, when his brother-in-law was in the legislature.⁴⁷ He became a trustee of the university in 1812 and served until his death in 1847.⁴⁸ Aside from these few public duties, his life was entirely devoted to his family and their concerns. He oversaw the Stagville store and the plantation management, not only of his father's large holdings, but of those of Duncan Cameron as well, whose frequent absences from home prevented him from giving any sustained supervision to his equally large landholdings. He went to Vermont to arrange for schooling for his nephew Thomas A. Cameron and attended his other nephew Paul Cameron's graduation from college.[49] He was a faithful Episcopalian and Whig, a quietly sociable man with many friends, an amused observer of men and events, a kind master to his slaves, a gentle and generous man, "a model of prudence and patience," as Paul Cameron called him.[50]

Unfortunately no portrait of Thomas Bennehan survives. His tailor's measurements, however, reveal his dimensions: five feet seven inches tall, a neatly made man who dressed with care if conservatively; he wore a wig long after wigs had gone out of fashion.[51] He enjoyed refurbishing his home and bought the latest fashions for it when travel in the North gave him the opportunity. In 1834, for example, he added venetian blinds "of the best quality" at $5 a window.[52] The next year he added an eight-day clock in a mahogany case costing $65.[53] In 1842 he bought a great quantity of carpeting for floors and stairs and one rug "of a drab ground with chintz colors in the figure."[54] In 1843 he bought a bureau, "a very neat article."[55] Two cane birch rocking chairs caught his eye in 1845, and more carpeting and another rug, plush, the next year.[56]

In later years "Mas Tommy," as his slaves called him, would seal himself up in his warm, comfortable, dining room, "his winter cell," and sit in his armchair and read his papers.[57] His housekeeper, Charlotte (Lotty) Rice, his favorite slave and general factotum, Virgil, faithful friends and overseers like James Leathers or Fendal Southerland, and once in a while passing friends from Hillsborough or Raleigh, kept him company.

Mary Amis Bennehan had died many years before in 1812 after a series of strokes. During her illness Charlotte Rice was recruited to help. She was the daughter of Thomas Rice of Granville County, who had worked for Bennehan and Johnston at Snow Hill.[58] After Mrs. Bennehan's death, Lotty became housekeeper at Stagville with wages of $50 a year which became an annuity after Thomas Bennehan's death.[59] She lived on into her ninetieth year and died in Smyth County, then Virginia, where she had retired in the 1850s to live out her life with a married sister and brother-in-law.[60] Miss Lotty or "Aunt Lotty" as she became to the younger generation of Camerons, was a beloved part of Stagville. Reminiscing again years later, Paul Cameron wrote to his sisters, "I think of and love Lotty Rice as a dear kinswoman true and stedfast to the end. . . . She acted well her part in life. I love to think of her and friends Richard and Thomas Bennehan and Stagville in my boyhood."[61]

3. The Cameron Connection

Virginia was the birthplace of the second principal as well in the Bennehan-Cameron history. The year after Richard Bennehan became a planter, Duncan Cameron was born in Mecklenburg County. A substantial Scottish Jacobite ancestry lay behind him through his father, the Reverend John Cameron, who had arrived in America in 1770 and in 1773 had married into a well-established and prosperous family of Southside Virginia, the Nashes.[1] Anne Owen Nash, his bride, was the daughter of Colonel Thomas Nash, a king's attorney, and his wife, Mary Read Nash, daughter of another king's attorney, Colonel Clement Read.[2] Anna Nash Cameron's uncles were Abner and Francis Nash, the former to become the second governor of North Carolina, the latter to die a general at Germantown in the Revolutionary War.

John Cameron was descended from Sir Ewen Cameron of Lochiel but as a younger son was without fortune or prosperity.[3] Nevertheless, he had been well educated at King's College, Aberdeen, and was admitted to orders in the Church of England in 1768.[4] He was able to support himself in America by his profession, which yielded a particularly meager sufficiency after the Revolutionary War when the established Church of England was overthrown along with British rule; but he was able to fall back on teaching, and wherever he lived he established and taught a classical school to supplement his income.[5] An advertisement in 1786 for the Petersburg Academy announced that the "Rev. Mr. Cameron will open the academy of Petersburg on the first day of next January in the buildings now erecting on that high, healthy, and agreeable situation near the Church; in which will be taught by himself and an able assistant, the English, Latin, and Greek languages; Writing, Arithmetic, Geography, Book-Keeping, and the practical branches of Mathematics. The greatest attention shall be paid to the morals of those sent to this Seminary of Learning, and every effort used to qualify them for their destined employment in active life."[6]

Such was the school which the Reverend John Cameron ran in Petersburg, then part of Bristol Parish, to which he had been called in 1784. His church and school were actually in the originally separate village of Blandford, but the growth of Petersburg was fast filling up the land once separating them. There the Camerons lived until the Reverend John

Cameron was transferred to Nottaway Parish and finally to Cumberland Parish, Lunenburg County, where he died in 1815.[7] Such was the school, too, in which Duncan Cameron, born 15 December 1777 and named for his Scottish grandfather, received his education.[8] Strict and authoritative by nature, the elder Cameron turned out good scholars from his various academies. The son inherited the mental and moral fiber of the father and became in turn stern and authoritative, yet a man in whom everyone recognized superiority of mind and character.

His choice of law as a profession was a natural one with his Read and Nash forebears as examples, but the fact that the law always provided far and away the best income in both the colonial provinces and the infant republic no doubt figured in his decision, for fame and fortune seem to have been from the first his goals.[9] He studied law with the Paul Carringtons, father and son, relations through his mother, whose aunt had married Paul Carrington, Sr.[10] For the younger Carrington in particular Duncan Cameron developed the highest respect, as was later reflected in Duncan's naming his second son for him instead of for his own father, as might have been expected since his first son had not received that distinction.[11] He also named his sixth daughter after Carrington's wife, Mildred Coles.

Duncan Cameron seems to have intended from the start to practice law in North Carolina, and soon after he became licensed in Virginia on 2 September 1797, he went first to Warrenton, North Carolina, to the home of James Turner, his sister's stepson-in-law and later governor of the state, and argued his first case at Wake County term of court in February 1798.[12] He next chose Martinsville, then the seat of Guilford County and the site of the decisive Battle of Guilford Court House, as his home base and set up an office there, a choice which dismayed his family, for Carolina friends had told them that Martinsville lacked refinement and Raleigh offered more advantage.[13]

A term at court in Hillsborough, the seat of Orange County, seems to have convinced Duncan Cameron that he would be better off there, and there he moved in 1799 to the satisfaction of his family, who had connections with that small but distinguished town.[14] William Kirkland, a Scots merchant and friend and customer of Daniel Anderson, Duncan's brother-in-law, operated a thriving mercantile business in the town. Amelia Johnston, by then married to Walter Alves and still living at Snow Hill east of Hillsborough, was a friend of Duncan's sisters. His great-uncles Abner and Francis Nash had added luster to the town's historical importance by their association with it, particularly Francis, who had settled there, practiced law, and served as clerk of the court before the Revolution. For Duncan Cameron, therefore, the move to Hillsborough was clearly a right decision.

Though technically in the Carolina backcountry, the town had been a center of trade and law. Its days of political tempest during the Regulator

Movement and the Revolutionary War were all behind it. In the past now were the coming of the army of the royal governor Tryon, three meetings of the General Assembly while the town served as temporary capital for the new state government, the encampments of the armies of Cornwallis, Gates, and DeKalb, and the raids of David Fanning. It continued to attract wealthy families from the older, eastern settlements to its pleasant, hilly terrain as a summer refuge from the coastal fevers. The recent (1795) establishment of the first state university at nearby Chapel Hill provided additional stimulus to economic growth and cultural improvement, factors which would have attracted Duncan Cameron. At the same time the town was located in the center of a large pioneer society with scope for a man hoping to make his way by his wits. Hillsborough offered a splendid combination of ripe refinement and raw opportunity.

At first Duncan Cameron boarded at various places: at the venerable Faddis's tavern, at Elizabeth Sharp's, and at Elizabeth Wilfong's.[15] Within two years, however, his foothold in his legal profession was sufficiently secure for him to invest in his first real estate. He bought from the town doctor and entrepreneur, James Webb, two town lots, numbers ten and thirteen, on Margaret Lane.[16] Whatever improvements they had once offered (there is mention of an old kitchen) were no longer habitable; Duncan Cameron set to work immediately to supply accommodations for himself, his clerk and step-nephew, George Anderson, and a slave, Jim, whom he had brought to Hillsborough from his home in Virginia, probably a gift from his father.

He built a dwelling of a storey and a half which contained a hall, parlor, shedroom, and endroom all plastered and underpinned.[17] An office was built at the same time, one room sixteen by eighteen feet with five windows of twelve lights each.[18] A new kitchen was added and the old one moved to a new site beside it.[19] Porches were added and the whole compound enclosed by a fence.[20]

Some idea of the artisans available in the area at the time may be learned from the bills they sent Cameron for their work. Bennett Watson, William Horton, Andrew Brooks, and Young Dortch were carpenters.[21] Horton also could do the finer work of cabinetmaking, as could William Palmer, Norwood Haskins, and John Adams.[22] They made various pieces of furniture for the new house: a china press, bedsteads, a walnut sideboard, a desk, a tea table, and book cases. James McCay was both a mason and a plasterer.[23]

During Duncan Cameron's next six years' residence in Hillsborough he continued to expand and improve his homestead. He bought three additional lots adjoining the first two, numbers eleven, fourteen, and sixteen.[24] In 1807, besides the dwelling, office, old and new kitchens, the little town estate of five acres comprised a corn crib, well-house, wagon shed, barn, dairy, smokehouse, carriage house, and stables — a well-built and well-equipped establishment, skillfully and durably constructed.[25] Duncan Cameron's dwelling later became the smaller wing of a house built by his cousin Frederick Nash when he purchased the whole property from Duncan Cameron in 1807.[26] Of the entire complex, only the law office remains, now enlarged by the addition of two rooms on the west side.

During his eight years in Hillsborough Duncan Cameron did much building of another kind. He laid the foundation for his career. He was tirelessly industrious, and in a very short time won a reputation as a skillful advocate and formidable adversary at law. One mercantile firm after another, first in Petersburg but soon as far afield as Philadelphia, wanted his services in collecting their debts.[27] One firm wrote him that they would retain him continuously rather than risk him as an adversary in any suit.[28] His oratory must have matched his skill. His sister Mary Anderson reported to him the testimony of an old man from his neighborhood who described Duncan as "'so clever he will be rich as a Jew,' for says he, 'this said Cameron bought a valuable tract of land the other day or so, & tho he did not get a good title to it I'll be bound he will talk them into giving him one, he really talks so pretty.'"[29] With this kind of reputation he could afford to charge high fees with impunity, and he did.[30]

The key words in his neighbor's description of him were *rich* and *land*, for they suggest where Duncan Cameron's interest lay — not in his profession as an end in itself but as a means to the acquisition of wealth. The businessman predominated. He was quick to buy up valuable land sold for taxes at bargain prices, to take deeds of trust on land and slaves on which he could later foreclose, to lend money at high interest rates, and to buy up promissory notes at discount from men who would rather collect partially on loans than be out of pocket entirely. Having still further cash at his disposal, he invested in commodities, too.[31] Probably his undisguised ambition and conspicuous success led to the difficulties of late 1802 and early 1803 when the confluence of political, professional, and matrimonial ventures, floated at the same time, threatened to swamp him.

Politics and government have always been purlieus of lawyers, and Duncan Cameron was ready to enter them. His interest in partisan politics his father recognized as a danger: "Let those who already possess property be watchfull over the Public Guardians thereof; — But do you who have it yet to acquire, learn, from the Example of the Bee, to collect Honey from every flower."[32] Young men are inclined to ignore advice from their fathers, and Duncan Cameron was easily persuaded by his Federalist friends, like William Cain and Walter Alves, to run for office. Again his father warned him, "You will soon find it to be a Step that will greatly tend to injure your private Interest — & with respect to the Public Good, your Efforts, though aided by the Powers & Abilities of Cicero & Demosthenes, will avail nought against a Host of obstinate Mules bent upon the Ruin and Degradation of their Country."[33] Duncan Cameron's first term in the General Assembly proved his father right. "I had to struggle against an overbearing tide of ignorance, stupidity, and prejudice. I have now done with publick Business and according to my present Impressions I shall never again be a Candidate for the Office of Servant to the sovereign People, in the execution of which, Ingratitude is the certain reward which the best service meats [sic]."[34] How little he knew himself! A staunch Federalist in a strongly anti-Federalist state, he soon recovered from his first fray and five times again was to serve as a representative and three times as a senator for Orange County in the state government, though he suffered abuse and frustration in being true to his principles.[35]

In his first term as a public servant, his private and professional life served as a butt for the usual political practices of rumor and insinuation. Two rumors concerned Duncan Cameron in relation to William R. Davie, a hero of the Revolutionary War, ex-governor of the state, the "father of the university," a lawyer of Halifax County, a man of wealth and erudition, and as has already been shown above, a friend of Richard Bennehan. One rumor was connected with the lawsuit of the Granville heirs against Davie and others in an attempt to regain the Granville lands confiscated during the Revolution. Rumor said that Davie had actually bought up the claim for the land from Granville's heirs and was eager to have the suit tried and himself convicted in order to cover up his true interest.[36] Cameron as Davie's lawyer was implicated in the supposed fraud and was further reported to have said he hoped the heirs would recover. At the same time another rumor circulated that Cameron's engagement to marry Richard Bennehan's daughter had been broken off by her father when he learned that General Davie was also interested in marrying her, for Bennehan could not refuse, the gossip went, the honor such a connection would bring him.[37] Obviously both rumors were false, but they led undoubtedly to much embarrassment and personal strain.

It was no rumor, however, that Duncan Cameron was engaged to marry Rebecca Bennehan. Although no record of how they met survives, conjecture supplies a number of answers. Duncan Cameron and the Bennehans were both friends of Amelia Johnston Alves, who with her husband still lived at Snow Hill. Cameron represented Bennehan in at least one court suit before his engagement to Rebecca. Both Bennehan and Cameron were members of the Federalist minority, and Cameron was actively soliciting interest in the party and promoting its principles. Perhaps most important of all their links was their connection with Petersburg which took them there regularly, Bennehan on business, Cameron on family matters. Cameron's brother-in-law, Daniel Anderson, knew the Bennehans although he had never been Bennehan's factor, and Mrs. Ebenezer Stott, the wife of Bennehan's factor, told Mary Anderson many flattering things about Rebecca, whom she had known since Rebecca's childhood.[38] Rebecca's and Duncan's meeting was inevitable.

Their engagement, however, was postponed at least once, and perhaps twice, because of Duncan Cameron's troubles with the rumor mills and with William Duffy, an eminent colleague and for a time a neighbor on Margaret Lane.[39] Professional rivalry seems the only explanation for the enmity that developed between them, although popular tradition has in this case as usual assigned rivalry in love as the cause.[40] Duffy was certainly responsible for the initial rumors that accused Duncan Cameron of perjury in a court trial.[41] Despite Cameron's efforts to clear up the allegations with Duffy personally, the slanders continued even though Duffy denied to Cameron any part in the charges. Finally, it was not Cameron but Duffy who brought the affair to a head by his challenging Cameron to a duel, the basis for which will now never be known.[42] Even Cameron, who wrote to his father about his troubles, seemed not to understand what lay behind Duffy's actions.[43]

While this troublesome matter suppurated, the postponed marriage finally took place on 24 February 1803 with the Reverend George Micklejohn performing the ceremony at Stagville.[44] Not quite two months later on a Saturday night, Duncan Cameron and his second, Dr. James Webb, made their way to the Virginia line and early the next day proceeded to an appointed place in Virginia, dueling having been outlawed in North Carolina. The adversaries met on Sunday afternoon, 17 April 1803. Duncan Cameron's shot hit Duffy in the hip and crippled him for life. Duffy's shot wounded Cameron only superficially in the chest. Having declared himself satisfied, Duffy yielded the ground; with a second shot, Cameron afterwards told Thomas Bennehan, he would surely have killed Duffy.[45]

With that cause for anxiety behind them, the young Camerons could start their life together with hopes for happiness. Unfortunately no pictures of Rebecca have survived to display her personal charm or to reveal her character. Other known assets she certainly possessed. She was the only daughter of a man of standing, respect, and substantial estate in the county. She was something of an heiress in her own right, having inherited from her uncle Thomas Amis over 300 acres in Halifax County and many slaves.[46] She had, moreover, been carefully brought up in a conservative, unostentatious home by frugal and prudent parents. Leading men of the state were her father's friends and guests at Stagville, where she learned to mix with ease in such company. Her mild temperament and devoted, obedient nature promised a dutiful and affectionate wife. Her letters show her to have been completely unselfish, outwardly pliable and yielding, but with a possible core of steel to bear the stresses life later laid on her.

Cameron's qualifications must have seemed impeccable to the Bennehans. Their staunch support of him through the harassment of slanders and potential danger confirms their respect for him and their belief in his eventual exoneration.[47] His skill at the bar and in the legislature, his reputation in the world at large, his family background, his own sterling character, his ability to provide a good home for Rebecca, and his rising prosperity — all were sound recommendations in a prospective son-in-law. To these must be added the man seen in his portraits — a tall, erect physique, attractive and intelligent face, and a lively yet compelling expression, all of which must have made persuasion in courtship as easy for him as that in the courtroom.

Cameron's marriage anchored him securely in the central Carolina planter scene where his father-in-law's land lay and in the mercantile base of the local economy. Although the law continued to be for many years his all-engrossing and lucrative occupation, he was a man of many talents, and in finance his true genius lay. The course of his career and the tenor of his letters suggest this inherent bent. He read dozens of newspapers, probably as much for the news of the markets as for politics. As soon as his profession began to return surplus cash, he began to invest in land, in slaves, in commodities, and in commercial partnerships.

The first partnership, called George Anderson and Company, he established in 1802 with his step-nephew to run a retail general store in Hillsborough while George was clerking for him in his law office.[48] It was decided afterwards that George Anderson did not have an aptitude for the law, and he devoted himself entirely to the business.[49] William Cameron, a younger brother of Duncan, also was put to work in the store after he had received some university education paid for by Duncan.[50] In an attempt to improve the flagging business, in 1806 George Anderson and William Cameron moved it to Martinsville in Guilford County.[51] There they were even less successful, and shortly after, both the business and the partnership were dissolved.[52] However, while the business was still being operated in Hillsborough, another Cameron brother joined the household. John Cameron, too, Duncan had first sent to the university, where he completed the course of study and then, reading law with Duncan, took George Anderson's place as clerk in the law office.[53] The store in Hillsborough was probably on the premises with the dwelling, the office, and all the other outbuildings of Duncan Cameron's five-acre estate.

Cameron's next partnership was on an entirely different scale, and it stemmed from his alliance with the Bennehans. Richard Bennehan's Stagville store had always been the basis of his prosperity, and seeing an opportunity to expand, in March 1802 he bought close to 600 acres on the north side of Neuse River ten miles downstream from Stagville.[54] There he built a second "storehouse" at a crossing called Fish Dam Ford on the Fish Dam Road and thereby appropriated another good location for a store on a well-travelled route.[55] In 1806 Richard Bennehan set up a partnership for his son and son-in-law to run the business at Fish Dam.[56] He conveyed to them for the purpose 2,283 acres in Wake County of which the Fish Dam tract was a portion; there they could "carry on trade and merchandise as co-partners in trade at the Store house. . . ." Any lands bought by either of them adjoining the tract would be considered as purchased for the partnership, and "all mills, distilleries and other useful works which may be erected and built" were to be maintained at joint expense and for joint profit. Richard Bennehan agreed to put in the stock, and each of the partners could add whatever he could afford. At the time of the contract in April 1806 the store showed a net gain of $5,574.30 since its commencement in December 1802.[57] This tentative agreement was apparently successful and proved to be merely a trial run for a much larger conception of combined operations. A year later Bennehan established the partnership which shaped and directed their combined efforts and resulted finally in the magnificent complex of plantations run under one management unique in central North Carolina and possibly in the state. The new articles of partnership encompassed all the lands, slaves, stock, and tools owned by Richard and Thomas Bennehan and Duncan Cameron and combined these assets with the two stores into one business enterprise, the Bennehans to be considered as one party to the contract and Cameron as the other, the profits to be halved.[58] This was large and efficient management. For Cameron the benefits were considerable; all would be managed expertly and diligently for him while he continued to be away much of the time engaged in his law business. The Bennehans would profit by the considerable contribution of land, slaves, stock, and tools which Cameron's still increasing professional income would make possible.

The earlier of the two contracts seems to have been the result of Richard Bennehan's inspiration and generosity. The second may also have been his ultimate vision for which the first was but a rehearsal. On the other hand, it may have been Duncan Cameron's scheme. The considerable lands he owned lay scattered far and wide, some in Granville, some on Little River north of Hillsborough, some on Flat River adjoining Stagville, some upstream on the Eno. Only part of the land was under cultivation, and an overseer was almost entirely responsible for its management because of Cameron's frequent absences. He may have realized that if his lands could be joined to the Stagville management and his and the Bennehan's efforts directed to consolidating their holdings to form one vast amalgam of adjoining plantations, all his land could become productive and efficiently worked for the benefit of all. He knew he could contribute the financial backing to further the plan. In all events the vision and the means to achieve it were the same for both men. The firm of Bennehans and Cameron was born.

One result of the new partnership, which must have been in the planning stage for a while before the signing of the contract on 30 July 1807, was Cameron's decision to sell his Hillsborough home and move to Stagville. For a number of years his obsession with his work had been a cause for concern and unhappiness in his own family. They must have hoped that at last he might slacken his pace and become a planter. Since his marriage his wife, brother-in-law, sisters, and father had chided him for his excessive industry. Such diligence was understandable in a young lawyer building a reputation and clientele to assure his family a comfortable sufficiency and to accumulate capital, but Duncan Cameron carried his efforts beyond these needs. The money, the land, and slaves increased apace and he never relaxed from his labors. His wife wrote to him in 1805, "I comfort myself with the pleasing hope that the period is not far distant, when you can spend more of your time at home, and that we shall enjoy more domestic felicity than if we had not been so often and so long separated."[59] His sister Mary Anderson wrote in 1806, "I see as usual your time taken up with a round of business, but I suppose you are like most men not know when they have enough to live comfortably on . . . but I think you do it at too great an expense of your own health & ease."[60] The same year Thomas Bennehan was even franker: "I hope now, your inclination will accord with our wishes, in giving up, as soon as convenient, all public or professional employment."[61] In 1808 his father was sharper: "I hope to hear in your next letter, that you are permitted to remain at home, to take care of your Family, & attend to your private affairs, — in my opinion — a much more natural way of employing yourself — than to engage with a feeble Minority, to stem a Torrent, which will certainly overwhelm those who oppose it, with Disappointment & Chagrin."[62] This last censure was of course for Duncan's running yet again for public office.

In the spring of 1807 the Hillsborough establishment, along with most of the Cameron furniture, was sold to Frederick Nash, a young cousin and beginning lawyer.[63] The Camerons moved out to Stagville with their remaining possessions in May of that year and there remained without any other prospect in view for the next three years. At the time of the move they had two children: Mary Anne born in 1804 and named for her two grandmothers, and Thomas Amis Dudley, born in 1806 and named Thomas Amis for Mary Bennehan's father and brother and Dudley for Richard Bennehan's father.[64] (Perhaps Thomas Dudley Bennehan also was meant to be honored.) The Bennehans must have been overjoyed to have Rebecca and her children with them, and Rebecca must have found that the arrangement somewhat assuaged the loneliness of her husband's absence. Her affection for her parents and brother was undiminished by her marriage.

The Camerons' move caught almost everyone by surprise. William Cameron, then back in Petersburg, clerking in another mercantile firm, wrote to his brother, "Your removal from Hillsborough was quite unexpected to me — I never heard that you had any such thing in contemplation until it had taken place — I can imagine to myself how gratified Mrs. Bennehan is in having you with her. . . ."[65]

A third child was born to them at Stagville on 25 September 1808. This was Paul Carrington Cameron, the only one of eight children to carry on the family line and name, the one who would survive them all, and the one in whom the entire Bennehan and Cameron fortunes would finally be united. Speaking of his birth in a letter to his sisters on his sixtieth birthday in 1868, Paul Cameron wrote, "This day 60 years ago in the little back room at the Stagville house about 5 o'clock in the morning I was born."[66] The heir was in the wings but the stage was not yet set.

4. The Building of Fairntosh

The building of Fairntosh was not the hopeful gesture of a young man who envisioned his future spread out before him and wished to approach it with an estate and house that matched his expectations. Duncan Cameron had already made a reputation and a fortune. It was, therefore, on a base firmly established — a lucrative law practice, several partnerships in commercial enterprises, and property in excess of 6,000 acres and sixty slaves — that Fairntosh was built. These were sound, diverse investments which were to continue and expand through the years. Begun in 1810, the main house and outbuildings of Fairntosh were completed by 1823, after which modifications to the house and additions of other structures were made from time to time over the next one hundred and fifty years. What precipitated the decision to build after so long a delay can only be guessed. The simplest explanation is probably that the Cameron family was outgrowing the Stagville house and needed quarters of their own. Richard Bennehan may have added moral suasion with his gift to Duncan Cameron of 300 acres which became the nucleus of Fairntosh plantation.[1]

Bennehan had taken this acreage, as the deed states, from two other tracts which he had bought in November 1796, one from the trustees of the university (to whom James Munro's original grant had escheated), the other from John Martin.[2] These two parcels together totaled about 700 acres, and the acres remaining after the gift stayed in Bennehan ownership until the death of Thomas D. Bennehan in 1847, after which they descended to Paul C. Cameron with all the other Bennehan lands in Orange County.[3]

The particular acreage of Bennehan's gift was undoubtedly chosen for two reasons: it lay close to Stagville and it comprised the highest portion of each of the two tracts, thereby offering a good location for a plantation house, the purpose of the gift. None of the land in the area, however, can be said to be high land; level or gently rolling, it occasionally rises to 350 feet. The rise on which the Fairntosh house and outbuildings are set is 358 feet, possibly the exact location of a diabase sill which at that place intrudes the sedimentary rocks of the Triassic Basin.[4]

The soil of this area, as Paul Cameron in later years frequently noted, is not good. Sandy and clay loams all formed from Triassic mudstone, they are notably infertile and lacking in organic matter.[5] They erode easily and require good ditching and heavy fertilizers to give good yields. Nevertheless with care given these matters, they can and do produce good crops of corn, tobacco, and small grains, and provide excellent pasturage.[6]

The deed of gift was dated 18 July 1810 but preparations for building had begun earlier. The first intimation of activity is an entry in April 1810 in Duncan Cameron's account book of a sum paid to Samuel Turrentine "for waggonage done by Lockhart & Thompson in hauling timbers for New House."[7] May of that year brought more activity; William Collier, the brick mason, arrived to make bricks for the chimneys and foundations, and the carpenters, William and John Fort, were building a carriage house.[8] Rebecca, in a letter to Duncan who was travelling in the north, referred to the new plantation, calling it Woodville. "I have not been to Woodvill, nor do I know what has been done there since you went away — I hope you will meet with agreeable company and be much pleased with your trip to the Northward, but I hope also that you will return better pleased with your Woodvill its sylvan scenes, and rural enjoyments."[9] For a man building a house he seemed rather indifferent: he had no business to take him north at that time, and even after his return he was absent from home during most of the construction.

By mid-June the brick was made and almost all of it had come safely out of the kiln.[10] Collier returned in October and resumed brickmaking. In December he was paid for making two batches of brick, 65,000 and 70,000, and for laying 150,000 bricks to build chimneys for the dwelling house, Mr. Sykes's house (the overseer's), and the kitchen, and for underpinning all of them.[11]

The building of the first section of the main house was completed by the end of 1810. During the next three months Henry Gorman plastered all the rooms on both floors with three coats of plaster "in good style;" the garret and part of the cellar received only two coats.[12] Gorman's bill in January 1811 enumerates the rooms, his designations for them probably reflecting Duncan Cameron's. There were five areas on each floor. On the lower floor were the passage, the hall, the breakfast room, the chamber, and the nursery. *Hall* was used there in its old sense of principal room, and *passage* in the present sense of *hall*. The second floor, according to the bill, contained a passage, a hall, the room over the breakfast room, an upper chamber, and the staircase room (the smaller, northeast room beside the staircase). Obviously the upstairs space had not yet been allocated in Duncan Cameron's mind. The number of rooms mentioned in this bill shows that it pertained to the plastering of what is today the front section of the Fairntosh house. This section is a large rectangle of two and a half storeys facing west with two interior chimneys. A central hall on each floor running east and west containing the staircase divides the space evenly. On each side of the hall on each floor is a pair of rooms sharing a chimney. The decoration throughout is distinctly Federal. Gorman's bill is important for its proof that the front section of the Fairntosh house was built before the back. It is of interest that Hardscrabble, the home of the Camerons' neighbors the Cains, may have been built in this way, in reverse of the usual later practice of adding a newer, usually larger and more elegant section to the front of the older, humbler portion, though the evidence here is mixed.[13]

The handsome woodwork of the mantels and overmantels was done by Elkanan Nutt.[14] He submitted his bill in May 1811 for eight chimney pieces costing $196.47. At the same time the Fort brothers were continuing to work on outbuildings, their progress reported to the again absent Duncan Cameron by his wife and his brother-in-law. Thomas Bennehan wrote in July, "Mr. Fort is endeavoring to close his business at your house in a week or Ten day's."[15] A week later Rebecca wrote, "Mr. Fort and all his family have left us, I do not know whether he has finished all he promised to do."[16]

At what date the Camerons actually moved to Fairntosh is difficult to determine. Mary Amis Bennehan was failing fast in those years after having suffered a series of paralytic strokes. Rebecca was probably fully occupied with nursing her mother and caring for her own four children, the fourth, Margaret Bain Cameron, having been born in April 1811. When Duncan Cameron was about to leave Raleigh at the end of 1812, where he had served yet again in the legislature, he wrote to Rebecca, "I hope you continue to bear in mind, my wish to remove home, soon after my return; and that you will shape matters accordingly."[17] Two weeks later Mrs. Bennehan died. Perhaps they had already moved to their new house the spring before and Rebecca was again at Stagville only because of Duncan's absence and her mother's illness. At the end of 1811 Mary Anderson had written to Rebecca enclosing a model of her own new window curtains and expressing a wish that she could be there to help Rebecca with putting up her curtains.[18]

In any case they were certainly living in the new house in the spring of 1813. By that time a new name had been chosen for it. Jean Syme, another sister-in-law, addressed a letter to Rebecca at "Farentosh," the first instance of this name in the family papers.[19] Fairntosh (Ferintosh) was the name of the Reverend John Cameron's birthplace in Ross-shire, Scotland.[20] It is noteworthy that Mary and Daniel Anderson had the name Lochiel for their new house in Petersburg thereby commemorating another Cameron place-name, the Cameron's direct ancestors having been lairds of Lochiel.[21]

After the move to Fairntosh, building still went on. A bill at the beginning of 1814 from John and Elias Fort itemized the materials and labor for building a schoolhouse, a dairy, "Jim's house," two small buildings the size of the dairy, and a stable well.[22] The two small buildings, of which no trace remains today, were possibly "necessary houses."

One of the most interesting of the present outbuildings at Fairntosh is the large, double-storey kitchen with its tall chimney and brick-nogged walls. This kitchen was not the one named in the Collier bill of 1810; it was not built until 1814. It can be dated so exactly by a letter of Rebecca's to the again absent Duncan in which she reports, "Mr. Coyler requested me to ask you if you wished the walls of the kitchen filled in with brick, he says you talked of it some time ago. I am afraid I shall hardly get an answer before he has finished the work he has on hand."[23] This evidence is important for more than the dating of the kitchen. It shows that the practice of using brick nogging in frame buildings at Fairntosh and Stagville was Duncan Cameron's, a technique he was still using in the much later slave quarters at Horton Grove and Shop Hill. (See Chapter 6.)

The main house was still not finished. James Courtis began painting it in the summer of 1814 and finished in September.[24] He also painted a fence and gates which the Forts had built to enclose the house and yard.[25] Cameron seems to have kept the Forts almost continuously employed from 1810 until 1822; when they were not working at Fairntosh, they did repairs and construction at other Cameron plantations, for there was no end of carpentry to be done. They also built furniture and coffins, including Mrs. Bennehan's coffin.[26]

When the Reverend John Cameron accepted his son's offer of the Brick House Plantation as his retirement home, more carpenters had to be found to put the old house in order.[27] Samuel Butler and John Gooch were hired to do the repairs, not a small job as their bills later showed.[28] Syphering the sheeting and shingling the house headed the list, which also included putting in new windows, building two small porches, applying new plaster in the upstairs rooms, laying new floors in both storeys of the kitchen, making new shutters and doors, constructing a dairy, repairing the smoke house, and erecting gates and gateposts. Unfortunately it was all done in vain; John Cameron died in December of 1815 of his old enemy St. Anthony's fire (erysipelas), a complication of another infection with which he was already ill.[29]

After adding a lumber house (storage space) to Fairntosh in 1817, the Forts were instructed to prepare for the addition of another section to the main house. "Bills of lumber got by John Fort for new building in 1818," the bill noted.[30] At the same time they were completing construction of a building to house the wheat threshing machine.[31] Again William Collier made his appearance and produced the required brick in twenty-eight days in the brickyard.[32] And again Henry Gorman came to do the plastering and whitewashing of the new interior walls.[33] His bill specified three rooms. The fine carpentry was done by John J. Briggs, who built the stairway and the mantelpieces.[34] This section of the house was completed by 1821. John Fort's bill headed "to framing add^n to dwelling H^o" contains the items ten large windows and two half windows, precisely the number in the back section of the house, identifying it unmistakably as the structure built at that time.[35] The bill also details the amounts of sheeting, shingling, flooring, cornice (plain and dentil) and "wainscoat" required for three rooms and two passages. This section of the Fairntosh house was originally separate from the front, about twelve feet to the east and centered behind it. Almost square, it contains one chimney in the middle of the east wall, one large room downstairs, one large and one small upstairs. A hall at the west side on both floors contains the staircase. The interior decoration of this back section, somewhat heavier than the front, suggests Georgian rather than Federal style, but the exterior exactly matches that of the front section.

John Fort's bill also mentions a colonnade, no longer extant, which, according to a much later bill, was twelve feet long.[36] It was an open-sided but roofed walkway connecting the two sections of the house and cost $75 to build. References to it occur in the family papers. Duncan Cameron's daughter Jean wrote to him in Raleigh in 1835, "I think you must be tired of Colonel Cook's by this time and anxious to get back to your quiet seat at the colonnade door, with your pile of newspapers at your side."[37]

Two other features of the house were added to complete the form in which Duncan Cameron occupied it. They were the stone steps to the outside entrances and the front piazza. The steps were built by McSweaney and Hennessey in 1823.[38] Their bill describes the exact size of each step of each set: five sets for the house, one for the office, the first mention of which appears in this bill. All these steps remain in place today except those for the front or west doorway. When the piazza was added to the front of the house in 1827, the front steps must have been removed and the present entrance stoop to the porch put in their stead. The stone entrance steps at the two front entrances to the Stagville house today are unquestionably those removed from Fairntosh. A view of the Fairntosh house today presents prominently a handsome front porch in the Greek revival style. In 1827 while Jean Cameron Syme was visiting, she wrote to Mary Anderson, "The carpenters are building a piazza in front of the house."[39] Unfortunately no bills disclose who did the fine carpentry of the cornice.

The last of Duncan Cameron's improvements to Fairntosh was the chapel, still standing today in a grove of oaks on a rise of ground between Stagville and Fairntosh. Built in 1825–26, it was a rarity few other plantations could boast of anywhere in the South.[40] Long narrow windows with paneled shutters were the only exterior decoration of the simple wooden rectangle. Inside, plastered walls, a gallery across the back, and pine pews were the only additions to its plain frame. Abraham Spencer did the plasterwork. The recessed chancel of the present structure was added by Paul Cameron in 1884.[41] Perhaps the beautiful triple stained-glass window which until recently filled the east wall of the chancel was also added at that time.[42]

The chapel was consecrated by Bishop Ravenscroft of the Episcopal Church on the first Sunday in October 1827; services were held there both Saturday and Sunday.[43] The Bishop wrote Cameron beforehand, "The Deed can be written after I reach your house and am able to describe the Boundary of the burying ground, if you remain in the mind to include it."[44] Of the celebration Duncan Cameron wrote to his son Paul, then away at school, "there was a great deal of Company here; and the occasion furnished much gratification to all present."[45]

Salem was the name given the chapel.[46] Arrangements for services always proved to be a problem. Apparently Cameron agreed to supply a salary of $100 a year to whoever discharged the duty of preaching there once a month.[47] The duty fell to the rector of St. Matthews Church in Hillsborough, the Reverend William Mercer Green, as long as he was in that post and for some time after his move to Chapel Hill.[48] The bishop visited the chapel once or twice a year for purposes of confirmation.[49] Duncan Cameron bought Bibles and testaments in 1828 for the chapel.[50] Very many years later, in 1879, at the time of Pauline Cameron's marriage, her aunts in Raleigh sent prayer books and hymnals for the chapel with "Salem Chapel Orange Co. November 6th 1879" inscribed on each; this was their offering "to the little chapel down in the woods," they wrote to Pauline.[51]

The first interment in the family graveyard at Fairntosh which adjoined the chapel took place in 1825, when Anne Owen Nash Cameron, Duncan's mother, died. Years later, Green, reminiscing about his long association with the Cameron family, referred to her midnight burial without explanation for the unusual hour.[52] Duncan's brother William was the second to be buried there, in 1826. The third was not a family member but Andrew Williams, the blacksmith at Stagville. Mary Anne at Fairntosh wrote to her sister Mildred in Raleigh, "Uncle will tell you that Mr. Williams is no longer one of us but is now in the quiet grave-yard of our little Chapel, I did not attend his burial."[53] No tombstone marks his grave.

The note of sadness in Mary Anne's remark reflected what was in the back of her mind: her sister Jean's death the previous August at Red Sulphur Springs, now in West Virginia, where she was buried. That same month, November, her body was brought home and reinterred at Fairntosh.[54] Two years later, in the summer of 1839, Mary Anne herself and another sister, Rebecca, were buried there, joined the following year by a fourth, Anne Owen, all four sisters victims of tuberculosis.[55]

The tombstones for these graves, and for those whose deaths would follow, were ordered from the firm of John Struthers and Son of Philadelphia.[56] At the same time that Duncan Cameron was ordering tombstones, he was planning to enclose the burial ground with a stone wall surmounted by an iron railing.[57] William Stronach, a local stonemason, was in charge of obtaining, dressing, and setting the stone wall.[58] Struthers provided the railing.[59]

The rock was quarried on the plantation. "Mr. Stronach is busily engaged with his work and you may say to my father," Paul wrote to his sister, "he has carried us to the Cain place to quarry our stone as we find the sand stone at this point of a *far superior* quality as regards firmness and uniformity of texture. We have great labour in getting the stone hauled requiring 8 oxen. My father has been very fortunate in getting so faithful a workman for he will not receive an inch of inferior material."[60] William Stronach began to lay the wall in August 1844, as the final pieces of stone were still being cut. The wall and railing stand to this day.

Other structures standing around the main house at Fairntosh today are the overseer's house, the music room or the teacher's house, and two buildings without chimneys in the kitchen row called the commissary or ration house and the weaving house, the latter mentioned in a letter of 1850.[61] Of the construction of the latter two nothing is known. Perhaps they replaced the earlier two unidentified structures the size of the dairy in the 1814 bill submitted by the Fort brothers. Each of these present buildings is larger than the dairy. The overseer's house was probably built in 1850 or a little before as it is not included in the inventory of buildings reroofed by William Lougee in 1850, but it is mentioned by Anne Ruffin Cameron in a letter in December of that year, referred to as Mr. Piper's house.[62]

The music room, too, is not included in the Lougee bill. Its earliest mention is in 1855, when Mary, Paul's daughter, got too near the fireplace in the music room and her dress caught on fire.[63] The music master, Antonio Di Martino, smothered the fire with his hands and saved her life. He was a Neapolitan who lived with Paul Cameron as early as 1853 to teach his daughters music and French, and was still with them in 1860.[64] Probably the music room was built for his use.

Beyond the few buildings enumerated, almost nothing is known about the construction in those early years of what surely must have been numerous farm buildings and slave quarters at Fairntosh and the other plantations. Tobacco barns, stables, cribs, granaries, and barns for animals and for storage of produce would have been vital components in the plantations' operation. Probably built by slave labor without any additional skilled workmen, they left no trace in the family papers. Construction of one sort or another went steadily on throughout Duncan Cameron's occupation, a condition reflected in a letter from Paul Cameron, away at college in 1829, to one of his sisters: "And Father intends to have a tanyard. What will he not have next. He has now as complete, I don't know what to call it so I will coin a word "Hodgepodgiana' will that one do — I hope you can make it out — Father wont get offended at the name that I have given to his various occupations. But I am often amused to think of some of his plans — He has made Fairntosh a little city and you dont know what you have around you until you think an hour — Yes I expect to see his man Luke declare it a regular incorporated city and himself mayor and sole sovereign."[65]

5. Duncan Cameron at Fairntosh

The fifty years that followed the building of Fairntosh form very much a unit, coinciding with the apogee of the antebellum epoch. A pattern of life was established that continued through two generations. Changes occurred, to be sure, many of them devastating, and although illness, anxiety, and grief sometimes clouded life there, the family afterwards looked back on their years at Fairntosh as halcyon days. The half century divides almost evenly into two cycles, the first from 1811 to 1836, when Duncan Cameron and his family lived there, the second from 1837 to 1860, when his son Paul Cameron and his family repeated the earlier pattern with minor variations.

The first decade at Fairntosh was one of expansion and building inside and out. To the four children who had moved into the new house with their parents were added four more: Rebecca Bennehan in 1813, Jean Syme in 1815, Anne Owen in 1817, and finally Mildred Coles in 1820. The Bennehans and Cameron partnership created in 1807 was continually bolstered by purchases of land and slaves and showed its efficient management by good returns. Slowly the boundaries of the home plantations moved outward as parcel after parcel, on becoming available, was added to the complex, and the Bennehans and Cameron patiently pieced together the moieties of the heirs of the Cain and Harris families who had originally owned much of the land in the neighborhood.

Certain broad outlines emerge from the series of purchases. All of Richard Bennehan's land purchases from 1776 until 1801, with the exception of one tract in Granville County, lay in Orange County. In 1801 he began to acquire parcels in Wake County. The land he bought was on both sides of the Neuse River, always bottomland, a policy followed by his son, Thomas, who continued to fill in the gaps in the Wake County lands and bought another large tract in Granville County.

When Duncan Cameron joined the family in 1803, his lands lay scattered in many areas of the county with the exception of three tracts in Granville County which he had bought in 1802 when his marriage to Rebecca Bennehan was only months away. In 1809 he began to acquire land in Person County to which he added periodically by the Bennehan system to form a final aggregate there of well over 8,000 acres.[1] Cameron Mills, a partnership he established with Lawrence Hargis there in 1808 to operate the mills and millstore, was absorbed the following year by the partnership of Bennehans and Cameron.[2]

The old Johnston Snow Hill Plantation was one of the last pieces to fall into place, a particularly large and important one geographically because it lay astride the main road, and on both sides of Little River close to Stagville and Fairntosh.[3] Thomas Bennehan wrote to his niece about the purchase in 1821, "We have almost ruined ourselve's by the purchase of Mr. Alvese's lands and I am in hope's you will exchange with pleasure the amusement's of the city for the rural economy, and will find much gratification in attending to the shuttle, the Distaff & Dairy until we get out of debt."[4] This purchase must have been particularly poignant to Richard Bennehan, then seventy-eight years old, and a crowning achievement: to bring the large plantation of his old partner and friend long dead into his own vaster land conglomerate at last.

The D. G. McDuffie survey, which purports to show all the lands held by Paul Cameron in 1890, was either left uncompleted or is incorrect. The first obvious omission is the Stagville tract acquired in 1787.[5] In addition, great areas of the map are not referenced to any record in the legend, or conversely, many tracts numbered in the legend are missing from the map.[6] The lands enumerated in the legend total about 20,000 acres, but a number of tracts acquired by both Duncan Cameron and Richard Bennehan recorded in the county deed books are missing from this list.[7] The Bennehans bought about 15,000 acres of the plantation complex of which a part was sold or given to Cameron.[8] Independently Cameron bought some 15,000 acres in addition, making a total of around 30,000. It is clear that the McDuffie map is based on incomplete records.

In 1810, at the beginning of his years at Fairntosh, Duncan Cameron compiled a list of his financial assets and liabilities and must have been comforted to see that his net worth then amounted to $100,000.[9] He owned sixty-six slaves worth $15,000; real estate worth $23,000 (Fairntosh is listed as "Woodville & houses"); stock in trade and business interests with the Bennehans and Hargis worth $16,892.54. The rest was money lent at interest.

If his family had hoped Duncan Cameron would become the typical planter, confining his interests to family and homestead, they were soon disappointed. He never separated himself from the world beyond his home borders, and he continued to engage actively in law and politics. Soon a third quite unforeseen occupation claimed his attention. In the War of 1812 as a major-general in the state militia, he was responsible for many local companies.[10] Company musters and related records fill many folders of family papers in the years 1812–1814. At the same time North Carolina appointed him to oversee the still unresolved controversy with Georgia over their common boundary in the mountains.[11] His participation in this effort was only administrative, however, for the problems of survey and negotiation were delegated to experts while he devoted himself to militia affairs closer to home.

The war had a financial as well as personal impact. The actual hostilities affected shipping and trade in general. For some years before war was declared, various disruptions caused by embargoes and seizure of ships seriously impaired the export trade of plantation products. Duncan Cameron, who had created still another partnership to set his brother William up in a mercantile business with Samuel Snow in Petersburg, was forced by losses to dissolve the business into which he had put $20,000.[12] William Cameron, whose health had always been delicate, went into the army and further undermined his constitution. All William's later attempts at trade in Virginia and North Carolina ended in failure, and his early death in 1826 left his wife and five children still on Duncan Cameron's hands and conscience.[13]

John Cameron, too, whom Duncan had educated and seen well established in a law practice in Fayetteville, North Carolina, suffered from the war. While he was serving in the army a paralytic stroke almost killed him.[14] He recuperated slowly and almost fully, but a lasting speech impairment precluded his resuming his practice, and for many years Duncan Cameron had his pecuniary problems to deal with.[15] Eventually John Cameron solved his own problems by obtaining first a consulate to Vera Cruz from President Jackson and soon after a judgeship for the District of Western Florida which effectively salvaged him and his family.[16] He died in the sinking of the ship *Pulaski* in 1838.

Duncan Cameron's war duties were interrupted by an appointment to the bench of the North Carolina Superior Court in February 1814.[17] His fee book recorded the end of his law practice and the beginning of his judiciary career with the words "a poor exchange," which referred no doubt to the size of the remuneration rather than to the character of the work.[18] He resigned from the bench in 1817.[19]

In 1813 Duncan served his last term as representative for Orange County in the House of Commons, but in 1819 he began a term in the senate and served twice more, in 1822 and 1823. Archibald D. Murphey, his friend and fellow attorney, handed over to Cameron the chairmanship of his own committee for internal improvements. Though he became very active in the senate, frequently amending the wording of bills, presenting petitions and memorials of his constituents and bills related to militia matters, his main concern centered on his internal improvements committee, which reported out bills on bridges, canals, roads, navigation companies and the like. He also played an active part in supporting legislation connected with improving justice and the courts.[20]

Duncan Cameron was also involved in the early efforts to establish a state bank, being one of the Federalists who believed that a state bank could repair the monetary damage which badly managed private banks and their unsound currency had caused in North Carolina.[21] After the legislature chartered the State Bank of North Carolina in 1811, Cameron was appointed a director and entrusted with the problems of the ordering and printing of bank currency.[22] He went to Philadelphia first to consult with bank officers there and then to Gilpins Mills on the Brandywine, printers of the currency for the Philadelphia banks. He was impressed by their size, efficiency, and quality of work; they were probably given the contract for the North Carolina bank currency.[23] From this time on Duncan Cameron was connected with the business of the bank.

In 1828 a huge deficit was discovered, and the results of an investigation implicated the cashier, M. C. Stephens, in the loss.[24] The bank directors were successful in December 1828 in urging Judge Thomas Ruffin, a man respected for his probity and wisdom, to take the bank presidency in order to restore confidence.[25] The anger aroused in the bank creditors and the public in general by its mismanagement threatened the bank with liquidation, a course which would have proved disastrous to the stockholders.[26] By February the next year Ruffin was already being spoken of as a candidate for a vacancy in the state Supreme Court.[27] His appointment was made in November 1829 and Duncan Cameron was named to succeed him in the bank.[28] Cameron's patient wife commented on learning of his presidency: "I was indeed very much surprised and concerned to hear that you had accepted the Presidency of the State Bank, you know that I never was a friend to Banks it has always appeared to me to bring trouble to those connected with them."[29] Her opinion, of course, counted for nothing with him.

Years before, her sister-in-law Mary Anderson had warned her, "He was ever one who did as he pleased."[30] Mary Anderson would probably have agreed that Duncan Cameron was also one who made others do as he pleased. In her later years she came to know the authoritative, even highhanded, streak in his nature. As the oldest child in the Reverend John Cameron's family, Mary was used to dealing with her younger brother Duncan without the constraint or deference which the younger children in the family used with him. Her marriage to Daniel Anderson had reinforced her independence, and as long as Anderson lived, her letters show, she felt free to speak frankly and as an equal to Duncan, even to chide or tease him as her mood might dictate. But Anderson's death put Mary at a disadvantage with Duncan Cameron by placing in his hands as executor of the estate and guardian of her two sons the control of her inheritance and, as a consequence, her life. She then had to submit to his decisions.

In one instance she appealed to him for advice and received the injunction that if she did not take it she was "never on any future occasion" to ask his advice again.[31] On a later occasion Mary suggested that together they erect a monument over the graves of their father and sister in Lunenburg.

She composed a text for John Cameron's grave which Duncan Cameron rejected, substituting one of his own composing with what can only be termed self-importance, as a comparison of their texts reveals.[32] Her proposed text read:

> Sacred
>
> To the Memory of
> The Rev[d] John Cameron D.D.
> Rector of Cumberland Parish
>
> Who after a well spent life
> Died on the 8th day of December 1815
> In the 71 year of his Life
> He was a native of Rosshire, Scotland,
> Studied in the University of Aberdeen
> Where he received the Degree of Master of Arts
> Was ordained by the Bishop of London
> and had a degree of
> Doctor of Divinity
> Conferred upon him by the College of William and Mary
> He was an excellent Classical Scholar
> And Able Divine
> An affectionate relative
>   And
> an Honest Man

Duncan Cameron countered with:

> Here lie entombed
> The remains of
> The Rev[d] John Cameron D.D.
> who departed this life on the 8th Dec[r] 1815
> in the 71 st year of his age —
> His life was spent in preaching the Gospel
>   of Jesus Christ
> This monument is erected to his
> memory by his son
> Duncan Cameron of Orange
> County — North Carolina

After the year as president of the bank, during which his talent for finance was challenged and proved in bringing the foundering bank out of its difficulties, he again resigned.[33] A new Bank of the State of North Carolina was chartered a few years later, and he became president in 1834 at the same time "winding up the affairs of the old bank whose charter had expired by paying its creditors and stockholders in full, together with a small surplus to the latter."[34] He served as president of the new bank continuously until his resignation in January 1849.[35]

Cameron's duties at the bank of course required his presence in Raleigh. His wife and daughters spent part of 1829, 1834, and 1835 with him in rented quarters. It must have been clear to him that he had at last found his métier. He began to build a house in Raleigh in 1835 to which the family moved in the spring of 1836.[36] A fine house with a double-storied, columned portico, it achieved a degree of elegance and comfort that Duncan Cameron had not cared to bestow on Fairntosh. Here he lived the rest of his life.

Life in Raleigh where the leaders and eminent men of the state were increasingly gathered was a milieu better suited to Duncan Cameron than the isolation and unvarying seasonal round of duties that agriculture imposed. His restless mind needed the distraction and stimulation which business and society in the city could provide.

By the time of the family's move to Raleigh, Duncan Cameron's six daughters had finished their education. Their relations looked on the move as propitious for the girls who had lived so much out of society and would now have a chance to bloom. They ranged in age from Mary Anne, then thirty-two years old, down to Mildred Coles, just sixteen. Since seven years separated Mary Anne from her nearest sister, Margaret, born in 1811, she had been educated alone. Her mother had taught her in the early years before she was sent to her aunt and uncle Jean and Andrew Syme in Petersburg, Virginia, for a few years. The Reverend Andrew Syme, like his father-in-law, had taught a small school to increase his earnings.[37] Following that, Mary Anne was sent to the respected academy in Warrenton, North Carolina, run by Jacob Mordecai, where she remained until 1818.[38] She was not a good student, but it worried the Camerons more that she was disrespectful to her teachers and untidy in her person.[39] Mr. Mordecai's decision to move from Warrenton saved her from further discipline, and at fourteen she returned home undoubtedly pleased to be relieved from what she had found a disagreeable experience.

All her younger sisters were educated together at home. In 1820 Duncan Cameron engaged Miss Mary McLean Bryant from Ithaca, New York, as their teacher at a salary of $300 a year.[40] In Miss Bryant the Camerons saw a lady of sound Christian belief and a good teacher. Her association with the Cameron family endured as friendship after her sixteen years as the girls' teacher were over. It was Margaret and Mildred Cameron who paid for her tombstone when she died in 1858.[41] Through all those years she remained a fast friend. Her voluble letters to the family, brimming with news and good advice, reveal the pious spinster. She took employment in a family named Spruill after she left the Camerons but was not satisfied and always looked back nostalgically to her years of teaching in the "little red schoolhouse" at Fairntosh.[42] For a few years she played a similar role in the household of Thomas Ruffin, whose daughter married Paul Cameron, and even taught Paul Cameron's oldest daughters for a year or two, so that she was able to prolong her happiness in the Cameron ambiance a little while.[43]

Duncan Cameron was not able to find a solution to his sons' education quite so easily. His eldest son especially presented a problem because of a mental handicap. Thomas Amis Dudley's condition seems not to have been apparent in infancy, or if apparent, not admitted, unless Rebecca's description of him a few months after birth suggests in the phrase, "in his mother's eyes," a qualification: "Our dear little Boy . . . appears well and is in his mother's eyes as fine a child as the Sun ever shone upon. . . ."[44] Whatever his condition, however, his schooling began early. When Thomas was five and Paul three in the fall of 1811, a tutor was hired for them.[45] Two years later Thomas was sent to school to his Cameron grandfather in Lunenburg County, Virginia, where he joined his youngest uncle, Thomas Nash Cameron, and his cousin William Anderson under what must have been an unsuitable if kindly meant discipline.[46] The Reverend John Cameron reported Thomas's progress from time to time. "I make them spell some lessons together, in order to put Tom in the way of getting or preparing his lesson by himself, a thing of which he had not the least idea before."[47] And later, "Tom now spells in words of four syllables & begins to read in words of one syllable — He also writes a little every day of which he is very fond."[48]

The next year Cameron hired as a tutor for his sons Willie P. Mangum, a neighbor and later a law student of Duncan Cameron, a local politician, judge, and finally senator in Washington, where he represented the state ably for many years.[49] Mangum reported of Thomas's studies, "Tom is now spelling; & it is probable his improvement is not commensurate with your expectations; the obvious reason of which is his indolence — when there are immediate objects of incitement, his attention becomes fixed, and he improves very well; but when they are removed or become stale by frequency of occurrence he relapses into inattention." By contrast Paul was improving very fast, making his brother's mental impairment obvious.[50] Paul wrote his first letter to his absent father in the spring of 1814 when he was not yet seven; Tom at almost nine years of age was mortified that he could not do so.[51]

Duncan Cameron, considering sending him away from home to separate him from Paul, made inquiries of his brother John regarding schools near Fayetteville. John Cameron wrote back, "As to the propriety of sending him from home, I can have no doubt; the truth is obvious, and I know it has not escaped your observation, that he is so aware of Paul's superiority over him that it discourages him. The remark is so often made, without his ability to do better, that from being at first mortified, he becomes callous."[52] No school was found, however, and the boys were tutored at home another year by Lotan G. Watson, who received $100 for the year.⁵³

In 1817 both boys were sent to the famous Hillsborough Academy of which the Reverend John Witherspoon was then principal.⁵⁴ In the fall of the following year Thomas was shifted to Miss Polly Burke's school.⁵⁵ Still another tutor was tried for both boys in 1818. He was Malbon Kenyon, who remained through 1820. His salary was $400 for teaching both boys, only $333 when teaching just Paul.⁵⁶ Kenyon was relieved of the problem of Thomas in 1820 when Thomas was sent to Elizabethtown, New Jersey, to the home and school of the Reverend John C. Rudd, where he remained over three years.⁵⁷

In 1821 Paul was sent to the Reverend William McPheeter's Academy in Raleigh, where he seems to have been taught by both William H. Haywood, Jr., and John Rogers.⁵⁸ When the latter became principal of the Hillsborough Academy, Paul was sent there once more until he entered the University of North Carolina in 1824. His cousin, William Anderson, who had preceded him to Chapel Hill, wrote that Paul was doing well and studying hard.⁵⁹

Unfortunately an ungovernable temper plagued Paul all his life, and he was always quick to take offense. At Chapel Hill, for example, he laid claim to a certain seat in the chapel in which a classmate unwittingly sat one day. When the boy refused to vacate the seat, Paul resorted to force. He was summarily suspended and sent home in disgrace.⁶⁰ Once more he went back to the Hillsborough Academy.

Meanwhile Thomas finished three years in New Jersey and was sent to Captain Alden Partridge's school in Norwich, Vermont (later to become Norwich University), which emphasized mathematics, science, and military drill.⁶¹ The choice of this institution becomes more understandable in the light of Rudd's description of Thomas's difficulties. "He has it is true improved in penmanship but he cannot without aid combine words and phrases. He enjoys good health, and makes generally a strong effort. Geography is his best exercise in which he is pretty familiar, being able to point out all places of consequences, on the Map of the World. His progress in figures is slow. In reading & spelling he does very well, and is more animated & active than formerly. His temper and intentions are good. He is seldom angry unless much provoked, which very seldom happens, and he seems impressed with a good degree of sensibility to what is right & wrong."⁶² While Thomas was still with Rudd, William Haywood visited him and reported to Cameron that Thomas expressed a desire to go to dancing school and to see his sisters, particularly the one born after he left home, whom he had never seen.⁶³

Thomas's situation must have given Duncan Cameron much anguish. The only writing of his which mentions Thomas's condition at all is a copy he saved of a letter written to Captain Partridge at the time he requested admission for Thomas to Partridge's school.[64] It gives in detail as much as will ever be known of Thomas's case history.

> Sir, my oldest son a youth in his 18th year has laboured under a species of muscular debility from his infancy which in this climate and under the influence of the warm weather in summer continued to increase on him until the spring of 1820, when I placed him in a private seminary at Elizabeth Town N. Jersey under the Rev. Mr. Rudd — [I did] this in the hope that a more northern climate where the weather was more settled and the winter steadily cold than with us could have a tendency to invigorate his constitution and relieve him from the inconveniences induced by the debility of his muscular powers. He remained with Mr. Rudd for three years and a half; and returned home in Novr last. The weakness of which I have spoken, appears in some degree to have reached his mental powers — for although his understanding in general is good & his memory acute and retentive, his mind appears on some points to be feeble, particularly in its efforts to combine numbers — on other subjects his proficiency under Mr. Rudd was perhaps as much as there was reason to expect — but he has almost totally failed in his application to Arithmetic. . . . He is amiable in his disposition, mild of temper docile & obedient, affectionate, and of morals most pure — in short I know no defect in his character, which is susceptible of self-remedy.

This carefully composed summary by Duncan Cameron of his son's deficiency was probably as much a protection for his own feelings as it was an attempt to provide the facts. Certainly there was no failure of comprehension on his part, as his will clearly shows: he left no property to Thomas outright. Paul, his sister Margaret, and Paul's wife Anne were appointed Thomas's trustees to handle his sizable inheritance.[65] His uncle Thomas Bennehan left him nothing at all.

Thomas spent his long life perfectly at liberty to come and go though he never handled any of his own business. He liked to read and he liked to oversee the plantation work on his horse from dawn to dusk with the workers in the fields. For a while he was postmaster at Stagville (1827–1830) but failed to make any returns to the government, for which failure the office was closed. The Camerons had the office re-established and Thomas replaced.[66]

Thomas was sociable and had friends among the neighbors whom he visited; he was a confirmed Whig, never missing an election. He lived most of the time at Fairntosh, but after Duncan Cameron and his family moved to Raleigh, he divided his time between the Raleigh household and Paul's family at Fairntosh, commuting between them on horseback. On one such ride he was shot by an unknown assailant from the woods, probably with the intent of robbery, but Thomas clung to the startled horse, which took flight and escaped. As a result he lost the sight in one eye and received shoulder and face wounds on the left side and in his right hand (he was eating wild grapes as he rode.)[67] Thomas was very fond of Paul's wife and children, who loved him in return. After Paul and his family moved to Hillsborough to live, Thomas made his home in Raleigh with his sisters. He died in 1870 of typhoid pneumonia at sixty-four years of age.

The great blow to the family hopes which Thomas's mental retardation represented probably shaped Paul's character as well as his destiny.[68] He was bright and intelligent, and because he venerated his father, accepted the role thrust on him and responded to its demands in the way his nature dictated — with every nerve and muscle. Duncan Cameron well understood the boy he was dealing with. "The best soil is rendered more productive by good cultivation," he told the planter-to-be, urging him to study harder. He also told him what to study. "I would recommend to you to cultivate composition and declamation — that is, to acquire the faculty of expressing your thoughts in writing, or by speaking, with ease, perspicacity and neatness and elegance — these acquirements will be highly useful to you through life."[69]

Whether or not they were useful to him Paul certainly found his father's advice congenial and later earned a reputation as a speaker, though his life offered little opportunity for practice, and wrote extraordinarily attractive letters in which his character and personality in all their colors are frankly revealed. Unlike his father, he found in words an outlet for his feelings and wrote and spoke with intensity and individuality.

After his false start at the university Paul was given more schooling and sent to Patridge's Academy with his brother in 1825.[70] After a year there he entered Washington College (later Trinity) in Hartford, Connecticut, where he completed the course in 1829. At both places his hot temper again got him temporarily suspended for fighting.[71] Derogatory remarks about the South had aroused his anger and led to one of the altercations. This attack resulted in a lawsuit which was finally settled out of court. For the junior exhibition in April 1828, Paul gave a eulogy on Lord Byron.[72]

For his graduation from college his Uncle Thomas Bennehan travelled up to Hartford and heard him deliver an oration, "English Travellers in America," and saw him receive his diploma.[73] But Paul's education was still not complete. He was set to reading law under his father's guidance. A letter from Paul to his sister hints that he found the subject somewhat less than absorbing. "Thursday last was quite a spring like day, and the larks seated upon their thrones in the forest-tops caroled forth their sweet notes, while the negroes in the 'cotton field' as if moved by a sympathetick emotion, gave their voices to the harmony of mingled sounds. And I, did what! Withal did sing an Elegy, to the memory of the 'Triune' of Blackstone, Lord Coke, and Cruise."[74]

Paul became licensed as a lawyer, was admitted to the bar, but was never happy in his profession.[75] His formal education was ended, but in the field where his true interest lay, Paul had not yet begun to learn.

His sons may not have been the most trying of Duncan Cameron's domestic troubles. About the time his sons were finished with schooling, his daughters, who had survived the perilous diseases of childhood, began more and more to complain of their health. In the 1830s the family letters teem with their symptoms: loss of appetite, digestive ailments, cough, headaches, neuralgia, and toothaches. Possibly their confined life at Fairntosh, though happy, serene, and uneventful, lacked social diversion and mental nourishment. Like their mother in their passive acceptance of life, they were pious, devoted to one another, dependent and doting on their father, overprotected and unnaturally timid. A letter from Anne Owen to her father in Raleigh is full of the affection they all felt for him. To his complaint in a letter of being homesick, she replied, "we are father-sick."[76] One or two vacations at medicinal springs temporarily improved their health and quite restored Rebecca, the one most ailing, for a while, but a tubercular tendency was already present. The move to Raleigh in 1836 to their new, comfortable, and handsome home may have been too much of a wrench for their delicate balance. Immediately one or another of them began again to ail, and little more than a year later Jean Syme, not quite twenty-two years old, died at Red Sulphur Springs then in Virginia.[77] Two years later both Mary Anne, then thirty-five, and Rebecca, twenty-six, died in Raleigh, two months apart. The Camerons made a desperate effort to save Anne Owen by travelling south in the fall and winter of 1839-40.[78] They spent time in Charleston, Savannah, and St. Augustine, seeking warmth and a miracle. After begging to be taken home, Anne Owen died in Raleigh in March 1840 twenty-two years old.[79]

Mildred Coles, the youngest, had been threatened, too, by the tuberculosis that killed her sisters, but the travel succeeded for her and she returned home restored to health, though not for long. The events of those harassing years must have weakened her in some other way; in 1844, in the spring after her mother's death, she suddenly began to suffer from attacks of muscle spasm and nervous excitement which continued to increase after periods of remission until she became completely infirm, unable to walk, emaciated, weak, and resigned to her lot. Repeated treatment year after year in Philadelphia, and once in Brooklyn, New York, produced only short-term improvement. An exhaustive medical report by Dr. Louis Bauer of the Brooklyn Orthopedic Institute gives many details of her life and that of her immediate family, but finds no single cause for what was always diagnosed as a spinal affliction, hysteria having been ruled out.[80] She died after thirty-five years an invalid.

Of the six sisters only Margaret Bain Cameron, named for her Scottish great-grandmother, lived anything approaching a normal life. Apparently always strong and unaffected by the illnesses her sisters suffered, she married George W. Mordecai late in life after her father's death in 1853 and a year later gave birth to a stillborn child, almost losing her own life in its delivery. Generous to all, including herself, she seems to have been the only child of Duncan Cameron able to enjoy the wealth he accumulated. After her mother's death she efficiently managed the Raleigh household to everyone's comfort, sheltering and mothering a host of nieces and nephews as well whom Cameron generosity brought to school in Raleigh. Year after year she left her husband to take Mildred to Philadelphia for extended medical treatment, never giving up hope that her sister's condition might be cured. The mainstay of her father, her husband, her brother Thomas, and her sister Mildred, she outlived them all. She died in 1886 of a heart condition at the age of seventy-five.

If the move to Raleigh in 1836 was disastrous for his daughters, for Duncan Cameron it meant salvation, for his mind desperately needed congenial employment. Though outwardly strong, invulnerable, and eminently successful, he was prey to his own restlessness. Previous long years of overwork, the burden of his son's retardation, and his brothers' and sisters' pecuniary plight — their needs always exceeded their resources — probably contributed to a mental crisis he suffered in 1823 that manifested itself in depression, emotional distress, and circulatory symptoms. His great friend Dr. James Webb wrote Thomas Bennehan of his consternation at Cameron's condition. "I recommend to him to unbosom himself to some divine and to seek consolation in Religion."[81] Duncan Cameron had confided his state to Webb, telling him of his intention to see the Reverend William Mercer Green, but Webb feared that Green was too young and of insufficient weight of character to console a man of such strength of intellect, age, and standing in the community.

His suffering seems to have moderated though it did not entirely disappear, becoming more or less chronic. Three years later a family friend, Dr. Lueco Mitchell, wrote Duncan Cameron his opinion of his case, describing it as a "morbid sensability of the brain itself inviting an unusual determination of blood to that organ." He advised Cameron to avoid all causes of excitement to mind or body. He recommended blistering of the thighs and legs, cold applications to the head, and a very restricted diet.[82]

Another friend, John D. Hawkins, who visited him in the summer of 1826 and witnessed his state, wrote to Cameron a long, explicit review of his own experience with tobacco, urging his friend to relinquish its use immediately as the cause of his illness. He enumerated the symptoms smoking or chewing tobacco had produced in himself: cough, bloody expectoration, narcotic and stimulant effects, prostration, sweating; "And dont you remember you offered me your hands when I was at your House to feel if one was not colder than the other? My dear Sir, it has often produced that with me."[83]

Another crisis occurred in 1833. This time Lueco Mitchell wrote to Bennehan that he had heard that their friend had become a melancholy hypochondriac. "He should find employment for his mind out of his family. I said when he became President of the Bank [in 1829] it would add 10 years to his life & was sorry he resigned."[84] Paul Cameron wrote frankly to his father-in-law, Thomas Ruffin, describing his father's condition; he contrasted the usual energetic and sanguine cast of his father's mind with the severe nervous derangement his father currently displayed which for a few days had even threatened to become a true melancholia. Paul attributed the condition to his father's strenuous but vain efforts in the previous year to save many of his Person County slaves from the disease which was ravaging the plantations there and to the continued deterioration of his daughter Rebecca's health. Paul was apparently unaware of his father's previous attacks.[85]

Possibly it is worth noting that all three of the episodes occurred in July of three different years, a time of oppressive heat, much plantation work, and worry about weather conditions that could make or destroy the year's crops and food supply for the entire plantation population. It is probably fair to conclude, since Duncan Cameron endured a series of strokes, that he suffered for many years from high blood pressure and its symptoms and a consequent depression of spirits and neurotic concern for his health.[86] It also seems clear that his obsession with work was more a means to sanity than to solvency. Hard work served to keep the neurotic tendency at bay, a tendency that idleness and domestic concerns exacerbated. This need of distraction explains his reluctance to stay at home and lead the retired life of a planter. When he followed that course he became distraught. The bank presidency was obviously his salvation. As Paul Cameron put it to Thomas Ruffin: "He wants mental labour for I think that I may with much truth and equal phylosophy remark that the year spent by him in Raleigh as President of the Bank was more beneficial to him than gallons of the most approved Panacea."[87]

Although the quarter century spent at Fairntosh seems in summary a depressing saga, the Camerons' memories of it were quite otherwise. Duncan's daughter Anne on a visit to Fairntosh after the family move to Raleigh wrote to her sister Mildred, "I went out this evening to see Sister Anne [Paul's wife] give out the work; it made me think of *old times*. Mildred, I did not think old Fairntosh held so large a place in my heart & I feel with dearest Mother that those were *happy, happy* days when we were all here together."[88]

6. Paul Cameron at Fairntosh

Events in the 1830s decided Paul's future (and that of Fairntosh, as is apparent in hindsight). He had dutifully read law after graduation from college, but as the time drew near to establish himself in practice, he was beset with doubts. In 1830 he fell in love with Anne Ruffin, a daughter of Thomas Ruffin, who like Duncan Cameron had left his native Virginia after studying law to settle in Hillsborough; there Ruffin, again like Duncan Cameron, had married the daughter of a merchant, William Kirkland, who had come there in 1790 to establish a business.

Duncan Cameron voiced no objections to Paul's choice, but he did think Paul too immature and professionally unsettled for so decisive a step as marriage. Paul was admitted to the bar, however, in March of 1832 and was allowed to marry in December of that year.[1] For over a year the young couple lived at Fairntosh while Paul debated what he would do. To Thomas Ruffin he openly confessed,

> I am still upon the horns of doubt and uncertainty as to my location. In truth I know not what to do. My father still urges me to locate in Hillsborough with no other object in view, but the prosecution of my profession. To this my judgment and inclination are alike opposed. . . . What in the present state of the profession am I to hope by a location in that place? What I to envy in the condition of those Gentlemen of the Bar who are now residents in our country town: and I have not the presumption to hope that I can do better than they have done. Besides to be honest and frank . . . I have ever honestly doubted my ability to advance in my profession beyond common mediocrity.[2]

He toyed with the idea of moving to the Deep South to become a planter there. To his wife's pleas for a hut of her own rather than the palace of anyone else, and to his father's urgings that he practice law in Hillsborough, he finally acceded.[3] He bought from Thomas Ruffin a few acres of a large tract of land just east of the Hillsborough town limit where Ruffin had lived before moving in 1828 to the Hermitage on Haw River, the former home of Archibald Murphey. When Paul was putting into repair the cottage already built there by William Cain, it caught fire and burned to the ground.[4] He was obliged to build from scratch a house of his own which very many years later he would greatly enlarge and improve. Burnside, as he called the completed house, was his first taste of construction.[5]

He and Anne lived at Burnside for at most two years while he diligently worked at the law. In an undated letter to his mother about this time, Paul revealed his state of mind: "No fees — and what is worse I expect none, this is a most miserable *trade* that I have taken up — or should better say that I have been *put at*."[6]

As the son of an outstandingly successful and imposing father, Paul felt a sense of inferiority and a desire to avoid the arenas in which his father's example could be used as a measuring stick for his own real or imagined inadequacies. Consequently he wanted to avoid both the law and public affairs. His reluctance for the latter he rationalized at that time: "I thank God, that I am free from what I esteem the greatest curse of the times, a thirst for office — of any sort."[7] In his old age he felt the same aversion, but time and observation had enabled him to externalize his repugnance with ironic humor: "I have observed," he was quoted as saying, "that when a man fails to take care of himself and family, he generally considers himself well qualified to manage the community."[8]

In 1837 Paul Cameron resigned from the bar and moved back to Fairntosh. He sold his house in Hillsborough to Cadwallader Jones, Jr., and turned his attention to what he really wanted to do — become a planter.[9] Here was a field in which his father had shown little interest. No family letters recount what led to this outcome or what reconciled Duncan Cameron to Paul's wishes. Possibly the family's move to Raleigh, which made Fairntosh available to Paul and Anne as a home of their own, was a first consideration. Possibly the loneliness of Thomas Bennehan and the size of the burden placed on him in superintending the entire plantation complex played a part. Thomas Bennehan had written to Paul's wife of the family's departure, "They all left poor Farentosh yesterday morning accompanied by Paul & Thomas for their new home, with I believe aching head's & heart's. . . . to me it has been a most severe tryal. I seam to be almost in the midst of a dreary solitude."[10] Perhaps also the fast deteriorating health of his daughters softened Duncan Cameron's heart toward his unhappy son. Whatever the reasons behind the change, in 1837 Paul and Anne took up their abode at Fairntosh and made it their home for the next twenty-three years.

Changes of many kinds had affected the plantations since Paul's childhood. It was impossible for him and Anne to duplicate exactly the pattern of Duncan Cameron and his family life at Fairntosh; the differences in them, too, dictated change. The area was no longer a frontier. The slow but continuous growth of towns and the concentration in them of all kinds of activity were changing the way men lived.[11] Raleigh as the seat of the state government was becoming a magnet for trade, the new railroad, and cultural and social affairs. Professional men and others who could afford it preferred to live in towns which offered all kinds of advantages and conveniences. Social lines hardened and differences became more marked.[12]

All the land had long since been taken up, and intense cultivation by the small farmers who made up the bulk of the population, ignorant or careless of the restorative practices of fertilizing and crop rotation, had impoverished the land's productivity.[13] Each year produced slimmer crops; this, combined with a national depression in the early decades of the nineteenth century, had caused an exodus of ambitious younger men; the sons of the old residents migrated south and west.[14] The Bennehan-Cameron plantations had swallowed up more and more of their lands and lay at last in splendid isolation. The Stagville store, once the cornerstone of the Bennehan wealth, was closed; country stores were no longer the moneymakers they had once been. Trade was centered in towns.[15]

Hillsborough, which had been so stimulating and professionally enriching for Duncan Cameron, had also changed. It had become a backwater when the tide of affairs and opportunity receded. Paul Cameron thus saw the town with very different eyes: "I don't wonder that the people of Hillsborough should be sick for it is certainly one [of] if not the very dirtiest [of the] villages in all the county. To say nothing of the decayed condition of the buildings."[16] At the same time new changes were taking place, and within the next twenty years the little town would regain some of its former prosperity after a period of stagnation.

Private schools were opening in many towns; people were beginning to reject illiteracy and ignorance, and cultural aridity was giving way to new efforts to improve the quality of life — changes in attitude soon to be reflected in legislation that instituted common (public) schools in 1839.[17] But the establishment of public schools, made private teachers harder to obtain. Governesses were going out of fashion. The teachers, too, were finding opportunity and better working conditions in the towns. Paul Cameron was to find it more and more difficult to educate his children at home.

Despite these changes, plantation life in general in the South was reaching its apogee. Plantation houses were being built larger, architecturally more imposing and elegant, with an eye inside and out to comfort and beauty. No longer required to tame a frontier, the planter was reaping the profits of greatly increased acreage under cultivation worked by a greatly increased slave force. Improvements in agricultural practices for wide-awake planters were beginning to result in increased production. Rich, new lands were opening in the Deep South where planters could invest surplus money and slaves for even greater returns. A country settled at last after a long period of peace was turning its attention to personal cultivation and enrichment.[18]

Though all these changes were to affect the life of Anne and Paul Cameron at Fairntosh, superficially it seemed to proceed unchanged. In Hillsborough, their domestic life had had its troubles. Anne's first two children had been stillborn.[19] Only in 1838 after the move to Fairntosh when she had a living daughter followed by another in 1840 did that particular problem seem to be solved. The years added eight more children between 1842 and 1856, when a second Mildred Coles completed the family.

Paul had already had a taste of farming, the real business of his life, before the move to Fairntosh. Both his father and uncle had given him plantations in Person and Orange counties as gifts at the start of his professional life.[20] These he supervised from his Hillsborough base, but their real management had been done by an overseer. When Paul could give his full attention to the subject, he brought to the job his usual energy and ambition, but his action was circumscribed by the long established practices of his father and his overseers. Still he read and thought and observed, preparing himself to be the scientific farmer he eventually became. Thomas Bennehan's death in 1847, which gave Stagville and Little River plantations to Paul outright, and his father's death in 1853, which added Fairntosh and its ancillary plantations, finally allowed Paul the scope to experiment, innovate, and change. He worked with enormous energy, conscientiousness, and skill, superintending all that went on, never resting from his work, and finding in it all a satisfaction and sense of accomplishment his father had never known there. He was always sensitive to the beauty of nature wild, but he found even more to admire in nature tamed and cultivated and cared for. Emotionally tied to the land through its long association with his forefathers and as the scene of his own happy youth, Paul Cameron came into his own and the fulfillment of his instincts and powers during his years at Fairntosh.

Soon after he began his work there he wrote to his mother, "It would do eyes good . . . to see our large wheat fields spreading themselves out, like the extended rich green, and untrodden savannas and prairies of the sunny south. Come up my good Mother and see them: you have nothing about Raleigh half so interesting to the eye: no, not your Dome crowned capitol!"[21] This reference to another achievement of his father, who had headed the committee that hired Town and Davis, leading architects in the nation, to design the exceptionally fine state capitol, was to point up his own preference for rural delights and to separate himself from his father's interests.[22]

The beauty Paul was creating was of another sort; he and Anne became interested in horticulture. For Duncan and Rebecca Cameron the task had been to impose order on a wilderness, make clearings in a forest, cut away the underbrush, keep back the jungle of undergrowth. Rebecca had set out a few calycanthus bushes a sister-in-law had sent her, some trees from Amelia Alves, a rose bush from another relation, a small garden with the family favorite, early peas.[23] Landscaping in the earliest days of Fairntosh had meant retaining some of the fine groves of trees around the house and chapel. But twenty-five years had accomplished the transition from forest to home place. Paul and Anne Cameron could become intensely interested in gardening and landscaping. Thomas Ruffin probably was largely responsible for encouraging their interest as he was for supplying many of the trees and plants that adorned Fairntosh. His specialty was orchards, an enthusiasm he easily communicated to Paul. In 1843 Paul planted an apple orchard at Snow Hill and a peach orchard the following year at Fairntosh.[24] Anne was actively involved too. When Paul was in Alabama in 1845 overseeing a new plantation he had established there, his sister wrote him, "Sister Anne has commenced gardening — and has Jem and Demps very busy in the front yard making a cedar hedge from either side of the piazza down to the enclosure around the grove — if they live they will look very pretty."[25] A few years later Anne wrote, "I wish when you have time you would have that tall China tree taken up and set out before the kitchen door, opposite the mimosa. Suppose you try and get some good large holly trees and plant between the greenhouse and kitchen; I think if they were taken up sometime when the ground was frozen, without disturbing the roots, they would live; and they would be the most effectual screen I know of, as well as an ornament."[26]

Thomas Ruffin sent her a tree she had long wished for, an orange tree.[27] He also sent peach, plum, cherry, and evergreen trees both from the nursery of Joshua Lindley, then in Greensboro, and from his own stock.[28] The same year, 1854, Annie Cameron wrote her father, "Mother is busy about the garden and front yard, where she has been framing her roses, and doing up her borders; the flowers in the greenhouse are blooming beautifully."[29]

A remarkable gesture of Thomas Ruffin occurred in 1863 when war was raging and retrenchment rather than expansion was the order of the day. He sent his grandson young Duncan Cameron, still a schoolboy, trees for an apple orchard for Fairntosh. His letter to Paul that accompanied the 557 trees of nineteen varieties showed his spirit and resolve that life must go on unchanged whatever the war brought:

> I hope it [the orchard] will thrive & afford him through a long life the comfort of good fruit for summer, autumn, & winter, & thus repay him for the planting, the pruning, the manuring & other care of it. On such a plantation as you will give him, with the number of negroes belonging to it & surrounding it, an orchard of only this number of trees will afford but slight security for his enjoying much of the fruit. *That* cannot be relied on, I suppose, with less than a *thousand* trees; and I rather think my nurseries will enable me to make up that number by another year tho' the trees are now too small to be raised. If I live, I shall with much pleasure endeavor to do so — I have only to say further to him, that he is not the boy I have taken him to be, if he does not go down with the trees &, if it can be done during his vacation, superintend the setting out of every young tree, or, at least, see how Mr. Piper does it: so that years hence he may look back with satisfaction to the rearing of his orchard as mostly *his own* work. That will be the great satisfaction to us all — Say to Master Bennehan,

that he must not be out of heart; for in due season, *his* orchard shall be forth coming too. As soon as the ground gets in order, I shall sow the *seed* for a new nursery *for his use* of exactly the same size & kind as his brothers, & I hope he will strive & with success to have one equal to Duncans."[30]

True to his word, the following year Thomas Ruffin sent the remaining trees to make up the thousand.[31]

Inside the Fairntosh house there were changes too. Duncan Cameron had furnished it with care but as frugally as possible. An undated list in his handwriting probably describes the earliest furnishings at Fairntosh.[32] It includes a mahogany sideboard, three beds and bedsteads, a child's bed, a crib, a set of dining tables with ends, a black walnut chest of drawers, a pine press, two carpets, one dozen chairs, and a lady's easy chair. The latter had been ordered from Petersburg in 1808.[33] In 1813 more bedsteads were also ordered from Petersburg.[34] In 1816, when Duncan Cameron's brother John was in England with his dying wife, he bought for Fairntosh glass bowls, casters, salt cellars, plate, and a piano.[35] Another piano was ordered from London two years later.[36] A bill for tuning these instruments sent by John Pike, the music master, describes them as a grand pianoforte and a square pianoforte.[37]

In 1821 Duncan Cameron bought an eight-day clock for $100 from the Raleigh firm of John G. Savage, and in 1822 yet another piano from Thomas and Robert Dunn of Petersburg.[38] May of 1830 brought a bill for four stained gumwood bedsteads with sacking bottoms, a set of mahogany dining tables, and two breakfast tables.[39] Possibly this furniture was bought for the family's sojourn in Raleigh in 1829, but it probably was taken to Fairntosh when they returned home the following year. In 1834 Cameron bought matting for the dining room floor. "I send you a piece of matting 1 1/4 yds wide 24 yds long," Cameron wrote to his wife from Raleigh; "it will make 4 breadths for your dining room — but will not cover the entire width of the room — a space on each side occupied by the sideboard and chairs will remain uncovered. I send tacks to put it down with — The pieces must be set down edge by edge — Jack Staples can do it very neatly."[40] Though possibly some of this furniture was moved to the new house in Raleigh after that was built, Duncan Cameron did buy a great deal of new furnishings for the new house, and probably left most of the Fairntosh furnishings intact.[41]

Meanwhile, Paul Cameron had been trying to assemble furniture for his cottage in Hillsborough as cheaply as he could.[42] Possibly some of this went with him to Fairntosh in 1837. In 1845 Duncan Cameron bought and sent to Fairntosh a sofa and a dozen mahogany chairs with hair bottoms, "as a present for dear Anne, which I desire her to accept for her parlour."[43] Paul afterwards bought two violins, two flutes, a banjo, and in 1850 added another piano. "I hope to have some good music at our lonely home in

Orange," he explained.[44] In 1853 the young Camerons were still trying to cover their floors; Paul ordered thirty-eight yards of matting and one good rug for Anne's parlor and sitting room.[45] Despite the quality of the woodwork and the furniture at Fairntosh in those days, the decoration would probably strike today's visitor as spartan. The walls were whitewashed if they were not panelled, and many of the floors were bare. Ornaments were few and the large rooms only sparsely furnished.

For the first ten years of Paul's life as a planter he could count on his uncle Thomas Bennehan's good advice and company and soothing presence through good times and bad. It was therefore understandably crushing for him when his uncle died in 1847. They had nursed the slaves together through many hard illnesses; they had ridden over the fields to inspect the planting and harvesting; they had suffered the damaging freshets that each year required repairs to the mills and milldams on the Eno River. They had enjoyed tax collectings, political hustings, auctions, and election days together. When his uncle's failing health took him away from Stagville in 1845, Paul wrote to his father, "Never have I felt the absence of my uncle so much from his Home — perhaps no man was ever more *sad* than I have been during the last week in riding out here and seeing no one to whom I could say 'We are brothers in blood.' The *only* one *here* of so many dear ones! God help us what a world of change!"[46] Two years later Thomas Bennehan's death stirred him deeply and continued to grieve him a long time. "I am very lonely here — the only one — of our once large and united family — here in the midst of the memory of the past — my very loneliness only makes every recollection the brighter — The very ride that I made yesterday along my uncles paths — now nearly a year since I gave up one who I shall ever regard as both father & friend — all make me feel very *sad*.[47]

At mid-century Paul Cameron was feeling more at ease psychologically and financially. He loved his work and recognized by its results his own capability. A son had finally been born to him in 1846 after four living daughters, and though this beloved child died in 1848, another boy arrived in 1850, large and robust and also named Duncan. In announcing young Duncan's birth to the elder, Paul wrote of his daughters' delight and added, "The word brother on their lips has opened a fresh, a long pent up grief for one that I loved perhaps too much; and I weep now — as I write — for that dear boy. Not a day has he ever escaped my memory!"[48] In these years William Garl Browne's portrait of the elder Duncan was brought to Fairntosh and hung over the mantel in the parlor; Paul told his father how the young Duncan stood below it babbling to his grandfather.[49] He then commissioned portraits of his two sisters and of himself and Anne. He found a roll of engravings among his uncle's possessions and these he had framed and hung as well.[50] The walls of Fairntosh were at last suitably clothed.

Pictures of another kind he supplied himself. He was happy and contented with his domestic life. In letters to his father and sisters he described the small details of their daily life with humor, delight, and pride.

> Anne & the children all keep *well:* & whilst the Mother is fully occupied with her household Matters: the elder little ones with their books betake themselves to the office & devote themselves diligently to their lessons — They seem very much pleased with the office as their study: and for a short time will continue to be pleased & to use it. Rebecca is making very handsome progress with her Geography — which seems better suited to her taste & fancy than saying 6 & 3 are 9 — or 7 & 3 are 10! This was the case with myself. In four months from this time she will have a pretty good knowledge of the surface of the world & will make both Mother & Father better Geographers. It will be a hard race between Anne and Mary but I think Anne will keep her distance just a little a'head. Her acquisitions are not rapid — but she holds what she gets. Her stock of Pigs & fowls occupy her thoughts to her disadvantage. But she enjoys her pets to such a degree & treats them with so much consideration that no one is inclined to shorten her pleasures. Mary learns quick — & like the prodigal who gets easily — lets it go as easily. After a while she will exhibit better powers of retention: she is capable of a very high degree of cultivation.
>
> Maggie & her maid & I may say her Shaddow pass the day on "a see-saw" in the yard — & at night like her grandfather is first off to bed — but unlike him in the morning — she enjoys her bed to the last — & after she is washed looks like a new bloom bursting into flower & glittering with dew. The little boy in the arms of his faithful Nurse delights himself out of doors under the shade of a wide hat — grows daily — & should He live will like his grandfather be a "six footer." You will say this is quite a family picture & a little flattered — but how could it be otherwise with the father for the painter & with *such subjects.*[51]

A general renovation of all the structures went on during the 1840s and 1850s. At Fairntosh the house and outbuildings were reroofed by William Lougee, who was astonished to find in what good condition the main house still was. "We find the sheeting on the house in fine condition and the shingles not much hurt. Lougee says *this House* was built on 'Honor!' That 'people had not then learnt how to cheat,'" Paul wrote to his father.[52] "We have to put an entire new set of sills under the front piazza as we find the old ones perfectly rotten — we have had to re-shingle the kitchen — & we are now covering the weaving House with excellent Shingles from the dwelling house — If the Tin Roof lasts as well & keeps us as dry as the *old Roof,* which in truth was *built* on *Honor:* we shall be very fortunate. . . . I am tired of the noise & dirt about us — & Anne is quite as tired of her boarders: 4 tin smiths & 2 painters!"[53] William Overby was repainting all the buildings.[54]

The greenhouse, probably an addition of the 1840s, and a portico added to the old office, were painted at the same time.[55] All these improvements accomplished and others still in contemplation made Paul feel sanguine.

He wrote in this mood, "after a while I shall have all matters here in a mighty nice fix — If then I had a good soil & good neighbors & in 10 miles of a T iron rail road I should smoke a Principe & take a glass of the Rich mans wine daily."[56]

The next decade saw improvements on the other plantations as well. Paul probably oversaw the building in 1851 of the unusually well-constructed slave houses standing today at Horton Grove, then becoming the center of farming operations for Stagville. They are important for their size and method of construction. Duncan Cameron's predilection for brick nogging in the walls of frame buildings is most fully demonstrated in them. A remark of Paul's in a letter to his father probably refers to them and thereby dates them. "I think it would be well to get some one else to calculate the quantity of brick in the walls of the houses," he wrote, "for it seems to me to be too much — tho it may be a correct estimate."[57] Each of these slave houses contains four rooms, two on each floor, each room almost seventeen feet square, each pair separated by a passage four feet wide. A stairway ascends from the passage on the first floor. The houses are built on high pilings which raise the wooden floors well above the ground. The walls with their brick fill are covered on the outside by board and batten siding and the roofs are tin. A chimney at each end provided a fireplace in each room (some chimneys are now removed). The interior walls were whitewashed.[58]

That these houses were built on Duncan Cameron's design there can be little doubt. In 1850 he drew a floor plan for tenements he was then constructing in Raleigh on the Bennehan Square which his daughter Margaret had inherited from Thomas Bennehan.[59] This plan shows exactly the same room layout as that in the Horton Grove houses except that the rooms are slightly larger, eighteen by twenty feet. The Raleigh houses were to have brick foundations rather than stone pilings, slightly wider hallways, and interior chimneys. No mention was made of brick nogging for them.

Brick was again being made at Fairntosh to supply all these building needs. The work went so well and so much brick was made that Paul thought it would amply supply them not only for the present but for all the years that would follow as well.[60]

Paul's most spectacular addition to the plantations, and possibly the only structure he built there entirely on his own plan, is the great barn at Horton Grove. That the plan and execution were his alone is certain, for Duncan Cameron died in 1853 and the barn was not built until 1860, the last building built on the plantation with slave labor. In March of 1860 W. F. Vestal, who became the overseer Samuel Piper's son-in-law and performed a variety of functions from miller to overseer, was then hauling the timbers and hewing them for the barn.[61] By September it was almost finished. Paul wrote of it proudly to Thomas Ruffin, "I have a great wish to show you the 'best stables' ever built in Orange (at Stagville) 135 feet long covered with cypress shingles at a cost of $6 per thousand."[62] He added, "This is Bennehan's affair — our boy." Obviously Bennehan Cameron, Paul's second son, was already manifesting the passion for horses that later characterized his own proprietorship of the plantation.

Paul Cameron could rightly feel pride in the structure. It stands today 135 feet long, just as he described it, and 33 feet wide. Its tri-part construction consists of a double-storied central section flanked by one-storey wings all painted white and covered with tin roofs, the central one hipped. Faced in board and batten siding, the whole is supported on a rock foundation. Two double doors opposite each other in the east and west long sides give access to the main block, which is divided by a spacious passage. This passage is intersected in the exact middle of the building by a long, narrow aisle which bisects the entire length of the barn. This structure served as stables, dairy, and storage for Stagville Plantation through the rest of its Cameron tenancy.

Paul's appetite for construction, whetted by the building of the cottage in Hillsborough, grew with the Fairntosh renovations and the slave houses at Horton Grove and found its first full gratification in the early 1850s when he contracted to build several sections of the new North Carolina Railroad then being constructed across the state from east to west.[63] He hired as superintendent for the job Robert Moore, who had long worked for Thomas Ruffin as overseer and in other capacities and possibly for Archibald Murphey before that.[64] Paul undertook to supply the materials and labor, the latter many of his own slaves, to set them up in encampments along the new railroad bed, and to keep them supplied with all their daily needs. In his usual style he worked them all to capacity and completed his sections, which lay just east of Hillsborough, in record time.[65] Durability and utility were ever his aims in whatever he built, and all the houses he later worked on for himself and his children display these qualities.

A tireless letter writer, Paul Cameron wrote to his family throughout his adult life long, detailed, and candid letters, "perfect family newspapers" he called them.[66] His letters are principally responsible for the coherent and comprehensive view of life on the plantations which the Cameron papers present. To his father he wrote fully, factually, and devotedly; to his sisters more playfully and humorously. To his father-in-law, too, he was equally devoted, and as a result the Ruffin family papers contain dozens of Paul's letters which fill in gaps or missing details in the Cameron letters. To Ruffin he could be franker and often was.

From all their letters the illness and death of Duncan Cameron comes through as one of the most important and emotionally trying events of these years. As noted before, Duncan Cameron suffered a few strokes which left him with progressively more severe paralysis before he died on 3

January 1853 of heart failure.[67] A friend's son wrote to Ruffin commenting on Cameron's death: "The family afflictions with which for many years he has been visited, seem to have perfected his Christian character and prepared him for what he long and patiently awaited, a peaceful end."[68] Thomas Ruffin, because of his long friendship with Cameron and the family alliance which gave them the same grandchildren, could speak for both friends and family in summing up Duncan Cameron's life.

> I have a large debt of friendship and gratitude to Mr. Cameron, which I would most gladly avail myself of any opportunity of saying to him or his. There are few men, if any, to whose beneficent regards and actual deed of kindness and consideration I owe more than to this excellent gentleman: who, indeed, has been largely the benefactor of a numerous kindred, besides his immediate family, and a still more numerous circle of unconnected friends, and also a most upright, active, intelligent, and successful depository of various and important public trusts.[69]

The death of his father of course affected Paul Cameron more deeply than any one else. Up to that time his life had been spent trying to win his approbation, trying to prove himself worthy of such a father. He had also leaned on him heavily, as he said himself, at the same time struggling to free himself of that dependence, psychological as well as financial. His confession to his sisters probably soon after his father's death reflects Paul's feeling of loss of direction and stability. "I feel so desolate that I cannot bring my thoughts into any sort of frame."[70] And in another letter to Bishop William M. Green he said, "All the other losses that I have suffered seem as nothing and I feel like a helpless child or pauper turned out on the world with no one to lean upon."[71] When his world righted itself, however, he found within himself a self-sufficiency and independence which released at last his talent and power to become himself.

All went exceptionally well with Paul's work and the maintenance of the plantations in the 1850s, but two problems vexed him through the last decades of life at Fairntosh — the ill health of whites and blacks and his children's education.

The Camerons lost their daughter Jean, their first live child, in 1842, when she was four years of age, and their first son Duncan in 1848. The 1840s were ravaging years for disease. In 1848 particularly it was so widespread and so severe that the overseers threatened to leave, fearful for their lives and those of their families.[72] Paul Cameron's letters in these years describe in detail the sickness of the slaves and his own exhaustion in nursing them. For example, his letter of January 1842:

> I trust my dear father that the *Storm* has spent its fury! But not without having produced an impression upon us all not easily to be forgotten. I informed you of the death of Jim Boge, My sister Magy carried to you intelligence of the

death of Ann (a daughter of "Nelly" and as likely a young woman as could be selected from your large family of slaves) and I have now to report the death of a third — little Amy, at Eno — aged about 12 — a daughter of Willies and Jinneys. I have seen all the sick to day: a hard days work having to ride to all the Bridges, in consequence of the fresh in our water courses. The old cases are all decidedly better, with two exceptions — Easter at Bobbitts and Sarah at Fairntosh. In the cases that have occurred this week — the disease (called by Dr. Webb — Pneumonia Typhoides) — seems to have lost all of its malignity. We have had 5 cases in which the disease fixed itself upon the brain — 3 have terminated in death — 2 convalescing slowly. I have never counted the whole number that have been sick — but it will exceed 40 of which nearly one half occurred at Bobbitts.

It is all a riddle to me! Why it should be confined to our family! (Uncle has had a few cases at two of his plantations) What made it so violent in the out-set! And what so quickly changed its character! One observation I have made and more than once called to the attention of those who have been with me — is this — that the disease has been chiefly confined to the junior members of the family — and of that class who suffered most from the fall fever, and who made most of the Christmas Holiday in dancing and frolicking. Dr. Webb who left me on Monday — expressed the opinion that the violence of the disease was greatly aggravated by the sudden and extreme cold of the first days of last week especially of Wednesday and that we should regard the mild weather that has succeeded as the chief cause of its assuming its milder form. Of the new cases this week the most important is that of Henry (Weaver) who has undergone a vast deal of labour and lost much sleep in blistering and administering injections. I hope it will be a slight case. Ned, Willie and a large list all I hope doing well — In truth I feel no anxiety about the cases that have presented themselves this week. I must not forget to mention that Luke who for five days was regarded in much peril is doing very well, as is Ben, Mason, Prince, Bob, Tom, Nelson, and others. Nancy one of our house servants was sent out of the house on Sunday with a very sore throat. She has had fever, but is better. A number of cases have been accompanied with sore throat. And one of the most common and earliest symptoms complained of was *pain in the ear!* I can only assure you and my dear mother that all that I could do has been done to temper the storm, soften the suffering, and administer to the comfort of the sick. I have been more than touched by the expressions of gratitude, sincerely felt and made by the sick and well. I trust I may never witness the like again.[73]

Paul Cameron was particularly apprehensive, therefore, when he saw on the plantation a renewal of the epidemic in the middle 1850s. His daughter Mary Amis died in the summer of 1855; the life of her brother, the second young Duncan, hung in the balance while he endured over forty days of fever before he began to rally.[74] Shaken by his daughter's death and son's illness, Paul Cameron took action. He reacquired the Burnside property he had owned during the early years of his marriage and received from Thomas Ruffin the large tract of which it had once been a part, on the Eno

River just east of Hillsborough.[75] He set about enlarging the house and making it comfortable for his numerous family with the intention of using it as a summer home and escaping the fevers at Fairntosh. This was his solution to the first problem.

The other problem, the education of his children, led him eventually to the same solution but only after attempting other measures. When his older daughters were ready for schooling, Paul Cameron was able to engage the services of their old teacher, Miss Mary McClean Bryant. She seems to have been at Fairntosh once again in 1850 and 1851 and perhaps even earlier.[76] Her advanced age and poor health were probably the cause of her leaving in 1851. As her successor Paul Cameron engaged a Miss Kingsbury, who had been educated in Utica, New York, and was a niece of Theodore Kingsbury, the Oxford, North Carolina, journalist. She was paid $300 a year, exactly the wages of thirty years before when Miss Bryant had first come to Fairntosh.[77]

Miss Kingsbury lasted only a year, and in 1852 Paul Cameron was advertising for her replacement. In answer to one applicant he described the position in detail. Eight students, he explained, would be the maximum. (He was including Samuel Piper's daughters in this number.) They would range from sixteen to five years of age. Three or four of them would take music and two or three French.[78]

Karl Petersilia, whom Paul Cameron had engaged in 1849, had been supplying the girls lessons in music and singing.[79] In 1853 he was replaced by Captain Antonio Di Martino, a native of Naples, Italy, who taught both music and French and was still with the family in 1860 after their permanent move to Hillsborough.[80]

That Paul Cameron wished his daughters to learn French reflected a viewpoint very different from his father's as to the proper subject matter of female instruction. When Duncan Cameron's daughter Mary Anne had had an opportunity to take French lessons in Hillsborough in 1824, he had written her, "I am pleased to learn that you have no inclination to join a class for learning French — your time can be better and more profitably spent in cultivating a more extensive acquaintance with Books published in your Mother tongue — and I hope you will not think of attempting to learn such gibberish."[81] Paul Cameron's attitude, was, however, in line with his grandfather's. Richard Bennehan had urged his son Thomas when a student at the university to arrange for French lessons with W. L. Richards.[82]

Following Miss Kingsbury's departure, a Miss Brown, again a relative of an Oxford man (A. G. Brown) and a product of the female academy in that town, came to Fairntosh to teach the children.[83] Miss Brown was a complete success. Her success, however, recommended her to the attention of Dr. Aldert Smedes, the principal of St. Mary's School in Raleigh, who offered her a post in the school the very next year. She resisted the offer in

1853 but succumbed in 1856, no doubt finding the location of the school, the association of other teachers which it supplied, and the salary too attractive to refuse.[84]

With the departure of Miss Brown in 1856, the problem of his children's education again loomed for Paul. The birth of another child that year and the arrival at school age of the then oldest son heightened his concern. Besides the two teenage daughters, Rebecca and Anne, the children then included five others: Margaret, eight; Duncan, six; Pauline, three; Bennehan, two; and the infant Mildred Coles.

The solution to the problem of schooling, though not immediately arrived at, was ultimately the move to Hillsborough. From the time of Miss Brown's departure until the permanent move, however, information about the children's schooling is sketchy. The family letters had another concern. In February 1856 Rebecca developed St. Vitus's dance (chorea), a convulsive nervous affliction related to rheumatic fever and often followed by arthritis, as it was in Rebecca's case. She was particularly ill during the following winter, 1857, which the family spent in Hillsborough, and during which the younger children undoubtedly attended school there.[85] In the summer they travelled to northern resorts hoping to restore Rebecca's health, visiting Nahant, Massachusetts, Newport, Rhode Island, and Cape May, New Jersey.

In the fall and winter of 1857–1858 Anne was left with her aunts in Philadelphia, who were again there seeking treatment for Mildred's condition. Anne was sent to the school of Mary L. Bonney and Harriet A. Dillaye.[86] The rest of the family returned first to Burnside and then in November to Fairntosh, where they spent the winter. It was a miserable winter for them, for Paul and all the children at home contracted an eruptive disease, probably chicken pox, which made them sick for many days and left them debilitated and scratching for many weeks afterwards. The summer of 1858 they were again at Burnside. With this kind of shuttling around the schooling of the younger children was no doubt frequently interrupted and sporadic.

Still another event added to the disruption of any routine existence for the family. In 1856 Paul Cameron decided to enter politics. He was elected state senator from the 30th district in 1856 and served one term, 1856–1857.[87] The senate *Journal* for that year shows that he was appointed to the committee on banks and currency. He took an active role in the session by introducing various bills and seeing them through to enactment. They concerned the clerks of the Supreme Court, amendments to the Hillsborough charter, and exemption from taxation of North Carolina Railroad bonds. He asked to be excused from the committee to fix a rate of interest on the bonds, probably because of his conflict of interest in owning some of the bonds. He added an amendment to exempt harps and pianos belonging to public schools from the taxation of musical instruments.

He introduced various bills of incorporation as well. They were to incorporate the Shepard's Point Land Company, the Historical Society of the University of North Carolina, and the Hillsborough Savings Institution. He introduced a bill to prevent the felling of lumber into the Eno River and to prescribe the duties of public treasurer. Although all this legislation was of comparatively minor importance, Paul Cameron made his point of view felt in the work of that session. He was also elected one of the university trustees for the first time, posts filled annually by vote of the legislature.[88]

The experience was apparently sufficiently rewarding for Paul to decide to run for another term in the senate in 1858. This time he was defeated by Josiah Turner, Jr. Both Paul and his friends were convinced that Turner's victory was the result of a liberal dispensing of whiskey, a ploy Paul had been unwilling to resort to.[89]

When Paul Cameron returned to Fairntosh at the end of his term in government, his years on the plantations were drawing to a close. During the almost quarter of a century of his occupancy, agriculture in all its aspects had been paramount in his life. So central to his character was his role as a planter and so important to the lands entrusted to his care that special consideration must be given it.

An objective and keen observer who saw the plantations at their peak under Paul Cameron's care has left a description that reflects the powerful impression they made. Benson J. Lossing came through North Carolina in the winter of 1848 collecting information for his *Pictorial Field-Book of the Revolution* and recorded what he saw and learned:

> Between the Flat and Little Rivers and filling the whole extent of four miles, was the immense plantation of Mr. Cameron, a Scotch gentleman. This plantation extends parallel with the rivers, a distance of fifteen miles, and covers an area of about sixty square miles. It is well managed, and yields abundant crops of wheat, corn, oats, cotton, tobacco, potatoes, and other products of the Northern and Middle States. One thousand negroes were upon it, under the direction of several overseers. Its hills are crowded with fine timber, and I observed several large flocks of sheep and herds of cattle upon its slopes. It is probably the largest landed estate in the Carolinas, perhaps in the Union.[90]

Paul summed up in a letter to his son Bennehan his philosophy of land management, but it accurately described as well his stewardship of the family land: "It is industry & intelligent care with fortunate locality that make a property either beautiful to the eye or valuable as an estate."[91] He had made it both.

7. Working the Land

The state of agriculture in North Carolina in the mid-nineteenth century was little changed from what it had been throughout the colonial period.[1] Men farmed as their fathers had done before them or by instinct, as women raised children, with no special training or experience for the job. New agricultural knowledge and practical improvements did not sift down to the common farmer. Efforts were made by the more informed, singly or in groups, such as agricultural improvement societies, to instruct farmers in better methods of farming and to disseminate the latest knowledge, but with little impact on the overwhelmingly rural and often illiterate population.[2]

Neither Richard Bennehan in the eighteenth century nor Duncan Cameron in the nineteenth had had any training or experience for their roles as planters. They became planters because that was how men of wealth in their time and place lived. For the routines of farming they relied on their overseers, who in turn, as sons of farmers, relied on the practices of their fathers. The longer farmers had been in America the more slipshod and antiquated their methods became, cut off by their isolation and illiteracy from all sources of improvement. The new land with its richly productive soils contributed to their laxity; every man could count on an easy subsistence and bumper crops with a little knowledge and effort and cooperation from the weather.[3]

With time the constant reuse of the soils without conscientious fertilizing, crop rotation, and prevention of erosion resulted in diminished yields. After an area had been completely settled and no new land was left to clear, the average farmer's income began to decline, and eventually he could no longer live off the land he held. The solution for many was migration to newly opened lands to the south and west. This opportunity attracted young, ambitious men in the older regions. Left behind were the old or the complacent or those, like the Camerons, whose holdings were large enough to make up for the declining productivity of the land.[4]

This was precisely the situation in Orange County when Paul Cameron began his career as a planter. Because the vastness of the Cameron plantations still allowed for the clearing of new land and for continually expanding farming operations, the decline was not yet apparent. At this crucial time Paul Cameron assumed the management. He was a planter of a different sort; committed to scientific methods in agriculture, he brought a new order to the Cameron plantations.

He was not so committed, however, from the start. He, too, had begun life as a planter by relying on his overseer to know the business. But he worked hard at learning. He was out from early morning to dusk riding from plantation to plantation, always observing and inspecting, quick to spot inefficiency and poor management. He was particularly fortunate in having Thomas Ruffin for his father-in-law, an association which fed and nurtured his natural bent. Thomas Ruffin had been influenced by his cousin Edmund Ruffin of Virginia and was in the vanguard of experimental and scientific farming in North Carolina, putting into immediate practice the best available knowledge.[5]

Besides what he learned from Edmund Ruffin personally, Thomas Ruffin was influenced by *The Farmer's Register*, a journal which his cousin published from 1833 to 1843.[6] Edmund Ruffin had already won a following by his pioneering article, "An Essay on Calcareous Manures," later expanded and published in Petersburg, Virginia, in 1832. It had far-reaching impact on Southern farmers. Ruffin himself was not, however, just a conduit for new ideas for the better management of farms, slaves, and overseers; he was an innovator in his own right and an authority on the soils and their relation to crop yields. He travelled widely throughout the South giving advice, gathering information, and cross-fertilizing the best thinking on agricultural subjects.[7]

The first volume of the *Register* contained articles with suggestions that both Thomas Ruffin and Paul Cameron put into practice. They recommended crop rotation, hillside ditching and deep plowing, and the use of lime, clover, and plaster of Paris as fertilizers, all practices that Paul adopted on his plantations. He also adopted the use of waterfences, described in that first volume, to eliminate his extensive fencing along the rivers that flooded so easily and so often.[8]

The first volume also contained Duncan Cameron's "Memorial of the Convention upon the Subject of Internal Improvement: held in Raleigh, November, 1833, To the General Assembly of North Carolina." Duncan Cameron had inherited the leadership of the Internal Improvements Committee directly from Archibald D. Murphey in 1819 and had been carrying on his efforts ever since.[9] Murphey had very early analyzed and given voice to the causes of North Carolina's backwardness and had concentrated on the lack of transportation in central regions of the state as the primary hindrance to economic vitality and independence. Murphey had formulated a plan for making the main rivers of the state navigable above the fall line by a system of locks and canals, a plan that was implemented only in part, so that twenty years later the problem was still unsolved.[10] Neither Murphey nor Duncan Cameron, who had headed a short-lived Orange County board of agriculture, organized in 1823, and had been concerned with the economic problems underlying the state's agriculture, had grappled with the more immediate and remedial causes of agriculture's decline: depleted soils, inadequate tools, and antiquated farming methods.[11]

A comprehensive analysis of the state of agriculture in North Carolina which incorporated economic, practical, and philosophical approaches to the problem was drafted by Paul Cameron in 1854 in his "Report of 'The Committee on the Best Farming in N.C.,'" for the first annual fair of the Orange County Agricultural Society, of which he was president. The undated text bears the unmistakable stamp of his personality: it is thorough and forthright though wordy and poorly organized, as though written in the heat of inspiration rather than in the light of reflection. It contains the same ideas he formulated in his presidential address in October 1854 before the Orange County Society for the Promotion of Agriculture, the Mechanic Arts and Manufactures which won him much praise and which was afterwards printed in the first volume of *Arator*, an agricultural journal published in North Carolina.[12]

The report noted the long-recognized absence of a home market for agricultural products and the difficulty of transporting them elsewhere. Paul Cameron saw the railroad just then being built as a partial solution to the problem. He treated the matter of soils and the need to reclaim swamps and bottomlands which were "fruitful nurseries of disease and death" though they were at the same time the "fatest earths of our state." Every acre of land, he recommended, should be fertilized with barnyard, marine, and mineral manures; "then & not till then will the ox & ass of No. Ca. know with proper familiarity his masters fields & cribs."

He decried the state's farmers' excessive dependence on Indian corn for feeding man and beast, a practice that could lead to disaster in years of flood or drought. He advocated instead diversity of crops. Farmers should plant more wheat, rye, potatoes, peanuts, and particularly clover and grasses, "silent and sure fertilizers." Cotton, he added, was not suited to this latitude and did much better farther south. If farmers insisted on growing it, however, he advised better selection of seed, better manuring, better tillage.

He next turned to the question of stock. It was foolish, he said, to import farm animals when attention to breeding and the development of pasture lands could produce native stock equal to that found anywhere. The breeding should not be left to the care of the Negro farmhand nor to random selection, for such practice resulted in the constant danger of the better stock's "being dwarfed & dwindled by the deformed runts of our fields."

As for the state's economy as a whole, Paul believed too much dependence on agriculture was a mistake. He advocated diversity of employment and encouragement of all pursuits; "the plough, the loom & the anvil" was his metonymical expression for agriculture, industry, and the mechanic arts. He saw opportunities for industry, for example, in the development of better tools and farm machinery; a man could make a fortune with a factory for their production.

He placed the responsibility for this kind of training on the schools. Better teachers and better schools were needed. He saw promise for these in the creation of two new professorships at the university to teach civil engineering and practical sciences and agriculture and analytical chemistry. Agriculture, he observed, required a combination of disciplines to master: every kind of knowledge played into it, "the earth — the air — the water — the leaf — stone and insects" — all should be a part of the farmer's study. Above all, he should read. Farmers must have good books and good tools, he proclaimed.

Finally, he explained the role that the legislature could play in bringing about these improvements. The next session, he advised, should establish an agricultural board to develop resources for testing and pronouncing on the capacity and usefulness of new tools and machines; the members should implement the collecting, arranging, and publishing of agricultural statistics and other information. They should prepare exhibitions of geological, mineralogical, and agricultural collections, and encourage competition among farmers. The State Fair, begun at this time, was to foster the last concept.

Paul Cameron saw farming as an honorable profession and condemned men who taught their sons that it was begriming and degrading. He wrote to his father of his own little son whose fondness for a new drum seemed to indicate a martial tendency, "I am not very anxious for him to be a 'Hero' — I would prefer to see him a distinguished ploughman."[13]

Through experience Paul Cameron came to learn another group of farm problems, quite immune to study and improvement on the part of the farmer. He came to know the fickleness of weather, the chanciness of nature. No expertise or ingenuity in management, no amount of industry and attention to business could counteract the effects of prolonged drought or destructive floods or infestation of insects or of disease. "No telling what is to be the crop as yet — the rust may blast it — the worm may eat it up — the frost may slay it in October — the wind & rain may give it to the earth to rot" was his poetical rendering of the uncertainties of farming.[14]

Some years were memorably worse than others. The years 1795, 1806, and 1847 brought particularly heavy floods.[15] In 1847 Paul estimated that the Camerons lost 1,000 bushels of wheat at Bobbitt's and Snow Hill, 100 stacks of oats at Stagville and Fish Dam, and half of the corn crop at Fish Dam and the Bullock field at the Brick House farm; 112 sheep were swept away at Little River. Miraculously, their two mills and their bridges on the Eno escaped damage, though the dam of their sawmill on Little River at

Snow Hill was destroyed along with all the other mills and bridges above it. All the bridges on Flat River were destroyed except the one at Stagville, and four or five milldams upstream, including their own in Person County.[16] Similar though usually less damage could be expected almost every year because of the sudden freshets common to piedmont rivers.

The Hessian fly made 1810 memorable for its damage to the wheat crop, while drought distinguished the year 1845. A year later Paul described to his sister Margaret its still noticeable effects: "In my ride from this [Hillsborough] to Judge Ruffin's I never saw so many poor Horses and cattle and the road is rendered very unpleasant by the dead hogs along it. It will be a long time before the County will recover from the fatal drought last year."[17]

The crops grown on the Cameron plantations were virtually the same as those Richard Bennehan had grown at Stagville in the earliest days: corn for subsistence, wheat and tobacco for export, cotton to clothe the large work force. Also grown were rye, oats, clover, flax, and alfalfa. Wheat was particularly profitable, for it could be processed in the Bennehan and Cameron mills. It was then hauled as flour to Petersburg (later, to Henderson to be sent by rail to Petersburg) or to Fayetteville. Paul constantly cleared new ground for wheat. In 1846 he wrote his father, "The new grounds cleared are the largest ever opened in one season on the plantations."[18] He had sown 44 1/2 bushels of seed in the previous October and November.[19] In 1854 he wrote that he was then seeding the largest crop of wheat he had ever put in as a farmer and using more costly manures than ever before.[20]

In 1858 Paul sold 1,033 barrels of flour to Rowland & Brothers in Norfolk, Virginia: the sale netted him $4,229.93.[21] At about five bushels of wheat to one barrel of flour, his crop would have been something over 5,000 bushels, which should have brought close to $6,000. In 1860 flour sold for $6.00 a barrel, and in that year Paul Cameron reported 3,400 barrels of flour ground at the Stagville mill and sold for $17,000, again a comparatively poor return but still a lucrative crop.[22] That figure, equivalent to 17,000 bushels of wheat, included in addition to his own crop those of his neighbors' which had been ground at Paul's mill. His own crop amounted to only 8,000 bushels, or 1,600 barrels of the total.[23]

Wheat continued to be grown at Fairntosh throughout the Camerons' tenancy. Paul's son Duncan sowed seventy-five acres in wheat in 1880 from which he got only 500 bushels, a very poor yield indeed.[24]

Though well aware of the limitations of the latitude for cotton production, Paul Cameron continued to grow cotton on his home plantations even after his purchase of the Alabama and Mississippi plantations. The former had been bought by Paul for his father in 1844; the latter he had purchased after his father's death in 1857, and both had been bought especially for cotton production.²⁵ His father and grandfather had grown cotton; since it could be ginned at home, carded, spun, and woven into cloth to clothe the slaves, it was a practical necessity as well as a staple. Figures for Duncan Cameron's cotton crop for the years 1829 through 1832 show that he produced 2,500 pounds in 1829 which sold for $50, or $.02 per pound.²⁶ His best year of the four was 1831 with 3,087 pounds of white cotton and 85 pounds of yellow. They sold for $.01 3/4 per pound for white cotton and $.01 for yellow, bringing a total of $54.87. The profit for the four years was $186.79, a trivial sum. Paul was able to increase production of this crop. In 1844 the crop from just two plantations, Snow Hill and Bobbitt's, equalled 34,628 and 24,293 pounds respectively.²⁷ It is difficult to compare crops calculated only in bales, for the number of pounds in a bale varied. The Alabama crop of 246 bales in 1846 weighed 123,740 pounds, or 503 pounds per bale, while the home plantations' crop for the same year was 200 bales, each weighing 300 to 400 pounds.²⁸ The cotton market fluctuated from year to year. The 246 bales in 1846 grossed $12,809.41, while 181 bales grossed $12,290.98 in 1850, and 241 bales grossed $15,065.14 in 1858.²⁹ From his Mississippi plantation Paul expected to reap a bale an acre. In 1857 he planted 100 acres in cotton there.³⁰

One of the variables of the cotton crop was the amount a hand could pick in a day. When the Cameron slaves first went to Alabama, they did not pick as well as the Camerons had expected. Two years later, however, they had improved. Paul sent his father a table showing three days' work by six Negro children all under fourteen years of age. The smallest child picked ninety pounds in a day, the fastest 176 pounds. Adult field hands, of course, did better than that. Charles, the best, picked 200 pounds in a day.³¹

Cotton continued to be planted on the home plantations throughout Paul's lifetime although the price was not always enough to make a good return for the farmer even when the crop was good. Paul's mature assessment was, "Any man who will plant cotton in N.C. should have a guardian!"³²

Tobacco was a staple crop of the earliest settlers in North Carolina. Richard Bennehan's earliest accounts show wages paid to men to roll hogsheads of tobacco to market, and later, the receipts for hogsheads hauled by his first team and wagon.³³ Tobacco was a product suited to slave labor because of the number of hands required in its growing and harvesting. The returns were always good, particularly when care was taken in its processing and when it received good grades from the inspectors. In 1826 Duncan Cameron sold 29,946 pounds of tobacco worth $374.32.³⁴ Five years later his sales netted $840.62.³⁵ New lands were constantly being cleared for tobacco; twenty-six acres alone were cleared in 1836 which promised to make good tobacco land.³⁶ In 1863 Mildred's and Thomas's plantations produced 33,894 pounds of tobacco which sold for $.20 per pound, yielding them

$7,778,80.[37] Though the expense of paid labor after the Civil War cut into the profits, tobacco still proved profitable. In the 1880s young Duncan Cameron told his father he hoped to put out 200,000 hills of tobacco, 100,000 on shares, the other half with hired labor.[38]

Far and away the largest crop grown on the plantations first and last was corn, which was planted on the rich bottomlands where it thrived. In 1850 the Cameron home plantations produced 6,000 bushels of Indian corn.[39] In 1860 Paul's plantations alone, not including his brother's and sisters' crops, totaled 14,000 bushels, an indication of the energy, experience, and expertise Paul was then bringing to his farming operations.[40] The yield per acre, though not noted in the family papers, amounted in 1880 to 20 bushels per acre, probably a common average for the Piedmont throughout the nineteenth century.[41] In the newer Mississippi soil, however, Paul planted 200 acres in corn in 1857 from which he expected 10,000 bushels, or 50 bushels per acre.[42] In the years 1956 to 1973 when Fairntosh was under N. E. Gilchrist's management for Paul's granddaughter and her husband, the yield on seventy-five acres planted in corn of 60 bushels or more to the acre shows the tremendous improvement that modern machinery, methods, and fertilizers brought to farm production in this area.[43]

More complete information on the products of the plantations may be found in the agricultural schedules of the 1850, 1860, and 1880 census figures.[44] (See Appendix E.) The 1880 table includes figures for only the small portion of the farms young Duncan Cameron could manage with hired help. Most of the land was either rented out or farmed on shares. The produce from this acreage was listed under the renters' or sharecroppers' names.

Paul Cameron always recognized the poor quality of the land he had to deal with. "I have devoted my life," he was reported as saying," to making poor lands rich."[45] For this reason he was more than usually careful about fertilizers. The Bennehans had used lime, obtained from oyster shells, in addition to stable manure. From the *Farmer's Register* Paul learned of plaster. In 1842 he informed his father, "For my own use I have ordered & obtained a Ton of ground plaster, which I intend to use chiefly on my tobacco crop."[46] The same year he began to plant clover. "As to the clover seed – I will be short, for I know the times are hard – but I will make it as good an investment as you shall make in any State Stocks or bonds – I should like to seed about 150 acres and a gallon to the acre is little enough."[47]

Ruffin too, introduced him to marl; he was elated when he thought he had found some at home. "I have very little doubt I have discovered Marl on your land in the Harris plantation," he wrote his father in 1845; "I have submitted it to the only test at my command, which confirms my impressions – I wish to be certain before saying more – But I am very confident of the result."[48] As he said no more about it, his confidence apparently had been misplaced. Later his interest turned to guano, an expensive fertilizer but one he continued to use in quantity.⁴⁹ After the war when all the usual supplies were shut off and money was scarce, he resorted once more to things close at hand: "I am trying shell lime mixed with plaster on my potatoes."⁵⁰

His last word on fertilizer is found in a letter to his daughter Pauline Shepard passing along his latest experiment's results: "Tell Mr. Shephard I have 'found the magic art,' of making poor land rich. The rye & oats & turnips of my lot & the clover lots of last fall now surpass *any thing* I ever saw — Deep plowing through tillage — 600 lbs of acid phosphate — 200 lbs of pulverized Kanit & 2000 lbs of cotton seed meal or as a substitute for the meal — 1,000 lbs of stable manure to the acre will on the Roberts farm give him 35 bushels of wheat to the acre — & grass equal to any in the valley of Virginia: yielding him 3 or 4 tons to the acre — worth 20 dollars to the ton if well saved — try an acre."⁵¹

The raising of livestock was another important aspect of farming: sheep for their wool and meat; cattle for their milk, leather, and meat; mules and horses for pulling plows, wagons, and carriages; hogs in quantity for pork, ham, bacon, lard, and leather; and all for the valuable manure they supplied. Hogs were particularly profitable. In 1806 Duncan Cameron produced 29,840 pounds of pork weight from the Brick House, Little River, and Fish Dam plantations.⁵² This total continued to grow through the years. In 1822, 334 hogs produced 843,181 pounds; in 1843, 484 hogs produced 58,343 pounds.⁵³

Hog killing was an important event at the end of every year. Good judgment and some luck were required to pick the right time for the killing: the weather had to stay cold, and the hogs had to be at their fattest. The killing, butchering, smoking, and lard rendering required the close cooperation of many workers at their special tasks. The lard rendering was managed by the mistress of the plantation, probably the most important plantation job she performed besides the making of clothing. All day long, day after day, she oversaw the rendering of the fat in huge pots in the kitchen, a supply both for market and home use. Many years after he had moved from Fairntosh, Paul remembered those December days: "Hog killing time makes things a little greasy still at my house, but not like it used to be when I sent in 9 or 10 hundred hogs at dear old Fairntosh."⁵⁴

Duncan Cameron's stock grew from 35 cattle, 63 sheep, and 90 hogs at the Brick House Plantation in 1808, his first stock list in the family papers, to the following numbers in 1845 on all the Cameron plantations but Fairntosh and Little River: 309 cattle, 203 sheep, 1,357 hogs.⁵⁵ These totals did not include Thomas D. Bennehan's stock with probably comparable numbers.

Because of Richard Bennehan's relationship to the Amises of Northampton County, North Carolina, and his interest and stake in the most famous horse of his time, Sir Archie, owned by William and John Amis, a misconception has grown up that the Bennehans and Camerons were interested in race horses. There is no evidence whatever for such a conclusion until after Paul Cameron's death in 1891 when Bennehan Cameron could finally indulge his own passion for racing and race horses. He then built new stables and bought, bred, and trained a string of fine horses at Stagville and Fairntosh plantations.

Like every other planter in the area, Richard Bennehan and his son attended the races at Petersburg and Halifax, where they went on business as well as on pleasure, and the elder Bennehan also attended the Hillsborough races, as his account books attest and as has been noted before. His investment in some of the finest horses of his day was not, however, for sport; he kept them at stud at Stagville and advertised their services so that farmers might bring their mares there to be covered.[56] Besides attracting custom to his Stagville store and adding stud fees to his income, they were used to improve his own stock. After the establishment of the partnership, Duncan Cameron joined the Bennehans in this investment in good horses.[57]

Paul Cameron, in fact, seems to have had an aversion to horse-racing. Twice he wrote to his father on the subject. "I must have a parcel of animals as pets, and I prefer a fat hog to a race horse," he said.[58] A few years later he wrote, "For myself I want nothing to do with the race horse — farm & harness horses is all I go for."[59] Still he well understood the importance of good breeding practices, just as had his father and grandfather. He suggested to his father, who was travelling in the north in 1847, that he go to Saratoga, where a cattle show was to be held, and invest in some good new stock, particularly a horse, "from which with some pains I might hope to breed a stock of Harness Horses and Farm Horses! We have bred from Archy and his descendants so *long* that our stock is now too small and light. It would be a good investment with a view only to improve our own stock of Horses: & he would be in demand through out the surrounding country. I want also a young bull of the short or no-horn Devons — No one can tell (even with our keep and I say it is improving) what can be accomplished by a little attention to these matters. . . . I am resolved if life last to have the best stock of farm animals in No Ca."[60]

Duncan Cameron did buy new stock but not at Saratoga. He went instead to the farm near Delaware City of a Mr. Reynolds and bought a bull and heifer, half short-horn Durham, half Holstein. He also bought an Oxfordshire ram. He was impressed by the farms of Mr. Reynold's six sons and their 1,400 acres of peach orchards and by "the truly great Practical Farmer of Delaware."[61]

Paul continued to buy new stock from time to time. From Bourbon, Kentucky, he obtained two large horse mules and three Morgan horses.[62] His removal to Hillsborough in 1859 and the outbreak of war shortly after disrupted his way of life and the plantation economy so that it was left to Bennehan Cameron very many years later to take up once more the interest in livestock which had been part of Paul's plan for the great plantation complex. Two years before his death Paul Cameron wrote his last words on the subject: "I have often said — that with mule power I would introduce a system of broadcast that should be saved by machinery as much as needed — and the remainder should fatten the animals of the land."[63]

The land was not worked without the aid of machinery. The invention of the cotton gin at the end of the eighteenth century gave farmers a glimpse of the utopia possible, but it was very long in coming. Improvements were made in farm machinery from time to time. The 1850s were particularly productive of new ideas and inventions as were the last decades of the nineteenth century when the loss of slaves made labor-saving devices crucial.[64] There was always a variety of tools to expedite the labor. Doc Edwards, once a Cameron slave, described some of the tools in a slave narrative recorded in the 1930s: "We had big work shops where we made de tools, an' even de shovels was made at home. Dey was made out of wood, so was de rakes, pitchforks an' some of de hoes. Our nails was made in de blacksmith shop by han' an' de picks an' grubbin' hoes, too."[65] Wagons and farm carts of many kinds became standard equipment on the plantations, the simpler models locally built and the more complex ordered from distant firms. Leavin Caulk of Guilford County made Duncan Cameron a wagon for $218 in 1805.[66] Eli Murray in western Orange County made wagons for both Duncan Cameron and Thomas Bennehan in 1842.[67] In 1840 Duncan Cameron ordered a particularly elaborate wagon with a baggage rack from John Holmes in Philadelphia costing $305, including delivery.[68] In 1844 Paul Cameron ordered three heavy wagons, each to be pulled by five mules, and one surrey wagon, to be pulled by six; all of these were bought through his Petersburg factor, Andrew Kevan and Brother, and built by a wagon maker named Van Pelt.[69] These were the large, strong wagons needed to haul the heavy produce packed in hogsheads and barrels, kegs and firkins, over the muddy red clay roads to the distant markets.

Plows were indispensable, the oldest and most important of farm tools and most frequently worn out, repaired, and replaced. The blacksmith did what he could to keep them in condition, but new ones were always being ordered. Robert Sinclair of Baltimore supplied them to Duncan Cameron in 1821.[70] In 1834 Paul suggested to his father that they try to obtain a plowmaker or a "good-at-all tradesman."[71] The number of plows used on the plantations along with all the other tools and the stock may be seen in the charts of Appendix F which tabulate the equipment in the 1840s on three Person County farms, five Orange County farms, and the Alabama plantation.[72]

The Bennehans and Camerons had their share of more sophisticated equipment as it became available. The cotton gin has already been mentioned. Four McCormick plows which Paul bought in 1853 were probably much improved over the colonial sort; they had wrought shares and lock coulters and cost $12 each. At the same time he bought a fifteen-inch screw propeller straw cutter for $45, an eleven-inch one for $30, and a double iron spout corn sheller for $16.[73] His increased investment in farm machin- over his father's, $1,500 in 1850, for example, compared with $9,000 in 1860, is indicative of both the increase in the availability of such machin- ery and of Paul's awareness of its importance.

The wheat crop required several different machines for its processing. In 1857 Paul Cameron bought a thirty-inch spiral thresher and separator from Borum and McClean in Norfolk.[74] Wheat threshers needed frequent attention; fortunately Paul Cameron had Ben Sears, a slave, who could handle these machines and make minor repairs. Often, nevertheless, he had to pay mechanics like Solomon Dixon and Wilson Woods to repair them.[75] Wheat also required fans to remove the chaff in the threshing pro- cess. They, too, had to be repaired and replaced from time to time.[76]

After the threshing, the wheat was taken to the mill for grinding. There another contrivance was brought into play after its invention in the 1840s. This was a smut machine which attempted to separate the diseased wheat (smut and smut balls) from the good wheat. John A. McMannen, who, like his father, had made barrels and kegs for the Camerons throughout the years, obtained the patent on a new smut machine in the mid-1840s and proceeded to manufacture them at his South Lowell farm.[77] The Camerons bought two.[78]

Carding machines for processing wool were part of the equipment needed for that crop. At first these were owned by the Bennehans and Duncan Cameron, but later their wool was taken to mills where carding service was offered.[79] For their leather-tanning operation they had a bark mill which had to be replaced by a new one from time to time.[80]

When young Duncan Cameron began to farm at Fairntosh in the late 1870s, he purchased a horse-drawn mower and reaper at the cost of $110.50, and ten years later a corn-planter which he calculated saved the labor of two men.[81] A striking social change had taken place, however; the machines young Duncan Cameron bought he operated himself, carrying his dinner in a pail to the fields, where he spent the day laboring. There were no planters anymore, for there were no more slaves.

It was the slaves or lack of them that made all the difference. Up until 1860 they had provided the farm labor and were the basis of the whole econ- omy. As the main responsibility of the overseer, they worked from dawn till dusk performing the manifold chores of the unceasing seasonal routines. Each plantation had its own labor force quartered on the plantation where it worked, and its own livestock, tools, and machinery. Each plantation like- wise had its own overseer, also housed there, responsible for everything and everybody on the plantation. It is not known whether the Bennehan and Cameron slaves worked in gangs or at task-work. Perhaps the methods were used simultaneously for different jobs or varied from overseer to overseer who assigned the work. As an assistant to the overseer the Camerons seemed to have designated a black foreman; they never used the word *driver* except in connection with a wagon or carriage. The slaves played so obviously large a part in the history of the plantation complex that they, like the overseers, must be considered separately.

8. Overseeing the Work

Although the system of labor changed dramatically after the Civil War because of the loss of the slaves, the management of the labor remained virtually the same. Overseers did not disappear with slavery but continued through the rest of the Cameron ownership of the land to perform their exacting and poorly compensated work. No plantation before or after the war could function without the overseer; it was he who coordinated all the efforts under the regulations imposed by the owner into a vast intermeshing of working parts, like gears in a machine, interacting at the precise moment and at a precise speed. The overseer oversaw everything. Ideally, his responsibilities required of him a game spirit, a hardy physique, and a nimble mind. That the historical stereotype of this man has been that of "a rough individual of humble background and dense ignorance who took delight in abusing Negroes placed under his care and in thwarting the wishes of his employer," is both unfortunate and inaccurate.[1] That the category included such men is doubtless true, but that they were either typical or predominant is certainly false.

A look at some of the overseers in the Bennehan-Cameron employ discloses their general characteristics. It is clear from the papers that each plantation had its own overseer, and though nothing is recorded regularly suggesting a post of superintendent over all the overseers, there are indications that the later managers of Fairntosh really held such a job. Actually, Thomas D. Bennehan and Paul Cameron filled the role of superintendent for their respective fathers. Some of the overseers under them were less than admirable, some merely unfortunate, but some were conspicuously successful in the performance of their difficult jobs.

An overseer for either the Bennehans or the Camerons was working for more than ordinarily conscientious employers in terms of their expectations, their attention to plantation matters, and their humane treatment of slaves. They indulged no one, not even themselves. Thomas Bennehan and Paul Cameron worked as hard as any overseer they employed, riding the plantation rounds, attending to trouble spots or to the sick slaves with a sense of duty that commanded respect and devotion. If they had a fault it was their unwillingness to pay more than the lowest going wages, $150 to $200 a year, yet they were able to find and keep men who performed ably and conscientiously.[2] They rarely increased an overseer's wages for long service, but kept them exactly as they had been at the start of employment.[3]

The earliest overseers, however, did not receive wages at all. Duncan Cameron's first overseer signed a contract drawn up after the old fashion by which an overseer received a share of the crops and certain supplies to oversee a plantation and work a specific number of slaves. This kind of contract had largely disappeared by the beginning of the nineteenth century, but in this respect as in many others Duncan Cameron showed a decided conservatism.[4] He hired Hugh Woods in 1805 to oversee his plantation north of Hillsborough on Little River, a tract of land that had formerly belonged to Governor Thomas Burke.[5] Woods was to receive one-fifth of the tobacco and one-sixth of the corn and other grain in addition to 300 pounds of pork and undoubtedly his firewood though it is not mentioned in the preliminary agreement which survives.[6] In return, he was to live on the plantation, take care of the stock, and work eight Negroes.

Comparison of this agreement with a contract made by Richard Bennehan with his overseer Hezekiah Ferrell twenty years before shows their similarity. Ferrell was to oversee Bennehan's Flat River plantation, with eight Negroes, four horses, and tools all supplied by Bennehan, to raise corn, tobacco, wheat, oats, flax, and cotton, and to take care of the stock and keep the fences in repair in return for 500 pounds of pork, eight barrels of corn, and a proportion of all crops.[7]

Hugh Woods was probably typical of the overseers who worked for the Camerons. He was a son of a family long established in the area, good, solid yeoman stock with more than the average education. His mother had been a daughter of James Cain, a member of the neighborhood gentry.[8] As early as 1804 when already working for Duncan Cameron he was feeling the pull of the western frontier with its wider opportunity.[9] Though he temporarily gave up the idea, he finally did leave the Cameron service about 1812 and move to Tennessee.[10]

Two Person County men named Cotheran worked for Duncan Cameron managing his Person County plantations. The first was soon dismissed for drunkenness after several temporary reformations.[11] The second, James Cotheran, remained in the Cameron's service for forty years. As Paul described him, "Mr. Cotheran is entirely destitute of what our farmers call 'niceness' alias taste; tho a man of honest purposes, and I think devoted to you and yours."[12] He managed two of the Person County plantations for which he received $150 a year for each.[13] He was apparently a thrifty man, for in 1859 Paul Cameron, who was always slow to pay his bills, owed him several years' salary amounting to $835.[14]

Cotheran's long service, very close to a record even by Cameron standards, was exceeded by Arthur Bobbitt's. When he was dying, Paul Cameron wrote to his sister Margaret, "He is now in his 94 year! He has passed at least 60 years in service of our family as an overseer. I have enjoyed many an hour in his recollections of the past."[15] As overseer at different times of the Leathers and Peaks plantations on the south side of Eno River, or at the Fish Dam plantation on the northeast side of the Neuse, his experience probably made him a valuable trouble-shooter who could be moved from place to place as needs changed. He had been hired on the old system of shares.[16]

Arthur Bobbitt created some interest in the family in 1835 by marrying a widow, Mrs. Woods, probably an in-law of the family to whom Hugh Woods had belonged. The Bennehans and Camerons were invited to the ceremony at Mrs. Woods's and to the entertainment afterwards at Mr. Bobbitt's.[17] Thomas Bennehan and Thomas Cameron accepted and found "upwards of fifty people."[18] Mrs. Woods's marriage with Bobbitt exemplified a tradition of intermarriage among overseers' families that lasted throughout the history of the plantations. Mr. Bobbitt's daughter Lucy married Philip Southerland, overseer of Stagville after 1849 and brother of Fendal Southerland, an earlier overseer there. The Philip Southerlands' daughter Orpah married William D. Turrentine, overseer of Fairntosh for Bennehan Cameron. William and Samuel Piper, also overseers, were married to Melinda and Ellenor Harris, daughters of Nathaniel Harris and cousins of Williams Harris, another Cameron overseer, a son of Colonel Robert Harris whose plantation adjoined Stagville on the north. Samuel Piper's son, Joseph G. Piper, married Annie Turrentine, a daughter of Samuel Turrentine and sister of William D. Turrentine, the overseer of Fairntosh noted above.

His long association with Arthur Bobbitt provided Paul Cameron with some of the amusing remarks he loved to quote. When Bobbitt was depressed he said, "I feel as though I'd been sold out."[19] After an accident he said, "The scare was as bad as the hurt."[20] It was Leonard Laws, however, whose land lay north of the Brick House Plantation and was eventually added to the plantation complex, who provided Paul with another favorite saying: "Drinks are so wide apart I get very thirsty."[21]

It was the practice for the Bennehans and Camerons to find their overseers in the sons of local farmers, usually families well known to them by some earlier contact, most often as neighbors. These families were not the neediest in the neighborhood as might have been expected but often, as in the instance of Hugh Woods, well provided with land and slaves themselves. Younger sons in families of small planters or prosperous farmers often found themselves landless because of the long lives of their fathers, or because of the partition into too many parcels of their father's estates, or simply because of general adversity. In these kinds of families the Bennehans and Camerons found their best overseers.

Two local families who supplied the Bennehans and Camerons with excellent overseers were the Leatherses and the Southerlands. Both families owned land on the south side of Eno River, tracts of which they eventually sold to the Bennehans or Camerons. Moses Leathers, who had been a Revolutionary War soldier, and William, probably his brother, had large families settled in the area.[22] Two of William's sons, William, Jr., and Fielding Leathers, sold their part of their father's land to Richard Bennehan in 1814.[23] Much earlier, William had become a kind of superintendent for Bennehan. Wages of $75 for the year 1797 are recorded for him, an amount raised to $100 the following year.[24] Moses's son, James Leathers, continued to manage his own plantation but frequently helped out as superintendent when the Bennehans found themselves shorthanded. He supervised the building of the New Mill, for example, in 1836 and its repairs in 1841.[25]

James Leathers's relationship with the family was always more that of a friend than a retainer, yet the Camerons felt a difference if not a superiority that separated them from the substantial farmers around them. Paul wrote to his father, "I have been invited with uncle and Thomas 'to dine out' on tomorrow — with our old friend and neighbor James Leathers whose youngest son has just been married — so to Waxhaw we go where I know we shall receive a *cordial welcome* and find an abundance of cheer. Tell Mother Magey and Milly that I will give them an account of all that I see, for I know it will afford them some amusement."[26] James Leathers dined at least once at Fairntosh and from time to time at Stagville with Thomas Bennehan, whose friend and contemporary he really was.[27] Leathers died in late 1844 or early 1845.[28] William Leathers had died in 1825.[29]

Fendal Southerland became overseer at Stagville in 1824, when William Leathers became ill. Samuel Yarbrough wrote of him to Thomas Bennehan that "he talks rough to his people but hasn't used the hickory yet."[30] Southerland's family owned land on Ellerbee Creek, a tributary south of the Eno. He was as faithful and dependable as William Leathers had been. When Thomas Bennehan drew up his will, he left Southerland, his "friend and manager," $500. Southerland's health failed before Bennehan died, however, and Bennehan retired him with a gift at that time and revoked the bequest with a codicil.[31] Fendal's brother Philip became overseer at Stagville in 1850 and proved just as capable and faithful; he was still overseer after the Civil War, having stuck by his post during those dangerous days.[32] Then he became one of a local group who rented Stagville from Paul Cameron and continued to live there many years more.[33] Young Duncan Cameron wrote to his mother in 1878, "I would not have father to ask Mr. Southerland to move. I think it greatly to his interest, to keep him, & I know if he makes another move, it will be to leave Stagville entirely, and I had rather see any man go, than Mr. Southerland."[34] He was still a tenant in the Stagville house when Bennehan Cameron hired a Scotch farmer, James

Smith, to come supervise his stock farm and dairy in 1886.[35]

In 1879 Southerland's son-law, William Daniel Turrentine, was hired by Duncan Cameron to oversee the farming operations at Fairntosh.[36] Turrentine's father, Samuel, had been one of the group associated with Southerland in renting Stagville and was a descendant of one of the earliest settlers in what is today northern Durham County. Two Turrentines, Alexander and Samuel, were already living on Buffalo Creek by 1760.[37] W. D. Turrentine continued as manager at Fairntosh up to the time of his death in 1924.[38]

James Smith, mentioned above, was the exception among Cameron overseers in not belonging to the local yeomanry. In 1886 Paul Cameron informed his wife that Bennehan was "expecting a Mr. Smith from Illinois who is to take charge of Stagville as overseer plant his butter dairy organize his cow farm — plant tobacco — make silos — do many new things. . . ."[39] Mr. Smith, a native of Scotland, brought his elderly father along with his own family when he arrived in the spring of 1886.[40] He stayed two years before moving to Minneapolis in January 1889.[41] The elder Smith died at Stagville, and Paul offered the family graveyard there for his burial place; the offer was politely declined.[42]

At the same time that Turrentine was at Fairntosh and Smith at Stagville, W. P. Durham was overseeing other aspects of the Stagville operation for Bennehan Cameron. His diary records the work done day by day, particularly the new building of barns then going on and the renovation of the older structures, including the Stagville house.[43] An entry in his diary reveals the respectability an overseer could enjoy: he recorded that he went with William Ruffin (a younger brother of Mrs. Paul Cameron) to take tea at Mr. Smith's.[44]

William Horner, an eminently respectable scion of a local family, was one of a few men who were clearly hired as superintendents over the overseers.[45] He was a son of Thomas Horner of Flat River, a colonel in the militia, a local politician of influence, a farmer, and a capable man. When his wife died in 1835, he was forced to resign in order to take care of three little daughters, but the Camerons found another position for him that he could fill without neglecting them.[46] He and Paul Cameron set up a partnership in September 1835 to operate the store at Cameron Mills in Person County.[47] Horner, of course, was the store manager and attended to every part of the business. Paul Cameron supplied the capital and building. This business was not dissolved until April 1841.[48]

One other family epitomizes the kind of men who were overseers for the Bennehans and Camerons and illustrates the overseers' relationship to their employers. The Piper family was not from the immediate neighborhood of Flat River but from many miles upstream on the north side of the Eno River where John Piper had settled in the 1760s by the ford at Few's

Mill.[49] It was John's grandsons who became Cameron overseers after their father's death in the 1830s and after their own marriages into the Harris family of Flat River.[50]

William Piper became overseer at Fairntosh in 1839. "He has some excellent qualities," Paul wrote of him.[51] William Piper had tried his hand at a number of occupations: hotel-keeping, milling, and later, schoolteaching.[52] Half a dozen of William's letters in the Cameron papers show that he was a man of some education and refinement and was apparently able to satisfy Paul Cameron's exacting demands for a number of years in his capacity of superintendent. "I take pleasure informing you that in one hour from this your three crops of wheat will be in shock, I finished my crop tuesday Bobbitts crop Wednesday Nichols crop today; fine crops both in quantity and quality. We are ploughing our hill corn with all possible speed. . . . We will stack our cradles and shoulder our hoes for a short time — our oats are almost ripe."[53]

His schoolteaching came about as a proposal from Senator Willie P. Mangum, who needed a schoolmaster for his young son. To this proposal Piper replied, "Your proposition in regard to a school was unexpected to me. I have thought upon the subject. I do not feel myself competent to teach a school as it ought to be done. I am willing if a school can be made to do my best, provided I can get a comfortable situation convenient for my Family. . . . It is true my situation in life is an uncomfortable one, through the mishaps of fortune. I am advancing in life, with delicate health, my children all daughters, and nothing but my efforts, upon which I can hope, to sustain myself and family. . . . I hope you will pardon me, if I propose too much, when I say, provided a school cannot be made, that if you divide your hands and plantations with Mr. Carrington and myself to manage, that with fortune in my favour I can so manage the part entrusted to my care, that nothing will [be] lost to you by the arrangement. Necessity has no law. I am anxious to obtain business, and submit this proposition. . . ."[54] For a few years from the time of this letter in 1845 Piper did teach school at the Mangums', but by the late 1840s he was again working as overseer for Paul Cameron.

The years 1846 through 1848 were particularly trying on the plantations. Everyone fell ill with malaria, and the Pipers and other overseers were not eager to renew their contracts; they felt for their health's sake and that of their families that they should not remain there.[55] Samuel Piper had come as overseer of Snow Hill in 1842 but had replaced his brother William as overseer of Fairntosh and general manager by 1846.[56] Paul Cameron had become disenchanted with William because of his delicate health. The year 1848 seems to have finished his time in the Cameron employ.[57]

Samuel Piper became the overseer to whom Paul Cameron was most closely attached, perhaps because he helped Paul through the trying period of Duncan Cameron's death when Paul felt himself forlorn and unequal to carrying his immense burden alone. Like his brother, Samuel was a man of some education, good intelligence, and integrity. He first lived at Snow Hill, but around 1850 Paul Cameron built the overseer's house at Fairntosh for him and his family where he lived the rest of his life.[58] Perhaps it was because Samuel Piper was so competent that Paul was able to make the move to Hillsborough in 1859 and leave the management of the plantations to him. Samuel Piper remained as overseer through the war years; he died in 1867.[59] During all that time, at least twenty-five years, his salary was $200 even though the worthlessness of Confederate money and soaring inflation during and after the war caused his expenses easily to outrun his income. He accumulated a debt to Paul, who felt compassion and affection for the man. As early as 1863 in their yearly settlement, which showed a balance due Paul from Piper of $249.18, Paul wrote on the account "For and in consideration of Mr. Piper's long and faithful services with me and my family I relinquish all claim or demand on him for the above balance of $249.18"[60]

Piper's health began to fail in 1866, and early the next year he suffered a fatal stroke. Paul wrote to Anne Cameron, "I am sick at heart and deeply depressed by the death of our friend Mr. Piper."[61] For Paul it was his father's death all over again, but this time there was no Mr. Piper to step in and help.

No satisfactory arrangement was worked out for the plantations after the war until in 1879 young Duncan Cameron hired W. D. Turrentine, whose long tenure and high capability maintained Fairntosh through the end of the nineteenth century and through the first two decades of the twentieth. Turrentine was also a county commissioner for many years.[62]

The Camerons were lucky in their overseers. With some exceptions, they were always able to find men who knew the business they were hired for and who had sufficient education, self-discipline, and dedication to give the kind of service the Camerons demanded. A few were incompetent, a few drank and had to be fired. Some were less than energetic. One came close to being charged with the murder of a slave. (See Chapter 10.)

The Camerons always maintained a semblance of equality in their relations with their overseers. They always addressed them as 'mister'; they dined with them on occasion and referred to them as 'friends.' The little Piper girls were taught in the schoolroom with Paul Cameron's daughters, and Mr. Turrentine felt free to consult with Bennehan Cameron on a school for his daughter: "Of course I cant send her to any fancy school and pay such high prices its useless for me to tell you this for you know how I am situated financially: but I would rather live on half rations & give my children an english education than raise them up in these times with no learning."[63] He sent her to the Oxford Female Seminary.[64]

The Cameron overseers, then, were with few exceptions all men of local families long established in the community and known to the Camerons: although they generally owned no land, they were acquainted from childhood with the routine and practice of farming; they had a modicum of education, a respectability that earned them a semblance of equality with their employers, and a dependability that kept them, once employed, throughout the rest of their working years in the Cameron service. Through long association, Bennehans and Camerons and their overseers developed a sense of gratitude and loyalty toward one another, and even in some instances, affection, not inherent in the relationship itself.

9. Mills, Stills, and Shops

Geared into the total complex of plantation operations were semi-autonomous industrial units: the blacksmith shops, the distilleries, and the mills. They performed auxiliary services on the plantations but were not indispensable to them. The Bennehans and Camerons might have used others' mills, smithies, and distilleries; it was, however, more convenient, efficient, and usually more profitable to use their own.

Although the date of its construction is unknown, the blacksmith shop at Stagville was undoubtedly an early addition to the facilities, possibly as early as the late 1790s. One of the first references to it is in a letter of Thomas Bennehan in 1807: "There is a large number of People now at the Shope haveing their Horses shod."[1] In 1818 the shop burned to the ground, but as the chimneys were unharmed, it was immediately rebuilt on the same site. He relates how the roof caught on fire while the Negroes were at breakfast, and though all rushed to the scene immediately, they succeeded in saving only the tools.[2]

For much of its history this shop was managed by a white smith possibly assisted by a slave. Richard and Thomas Bennehan's system was to form partnerships with the smiths for the running of the shop, which served both the family and the community. The Bennehans provided the tools and building while the smiths managed the work and kept the accounts. John Green, John Wilkins, and Andrew Williams were smiths at Stagville during the first four decades of the nineteenth century. Green had in fact come to Stagville as early as the 1790s, possibly as a clerk in the Stagville store, but it is clear that by 1804 he was the smith in partnership with Richard Bennehan.[3] By 1814 it was Wilkins who was smith; in that year Mary Anderson wrote Duncan Cameron about her slave Fred: "If you could get Johny Wilkins to make a good black smith of him I would send him to Stagville."[4] In 1817 Wilkins's agreement with Thomas Bennehan stipulated his wages as $130 a year; apparently at that time he was not a partner.[5] Andrew Williams, who died in 1837, was buried in the Fairntosh cemetery. His will speaks of his partnership with Thomas Bennehan in the management of the shop at Stagville[6] The employment of these men seems to have overlapped; Green and Wilkins were employed in some of the same years. Perhaps one was smith at Stagville while the other was employed at the Fish Dam plantation where there was another shop.

After Paul Cameron inherited the Stagville plantation from his uncle in 1847, his system was to rent the shop to a man who either did the work himself or hired a smith to do it. Willam F. Vestal, Samuel Piper's son-in-law, rented the Stagville shop after the Civil War, for example, and lived in the Stagville house.[7] In 1874 Philip Southerland consulted Paul Cameron about obtaining a smith for Stagville since Meredith, the current smith, was moving to Durham and Leonard Ray, a former smith, wished to come back.[8] A third offer, from W. A. Southerland, who wrote to Paul the very next day asking to rent the shop himself, suggests it was clearly a money-making concern.[9] Though nothing now remains where the shop once stood, the name Shop Hill survives for the general area, which is still marked by the presence of two slave houses exactly like those at Horton Grove and a few miscellaneous farm buildings.

Fairntosh, too, is known to have had its own shop, but it seems to have been only a private facility for the Cameron plantations. Mention of it occurs in an undated letter of Paul Cameron to his sister Mildred that also gives a glimpse of the Cameron's domestic life:

> The little ones are very well and as wild as anything in the wild woods of the west. I gave them a concert this morning. Meeting "Frank Johnson" in the road near Stagville with his band I thought Anne & the children would be delighted to hear them, so I invited them over — They gave us several very fine pieces of Musick in the piaza and after your sister Anne had given them breakfast they went off to Oxford — As they drove off from the gate seated in an open wagon they gave us a most delightful tune which we listened to until they had passed the blacksmiths shop.[10]

Information about the distilleries is equally fragmentary. A bill from Young Dortch in March 1807 is for building a stillhouse at Fish Dam plantation thirty feet by twenty-four feet with a fourteen-foot pitch in the roof and made of logs hewed all round. It had two doors and a trough to convey water to it.[11] An undated bill from John and Elias Fort shows that they built a distillery on Cameron's Person County lands. Fairntosh, too, had its own still. Paul wrote his father, "I have beged Mother to send you a bottle of your Fairntosh whiskey, and not doubting that at times you will find it an excellent cordial, and as well satisfied that the city of Raleigh contains no such spirit."[12] The following year, 1836, Paul wrote that he greatly needed a labor-saving machine to shell corn for his own distillery in Person County. He asked his father to look into the possibility of obtaining Parker's Patent Corn Sheller.[13]

Some idea of the size of production and of the wages of a "stiller" may be found in Duncan Cameron's accounts for 1828–1829. Alexander Carrol, the stiller, had used 180 bushels of corn, 84 bushels of rye, and 16 bushels of corn malt to make 437 gallons of whiskey, of which Carrol's part was one-tenth of the whole.[14] Not all their stillers had to be paid, for not all were white men. The Camerons had a slave identified as "Jim the Stiller."[15]

Both shops and stills produced revenue for their owners and were not expensive to run or maintain. The mills presented a different situation entirely. The capital outlay to build a mill was on the average $3,000 to $4,000 and sometimes costly repairs were required to maintain it.[16] In addition, miller's wages had to be figured in with the cost unless, as was often true at the Bennehan and Cameron mills, the miller was a slave.

In the early days of Stagville Plantation the nearest mills would have been Hicks's mill on Eno River, petitioned for in 1791, and the old William Johnston mill on Little River if it continued to operate after his death. Neither location was far from Stagville. Nevertheless, Bennehan wanted his own mill for the convenience and the profit he hoped it would provide. He first built a mill on Panther Creek on his Peeksville plantation on Neuse River, but the mill was small and the water power undependable.[17] Rebecca wrote to Duncan Cameron in 1805, "Papa's little mill begins to fail."[18] Consequently, in 1806, he bought the old Hicks mill from the current owner, Charles Kennon. Actually, he effected a swap with Kennon, trading his Panther Creek mill for the Eno River mill and paying an additional sum for the hundred-acre tract on which the mill stood.[19] From that time on, for one hundred years or more, the mill remained in the family. It was known as the Bennehan mill until after the Civil War, when it became known as the Red Mill and the road leading to it, Red Mill Road. From the first it had been a public mill, and it continued to grind grain for the neighborhood as well as for the family.

The terrain where it stood is low and the river makes many turns and creates almost an island of the land on which the mill was situated. A wash or drain or gut (the deeds describe it variously) had formed at the site, too, so that when the first bridge across the river there, built in 1816, needed repair, the county court appointed a commission "to let the repairing of the Bridge across Eno near Bennehan's Mill and to erect a Bridge across the Wash south of said Mill."[20] These bridges made Bennehan's mill accessible from either bank at any time and for many years provided the only dry crossing of the river for a distance of eighteen miles upstream where there was another bridge at Hillsborough.[21] The bridges gave the mill a real advantage over other mills along the river, because many days of the year the river was in spate and could not be forded.

It was not a particularly good site for a mill, however; the land lay in the Triassic Basin and was easily and frequently flooded, and a good rock footing for the mill foundation was difficult or impossible to find. Still, there was a considerable population of small farmers south of the river to utilize the mill's services; and roads on both banks leading in the early days to a good fording place and later to the bridges brought customers readily to the mill. Business was always brisk. Thomas Bennehan could well tell

Duncan Cameron a year after the mill's purchase that it "now has a handsome run of business."[22] Long years of experience were needed to prove that the mill's geographic deficiency exceeded its demographic advantage.

Wheat and corn grown in the quantity that the plantations produced it, ground at the Bennehan mill, and carried by their teams to market comprised a large, self-contained, and efficient undertaking. Duncan Cameron was naturally eager to tap what seemed so good a source of profit. He decided to build a mill on a fork of Flat River which ran through the Person County land he had recently acquired. He hired Joseph Terry, a millwright, and John Fort, the carpenter, to build both grist and sawmills at that plantation.[23] Millstones had to be ordered from Petersburg, but two local creeks, Ledge of Rocks and Knap of Reeds, may have supplied the flintstone used as gudgeons for the waterwheel. They were known as a source of this stone.[24]

In 1819 Cameron built another mill in Person County on the other fork of Flat River. This millseat was rocky and required "rock blowing" (blasting). James Means blew the rock, Francis Epperson did the masonry, J. Seawell supplied the millstones.[25] Conard Staley of a family of millwrights built the mill and set up the machinery.[26] Isham Malone was one of the Person County millers from 1823 to 1834 or longer and kept the accounts for the general store located at the mill, where a post office also operated.[27] These mills could handle the produce of the vast Person County tract, but Cameron had large holdings in Orange, too, and the Bennehan mill could not handle all the family's grain and the neighborhood's as well. He decided to build a mill on the Eno River upstream from the Bennehan mill at a place called Buck Shoals which bordered the Snow Hill plantation. In 1834 he obtained permission from the court for a mill and the necessary acreage on the opposite bank. In 1836 Abraham Staley constructed there a three-storey millhouse thirty-five by forty feet with two waterwheels each fifteen feet in diameter.[28] A sawmill, also built at this time and place, was forty-two by fourteen feet.[29] To finish the job properly Cameron built a bridge at the site. The court cooperated by opening a road from the bridge through the Bennehan and Cameron lands to the Wake County line.[30] The site of Cameron's New Mill, as it was called, was just upstream from the present bridge across the Eno on the old Oxford highway, state road #1004. The first road that led from the mill to Wake County may still be traced as it enters the old Eno plantation and curves down to the river a few hundred feet upstream from the present crossing. James Leathers superintended the building of this mill complex.[31]

Cameron had already built two other sawmills many years before, both on Ellerbee Creek. The first was on a tract south of the creek. After a land swap with Samuel Southerland for a tract on the north side, he built another sawmill there.[32] The very next year, 1822, they made the same swap in reverse except that Southerland then had to pay $1,000 extra to Cameron for the newly built sawmill on the north tract.[33] Conrad Staley built this sawmill at the same time he built a new millhouse for Bennehan's mill.[34] Nimrod Ragsdale did the masonry for the rebuilt Bennehan mill.[35]

Unlike the stills and shops, the mills are fully documented. For one reason, they were always needing attention; the floods to which piedmont rivers are prone repeatedly damaged all the mills and milldams up and down the rivers. A recital now of the repairs year after year, first in one place and then in another and back through the cycle again, creates an almost farcical tale of disaster. The reality then must have been only disheartening.

Cameron built his mills for an investment as well as a convenience, but as regards his Eno mill he must have been disappointed. Paul Cameron, who was as vocal on this subject as he was on every other, had much to say about the problem and expense of maintaining this mill. "I have a good portion of our efficient hands at the mill extending the south abutment and making it higher, so as to prevent the break of water around, which is fast washing away the South Bank. This job is entirely of stone and is not half completed — Never was a mill sustained and maintained at so much labour and cost in our part of the country."[36] Only two years before, in 1841, the milldam there had been repaired by Laban Collins. The repairs then were lengthy and costly. James Leathers was again called in to supervise the work.[37]

Ten years later, again working on the New and Bennehan mills, the latter of which he had inherited from his uncle, Paul characterized for his father the repairs going on as "at all times to me the most unpleasant and as far as my experience extends unprofitable sort of work."[38] His experience was by that time considerable. Milldams were particularly vulnerable. In 1830 Isham Malone wrote Paul of the rebuilding of the dam across Flat River at one of the mills.[39] The same year James Ball was rebuilding the dam at Johnston's old mill on Little River, which, two years later, again had to be rebuilt.[40]

Most of the rebuilding and repairing could be done by the slaves with the help of neighborhood carpenters, but when the machinery was damaged, millwrights had to be called in. One of these, employed in 1846, was Caleb Dixon of the Quaker family of millwrights and millers on Cane Creek, Alamance County. Paul Cameron was shocked by the size of his bill and was still seething four years later when he needed to call in another expert to replace the waterwheel at New Mill: "I will keep clear of those free soilers & blood suckers Dicksons."[41]

Paul had the mill wall at the Bennehan mill rebuilt in 1848, and two years later was lamenting, "I have to rebuild the mill dam at my mill on Eno as it is about to fall down!"[42] In 1854 William G. Dollar, a local millwright, was brought in to work on Cameron's New Mill.[43]

Less information pertains to the millers. After Malone left the Person mill, he was replaced by a slave, Cyrus.[44] This same Cyrus, seven years later the miller at New Mill, was surprised by a Sunday visit of Paul's to the mill where Paul found him so drunk he did not recognize Paul.[45] That same month another slave, Daniel, was selected to be the miller in Person County. Cyrus, who, despite his failing, continued as miller at New Mill, was sent up to Person County to train Daniel and get him started in the job.[46] As so little is said of the millers, the Bennehan and Cameron system of using slaves for millers must have worked well enough. Nothing is known of the millers at Bennehan's mill from the time it was purchased, when a Mr. Dockary was miller there, until 1846, when the slave Matthew was running the mill.[47]

The New Mill caused Paul Cameron other kinds of trouble. A daughter of their neighbor William Cain owned land adjoining the mill tract, and in 1851 she complained that the dam flooded her land and ruined her crops. She finally withdrew the charge and a threatened lawsuit, but the experience strengthened Paul's antipathy to mills.[48]

When Duncan Cameron died in 1853, he left the New Mill along with the Snow Hill plantation to Thomas A. Cameron. Paul, his sister Margaret, and his wife, Anne, named in the will as trustees for the retarded Thomas, apparently decided to hire a white miller for the New Mill and obtained Wilson Woods to run it for $200 a year.[49] After the Civil War, however, Paul as trustee leased the mill to a Mr. Green and his son J. R. Green for five years at a rent of $600 a year.[50] Again a controversy arose; sometime during the Greens' tenancy, possibly in 1870, a severe freshet washed out forty-eight feet of the dam, and despite the terms of the lease, which required the Greens to return the property in good repair on termination of their lease, they did nothing towards its repair. The family papers do not disclose how this problem was resolved. J. M. Clark, who had been acting as miller for the Greens, was kept on after the Greens' lease expired until about 1880.[51]

A letter from Clark reveals some details of the mill at that time.[52] He explained to Paul that the river was so often "past fording," maybe eight or ten days at a time, that business was interrupted. He said the time was not far distant when a bridge would be built at the site. Apparently the bridge the Camerons had built in 1837 had long before washed away and had never been replaced. George P. Collins, Paul's son-in-law, who was eager to rent the mill himself, had a different explanation for the slack business.[53] He told Paul that Clark hardly ever went to the mill and his employees did not do what they should. "His mismanagement & neglect have driven off all custom so that the mill stands idle three-fourths of the time, the grinding from these places going up to Tillys where they can get better flour."[54]

George Collins finally got his turn in 1881 and went to work to repair the New Mill once again.[55] And again, five years later, another freshet seriously damaged it.[56] Collins continued to make repairs and run the mill until he inherited it from Paul Cameron in 1891, when information about it disappears from the Cameron papers.[57]

The Bennehan mill was rented out, too, after Duncan Cameron's death. Mr. Vestal, who had rented the shop at Stagville, took a lease for the mill as well, though it is not certain just when he ran it. An undated letter from him to Paul reported that Boyce's Mill in Wake County downstream and Green at the New Mill had reduced their prices for grinding. They charged only one-twelfth as their toll. Vestal suggested he could undercut them by charging only one-fifteenth.[58]

D. J. Ellis, who was living at Fairntosh in 1894 while he was repairing the Bennehan mill, offered to lease it.[59] He agreed to be miller for $10 a week, to pay his own board, and to sleep on a plain mattress in the mill, where he could keep a wash tin and towels. He wanted a helper with a salary of $5 a month. He himself would do the repairs and operate the sawmill. He planned to put in elevators to take the toll corn to the second floor to store. He estimated the mill was capable of grinding six bushels of corn per hour and the same amount of wheat; consequently Cameron's toll would be $9 or $10 per day and his expenses just a little over $2 per day if both mills were to run all day. He calculated they might lose three and a half days a month for various reasons, one of them undoubtedly repairs.

Despite this dismal record of breakdowns, altogether different forces caused the river mills' final downfall. Technological improvements doomed them. In the 1870s the old over- and undershot waterwheels had been replaced by turbines, and in the 1880s steam mills were coming more and more into use because they did not require a seat on a stream but could be located in towns where industry was gathering. They very soon cut into the business formerly enjoyed by the old river mills.[60] Paul Cameron saw clearly the drift of the times and advised his son Bennehan against repairing the dams after a severe flooding in August 1889. A newly built railroad bridge across the Neuse had augmented the damage by backing up the water.[61] After ordering Bennehan to bring suit against the railroad, Paul discussed the problem the mills had always been for him:

> Now as to the reconstruction of the Red Mill dam & the Saw Mill on Little River! I have the same opinion that I have ever had — but for the enormous family of slaves my father & uncle had to bread: & the large crops of wheat on the plantations, the mill maintained at constant cost in building dams & other repairs did not pay — the customwork was never worth the cost of maintenance. As I thought then so I think now. Besides — I was fully convinced that it would [be] a hard sum to work to say to what extent the Mill pond poisend the land, & shortened the product & destroyed the health of the neighborhood. The Harris Hill & the Little River Grave yard can make the best response; & yet

nothing ever increased so rapidly. Under my rule it doubled in 20 years. But you ask how can farms be used without a Mill! My own belief is that the Mills will never be wanted to grind up large crops of wheat again & that those who will run them will not be able in about 7 years to rebuild the dams and the water wheels. After much reflection I say it seems best to me to let the dams be taken down & put up a steam Mill at or near the R.Road Station in the Little River field or below the crossing of the RR of the Hillsboro & Oxford Road. The Mill on Eno or New Mill might be taken down & made a Mill house for grinding corn & wheat on a large scale if it should become desirable & the Red Mill might be made a fine wheat barn at Eno associated with a cotton gin — or be used at Fairntosh or at Stagville for a large cotton House or tobacco Storage or Manufactory. I cant say which would be best.[62]

In a follow-up letter Paul added to what he had said by reporting that various owners of large mills had told him they were no longer profitable and many had ceased grinding.[63]

Apparently Bennehan did not accept this advice immediately; during the mid-1890s he was still making repairs to the mills.[64] Severe freshets in 1904 and 1908, however, probably ended the Red Mill's service as a mill, if it in fact had continued that long. It was possibly at that time that Bennehan finally acted on his father's advice and moved it to Stagville. The large farm building standing at the entrance to Stagville today, last used as a tobacco packhouse, was certainly not built for that use. Its roughly twenty-four by thirty feet, three-storey construction strongly resembles a mill. It cannot be the New Mill for the Collinses inherited that. Furthermore, it was the Red Mill that Paul Cameron suggested be moved to Fairntosh or Stagville to be used as a tobacco storage or manufactory. The packhouse building is almost certainly the old Red Mill.

Mention of the Red Mill dam is the last vestige in the family papers of the mills and milldams that once occupied so prominent a place in the plantation's economy. In 1922 the railroad bridge again caused the waters of a freshet to back up into the Eno River and wash away the Red Mill dam forever.[65] Nothing now remains at either Eno River site of the vexatious mills that exacted such costly attention and heavy labor over so many years.

10. Masters of Slaves[1]

The economic basis of the southern plantation system was slave labor. The social dominance which the planter and his family enjoyed, with its aura of privilege was, however, not derived solely from economic advantages; in addition to providing release from manual labor, it became a way of life and a point of view that died very hard. Therefore the changes which the Civil War effected were for the Camerons and their kind very deep and all-encompassing and were not only the result of the loss of the slaves; the changes were social and psychological as well as economic.

While slave labor was ostensibly free labor, there were expenses connected with it that any slaveholder recognized. The slaves had to be housed, fed, clothed, cared for when sick, maintained in childhood and old age when they could yield no service, and finally coffined and buried. Still these expenses were more than offset by the gains of a plantation efficiently run on a large scale and by the other more subtle advantages the system carried with it.

Although the economic profitability of slavery is still being argued, it seems obvious that if large-scale commercial farming with slave labor had not been lucrative, the Bennehans and Camerons would not have continued it. They had not been born planters; with money made in other pursuits they had deliberately chosen to invest in land and slaves. Admittedly an element in their choice would have been the social one: land and slaves were the hallmark of success and prestige; the planter's was a way of life any white man might well have aspired to in that time and place. Although they had other options, they deliberately chose to pursue and ever expand their agricultural efforts.

As they accumulated more and more land around them with more and more slaves to work it, the Bennehan-Cameron family became a small white minority of the population where they lived. The history of the black majority is partly found in the family papers. In them are revealed the origins and growth of that work force of slaves, their location and housing, their working conditions and welfare, and their relations with the overseers and masters in whose hands their well-being rested.

The large "black family" (as the Camerons always called their slaves) numbering at its height around 900 men, women, and children on the North Carolina plantations was assembled in a variety of ways over a

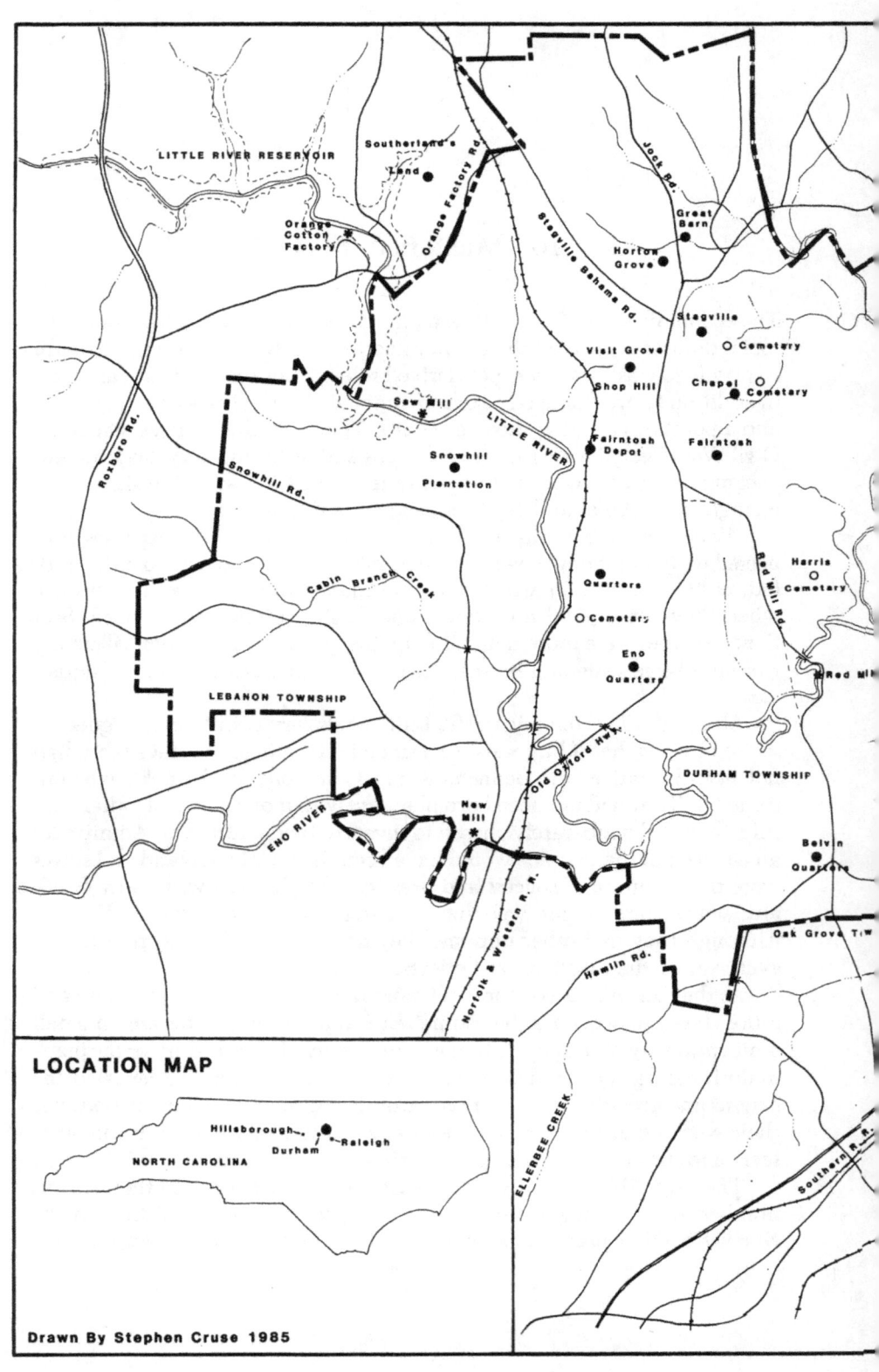

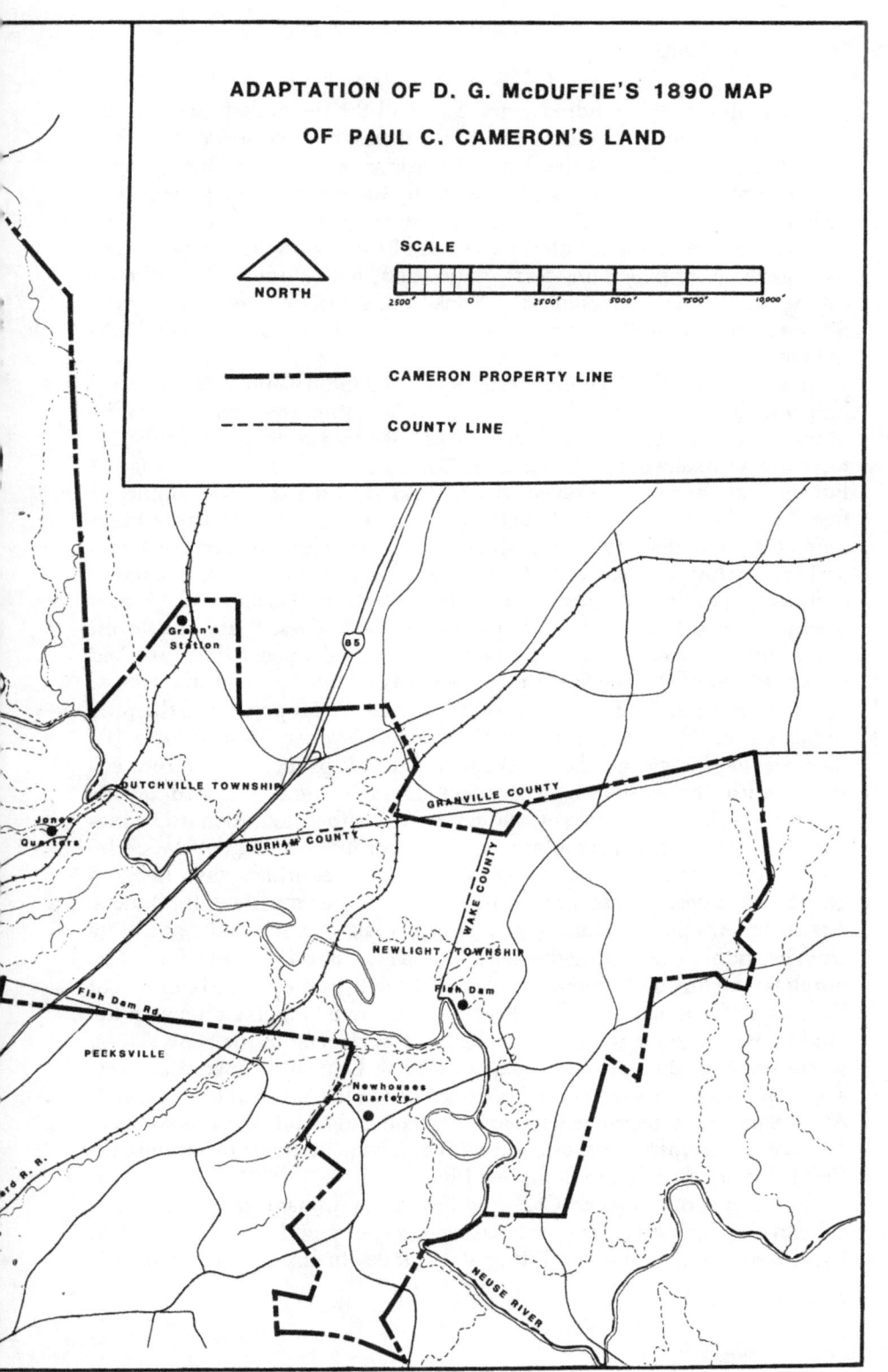

period of almost one hundred years. Since all the slaves despite their different origins were knit ultimately into a widespread network of kinship through intermarriage of the disparate groups, a history of their growth must begin with the earliest slaves owned by Richard and Mary Amis Bennehan at the time of their marriage in 1776 or 1777.

Natural increase accounted for much of their growth, but purchase, too, played a large part in their composition, both through a small continuous flow of new slaves into the black family and by several sizable additions from time to time, resulting in a steady infusion of new blood into the older stock.

The black family of Thomas Amis of Northampton County, North Carolina, was the main source of these slaves. By her father's will written in 1764 Mary Amis inherited five slaves whom with their increase over the twelve intervening years she brought to Orange County at the time of her marriage.[2] For his part, Richard Bennehan contributed at least two small families of five slaves in all whom he bought in 1777.[3] There were probably other sources, now unidentifiable, for Bennehan's 1778 tax list included the names and ages of thirty-one slaves.[4] At least one of these, that of Scrub, is found as early as 1771 in the accounts of the Little River store.[5] He had undoubtedly been purchased by Bennehan at some earlier date. These thirty-one slaves, then, formed the nucleus of the group that eventually peopled and worked the broad plantation lands of the Bennehans and later of the Camerons.

The Amis family slaves formed an even larger proportion of the total number after 1797 when Mary Amis Bennehan's brother, Thomas Amis, Jr., died leaving his niece Rebecca Bennehan all his property, real and personal, with the exception of $1,000.[6] Thomas Amis, Jr., had owned twenty-five slaves, only two of whom were to be liberated. Richard Bennehan, as executor of Amis's estate, in 1803 recorded the result of the settlement which, because of children born in the meantime, gave Rebecca twenty-six slaves in that year, a month before her marriage to Duncan Cameron[7] Another account a year later reveals that she had 1,200 acres from her father comprising the Brick House Plantation, already deeded by purchase to Duncan Cameron, and that Bennehan himself had thirteen of the slaves of Thomas Amis, Jr.[8] Perhaps Bennehan had given Rebecca the land in exchange for the slaves. Rebecca kept the rest of the Amis slaves, who from that time on were counted among Duncan Cameron's slaves. Thus Amis family slaves formed the nucleus of the Cameron force as well. At the time of his marriage Duncan Cameron had acquired a few slaves of his own. He seems to have brought with him from his home in Virginia the first slave he owned, a man named Jim.[9]

From 1803 on, Duncan Cameron began to purchase slaves systematically to keep up with his ever-increasing acreage of land under cultivation. By November 1810 he was listing sixty slaves in his personal financial record.[10] A similar account in 1816 showed ninety slaves.[11] By 1839 the number had grown to 347 slaves, and in 1841 to 405 slaves.[12] In 1846 they numbered 514 and the year following, after Thomas D. Bennehan's death, Paul Cameron calculated that the combined Bennehan and Cameron force was then 890 slaves.[13]

The number of Cameron slaves at the time of their emancipation is difficult to estimate. The Orange County census for 1860 listed 592 slaves for Paul, Thomas, and Mildred Cameron combined.[14] Paul's Person County slaves were listed under the overseer's name, Nathaniel Walker, and numbered 114.[15] Margaret Cameron Mordecai's inheritance from her father of over one hundred slaves would have increased during the seven years since his death, but all of them were by 1860 merged with her husband's slaves and listed under her husband's name.[16] Then there were the just about two hundred slaves in the Deep South to be added to the total and twenty or more house servants whom Mildred and Margaret owned jointly.[17] A conservative estimate of the total number of slaves owned on the eve of emancipation by the four remaining children of Duncan Cameron would be well over 1,000 persons. Though he does not give their number, Paul Cameron estimated in 1859 that his slaves were then worth $443,000.[18] Yet in his plea for a pardon at the end of the war, Paul Cameron stated that he had had about 650 slaves on his lands in Orange County before the war, a figure at variance with the census figures.[19]

The list in Appendix B contains the names and former owners of the original Bennehan and Cameron slaves and all slaves purchased by them as revealed in the family papers. It does not contain the names of children born on the plantations. The family papers record the last slave purchase in 1842; they include none made by Paul Cameron. But Paul Cameron's plea to the military authorities in 1865 requesting a guard for the plantations states that he had made two purchases of slaves for the purpose of uniting husband and wife.[20]

No one can now testify to the mental and physical suffering borne by the participants in that uneasy bond of master and slave. The Camerons' papers, however, provide much evidence about the slaves, if largely from the white viewpoint. Half a dozen letters in which the slaves speak for themselves together with voluminous writings, lists, and financial records of the white family make up a mass of material from which a kind of history of this large group emerges.

More than likely the Bennehans and Camerons would have been judged good masters by both whites and blacks in their own time. Although admittedly not the best evidence, Paul Cameron's description in his letter to the military authorities of the regimen under which the slaves lived is the only comprehensive statement on the subject in the family papers:

Heretofore a mild & humane care & control of the family of negroes has been observed for a long period of time — that they have been as docile & free from violence & vice as the same number to be found any where in the South. The entire labour of each farm has heretofore been directed by a white man in the office of an overseer whilst he has had the aid of former master & well educated physician, in the police & sanitary supervision of the property & population. Supplies of food have been regularly distributed from the mills & store houses every seventh day. The females have been employed in the domestic manufacture of clothing suited to all classes & distributed to all equally. That from infancy old age & other causes not one half of the entire population have been available in the field or house for any useful purpose — whose wants in food & clothing constituted a heavy burden on those that had capacity to labour.[21]

Food, clothing, housing, working conditions, treatment, and overall experience must have varied considerably for the slaves according to their occupations. The house servants would have been close to the white family and under their immediate supervision most of the time. Treated almost as members of the family, they probably were dealt a share of verbal chastisement and criticism because of their proximity, but there is no evidence of their having been mistreated. They would also have received better food and clothing than field hands: left-overs from the whites' table and cast-offs from their wardrobes. Family letters frequently contained affectionate comments about them and their faithful performance of their duties.

The whites in general considered house servants superior to the vast rank and file of the black force and probably chose them for their intelligence and dependability. The Cameron papers confirm this impression though nowhere is it actually stated. Children of house servants became in turn house servants, perpetuating and accentuating through the years the qualities their masters desired in them. That house servants were preferably mulattoes the Cameron papers also confirm. Mary Walker, her mother and children, the Umstead slaves, Virgil Bennehan and his kin — all house servants — were mulattoes. The census records of 1870 and 1880 show a high proportion of mulattoes among the Camerons' former slaves.

Among the favored slaves should be numbered those with special skills or responsibilities: the wagoners, coachmen, tanners, carpenters, millers, blacksmiths, shoemakers, coopers, and gardeners. This class of slaves, like the house servants, could take pride in their work and in their masters, whom they knew well.

Field hands fared less well; under the supervision of overseers, they were only infrequently in the master's presence, and were imperfectly known to him. Overseers knew it was to their advantage to get as much work as possible out of the slaves short of maiming them, and they usually did not spare the whip for malingering and idling on the job. Very little is found in the Camerons' papers about physical punishment, but it was certainly not unknown. George Anderson, when he lived in Hillsborough with Duncan Cameron, reported to him that he had had to whip Jim once or twice for disobeying or for staying out at night against Cameron's wishes.[22]

The most notable case of cruelty on the Cameron plantations occurred when William Nichols, an overseer, struck a slave named Jim a blow on the head. "I fear that we have a case of murder on our plantation," Paul Cameron wrote to Willie P. Mangum.[23] Dr. James Webb was sent for, however, and trepanned Jim, who recovered.[24]

Suffering could take other forms. For the Cameron slaves possibly the most widely felt blow was the large-scale removal of 110 slaves from the plantations in North Carolina to the new plantation in Greene County (now Hale County), Alabama, in 1844. For those who went and for those who remained, the move meant heartache and separation from family and friends. Taken away from the only environment most of them had ever known, they well knew they were going so far away that they would never see home and friends again. This was the worst pang that slavery could inflict. The Camerons were quite aware of what they were doing, and Paul dreaded it.[25] Yet expedience prevailed; heartache was built into the system.

After Paul Cameron decided to buy a plantation in Alabama, he began preparations for the removal of the slaves, animals, and supplies. Clothing, including shoes, had to be made, and blankets and hats and a thousand buttons of iron or horn had to be purchased from Petersburg.[26] Two large tents were made measuring thirty by forty feet to shelter the women and children during their nightly stopovers on the long trek.[27] Wagons were bought for the trip from Eli Murray of the Cross Roads Church area, now in Alamance County.[28] Most if not all of the slaves were chosen from the Person County plantations, probably because they already had lived apart from their master and would find their existence in Alabama little different from their old except as to location and climate; the move would be least hard on them. Before the final parting, the people were to be brought down to Fairntosh by Mr. Bobbitt, a long time and trusted overseer, with the help of Squire, a slave.[29] George Laws was hired to take the caravan to Alabama. He was to receive $600 to cover his wages of $140 and the expenses of the group. The caravan was to include two wagons, twenty-one mules, and one horse besides 110 slaves.[30]

They left on the first of November accompanied part way by Paul to make sure all went well. They walked about twenty miles a day, and all had arrived at the plantation in Alabama by December 7th. A letter from Paul on that date tells of concluding terms with Colonel Armistead, the seller; 1,680 acres cost Duncan Cameron $29,400. The plantation included 1,100 acres of open land, two new cotton houses with gins, a cedar log house of six rooms for the overseer, cabins for the slaves (the condition of which disappointed Paul when he saw them), and four wells. Paul secured the services of Charles Lewellin as overseer, paying him three times the annual salary of an overseer in Orange County: $600.[31] One infant died on the way to Alabama and another slave, Edmund, a young man, died on arrival. The latter was a brother of Jenny, a Fairntosh slave then dying of tuberculosis.[32] Reports of the property — crops, stock, slaves, and equipment — are frequent in the Camerons' papers from 1845 on, but individual slaves as persons pass out of the Cameron history forever.

Because these slaves were separated from their masters, who consequently could not oversee the overseers on the Alabama and later the Mississippi plantations, they endured the worst conditions of all. They included probably more than the usual number of runaway slaves. One runaway when caught said that he belonged to a man in North Carolina named 'Camron' and that he was on his way home to him.[33] William Lamb, a later overseer in Mississippi, wrote to Paul Cameron, "Len & Nat missing I suppose they had rather try the woods than pick cotton. Len is the leader as usial he was whiped Saturday at noon for not having cotton enough is the only cause I know of, Supose he was offended for being whiped."[34]

At least one was recovered, for Lamb again wrote, "Len is at his work with his shackles on and I have him confined at night under care of a trusty fellow (Daniel Low) he is very little trouble but to all apearances there is but little if any change in him I would suggest the Idia of exchange him for a carpenter for this place."[35] As a rule the Bennehans and Camerons did not sell their slaves unless they were unruly or attempted to run away.

Ironically, it was not in the Deep South that the Camerons had the most serious case of runaway slaves, but in the Raleigh family of slaves right in their own back yard. An old slave, Siller, her daughter Mary, and her grandchildren Frank, Agnes, and Bryant, were involved in the story. Mary was the first to run, sometime before 1851.[36] The Camerons knew she went to Philadelphia but seem not to have tried to get her back. After Duncan Cameron died in 1853, Frank, too, ran away, but they made every effort to retrieve him. A letter from Frank to his family told of his working in Trenton, New Jersey, for $1 a day. Paul advised his sisters to sell the rest of the family to forestall losing them all. When another letter from Frank to his grandmother asking his mother's address again revealed his whereabouts, Paul took measures to get him back. He engaged Joseph Woods, a neighbor with experience in the slave trade, to go north with Philip Southerland, the Stagville overseer. Paul procured letters of introduction for them from George Badger and Willie P. Mangum and gave Woods a power of attorney to act for him in bringing back the fugitive.[37] He wrote out a detailed description of Frank, also known as Francis Walker, probably the most interesting document in the case. Frank was described as about twenty years old, "so nearly white that with ninety-five men in a hundred he will pass for a white man." He was five feet eight to ten inches tall, with straight black hair, blue eyes, and freckles. A horse had bitten off the tip of one finger on his right hand, and he was fond of whiskey and likely to be found in "such places."[38]

In spite of all that the Camerons knew about him and all the care they took to retrieve him, he was never found. Instead, some five years later Mildred Cameron received a letter from a professor of mining at the University of Pennsylvania, carefully worded to move even the hardest heart, pleading with Miss Cameron to allow her former slave Mary Walker to buy her children Agnes and Bryant.[39] "Her mother-heart yearns unspeakably after them," he wrote, "and her eyes fail looking towards the South, over the dreary interval which separates them from her. She has saved a considerable sum of money to buy them, and will sacrifice anything to see them once again and have their young lives renew the freshness of her own weary spirit." He described Mary Walker as "a lovely person," "a sincere & elevated Christian" with a "ladylike & conscientious carriage" that "has made her a large circle of friends." It is a long letter but did not achieve its aims; both slaves were listed on the Mordecai slave lists right up to the beginning of 1865.

Long pent-up anger and frustration or sudden passion caused by punishment could make the slaves erupt into violence. Just before the outbreak of the Civil War, word reached Paul Cameron that two slaves he had hired for the Mississippi plantation had tried to kill their overseer.[40] He went south immediately to handle the situation.

Although the Camerons of Fairntosh never personally experienced violence of slaves, some of their relations did. The Reverend John Cameron was the intended victim of a poisoning attempt fortunately frustrated in time by inadvertent disclosure; and Thomas Ruffin's house was set on fire by a house servant while Anne Cameron was there recovering from childbirth.[41] The alarm was sounded in time to save all the family.

The Camerons encouraged capable slaves to learn skills, primarily to save them the hire of white artisans. A number of this slave elite are known from the records. Old man Coxe, Jim, Lewis, and Soloman were coopers engaged in making barrels in which flour was transported to market; they also made lard kegs and the smaller butter firkins. Jim was for a time distiller.[42] Cyrus was the miller in Person County and later at the Cameron New Mill on the Eno in Orange County, where he fell into the habit of drunkenness.[43] Cyrus trained a fellow slave Daniel to fill his old post in Person.[44] The Bennehans had a slave Matthew for their Eno mill, and many of the mill repairs could be done by Dandridge, who was also a good carpenter and furniture maker.[45]

One of the most responsible jobs of all was that of wagoner. The wagoner not only had to guard the produce on its way to market, manage the horses and wagons to see that they arrived home again safe and undamaged, but carry money to merchants in Petersburg or Fayetteville and bring home the receipts, having made sure that his master was credited for all that he had delivered. It was a job for independent action and thought, and a few of the wagoners took occasion to use them. Pompey and Lewis, Cameron slaves, each in turn had to be relieved of the job after they were discovered bartering plantation produce on the side and bringing home whiskey and coffee to sell to the other slaves or hauling for pay goods from Petersburg to Oxford on their return trips and pocketing the money.[46] Lewis later became a blacksmith.[47] The Bennehans were luckier in their wagoners. Their slave Jerry was managing the wagonage as early as 1810, and twenty years later he was still on the job.[48] Following Jerry, Norvel took over that responsibility.[49]

One of the most valuable of the skilled slaves was the tanner, Ben Sears, who was badly missed when he died.[50] He was something of a mechanic as well and managed the threshing machine in the barn at harvest.[51] Paul attributed his illness and that of other slaves to the damage their health suffered through exposure to the heavy dust in the barns at wheat-threshing time.[52] A slave narrative collected in 1937 from an ex-slave of the Camerons, Doc Edwards, describes the threshing process.[53]

> We had a han' thrashing machine. It was roun' like a stove pipe, only bigger. We fed de wheat to it an' shook it 'til de wheat was loose from de straw an' when it come out at de other end it fell on a big cloth, bigger den de sheets. We had big curtains all roun' de cloth on de floor, like a tent, so de wheat wouldn' get scattered. Den we took de pitchfork an' lifted de straw up an' down so de wheat would go on de cloth. Den we moved de straw when de wheat was all loose. Den we fanned de wheat wid big pieces of cloth to get de dust an' dirt outen it, so it could be taken to de mill an' groun' when it was wanted.

Paul Cameron was hard put to find a replacement for Ben Sears. "I would as soon look for a mass of pearl in the bed of Flat River as a currier in Orange County."[54] He finally employed a white man, Mr. Blakely, to do the job and to train some of the Negroes to do it. At first Mr. Blakely refused to allow the Negroes to hold a knife. Paul wrote to his father, "I thereupon told him I had no further use for him or any man who had such narrow views. This soon brought him to his senses & he now promises to instruct them & as far as I can see very much ashamed of himself."[55]

Ben Sears was not unique among Bennehan-Cameron slaves in having a surname. That slaves had surnames often came as a surprise to many ex-slaveholders when the Civil War was over, and names that on some plantations the slaves had kept like contraband through generations of bondage were then brought out into open use.[56] This had never been the situation on the Bennehan-Cameron plantations, where as early as the 1803 list of Rebecca Bennehan's slaves at least two are shown with surnames: Esther and Jim Dickenson.[57] Through the years more and more of the slaves' surnames were used, often to prevent confusion of slaves with the same first names. A descriptive word or place name was also often used for the same purpose: Yellow Daniel and Fish Dam Sam, for example.

It is not possible to explain the origin of many of their surnames with certainty, but it is safe to say that most of the names they bore belonged to a master, former or current. Ben Umstead and his children, for example, were originally slaves of Dr. John Umstead from whose estate Thomas Bennehan obtained them.[58] Many Cameron slaves took the Cameron name, as is easily proved by the 1870 census. Thomas Bennehan's favorite slave took the name Bennehan.

Some of the other surnames found in the slave lists are Alves, Amis (and its variant Amey), Bell, Cain, Dunnagan, Justis, Latta, Laws, Parks, Ray, Walker, Watson, and Yarbrough. Other names of blacks which show up either in the neighborhood in the 1870 census, in the Cameron papers, or in the cemetery at Little River farm are Brandon, Haskins, Hart, Meaks, Peaks, Sowell, and Veasey.

The Amis family name undoubtedly conferred on its owners a certain distinction and prestige if only in length of service in the family. The white family was aware of the different origins of their Negroes and of this group within the larger black family. Paul wrote of his dying Amis slave Luke, "I am not without a strong attachment towards him — from his association with my father & family and the many acts of kindness towards myself."[59] Another Amis slave, old man Ned, certainly showed pride in his origins. When Thomas Bennehan wished to breed his mares, he was considering where to send them to be covered. "I have consulted the old man Ned this morning to ascertain if he would go with the mare's, in reply he said it would depend upon his health & sight, what compensation he was to have, that it would be only to oblige if he traveled to the mountain's, that the mare's had best be sent to NoAmpton [Northampton County, N.C., where the Amis family lived] & that he would be reddy to go there at any time, that in that country was the best blood."[60] Obviously Ned had status to bargain thus with his master. He also made it quite clear that whether of horses or men Northampton blood was superior.

Of still another slave, old Aunt Hannah, who received respect because of her long association with the family, Paul wrote, "She was ever a favorite of our dear Mother — and deserved it for her integrity & fidelity — one after another the old set is passing away."[61]

The question of emancipation for slaves must have been ever present in the minds of the white family, who had been closely involved with it all their lives. Nowhere in their papers, however, is there a statement expressing their views on chattel slavery in general. The will of Thomas Amis, Jr., which gave Rebecca Bennehan many slaves, also freed two: Grace, his mulatto woman, and her son Harry.[62] In his office as executor of this will

Richard Bennehan was involved in carrying out that wish of his brother-in-law, but Richard Bennehan liberated no slaves in his own will.

Duncan Cameron was early brought into the emancipation problem by the will of Absalom Tatum which gave to Duncan Cameron and several other friends instructions to free his slaves.[63] These slaves were freed early in the nineteenth century, but almost fifty years later a disgruntled Tatum heir attempted to re-enslave and claim possession of them.[64] Paul Cameron felt obliged to take up their cause because his father, the last of the men involved with the action, was then dead. Thomas D. Bennehan and, later, Paul Cameron, had already had experience with manumission. The old Bennehan family doctor, John Umstead, left instructions in his will that Dicey, a slave, and her two daughters, Emiline and Harriet, were to be freed.[65] Catlett Campbell and Thomas Bennehan were to superintend their manumission. Certainly they effected Dicey's liberation, but not that of her daughters. When Bennehan died in 1847, his will referred to these two rather cryptically.[66] He left to Duncan Cameron his man Ben Umstead, Ben's wife Mary, their six sons, and a daughter, asking him to "place them in as comfortable a condition as may be in his power" along with "the slaves given me by Dr. John Umstead of Orrange." He then described the latter as "the daughters and their increase of the woman Dicey who has been emancipated." He added that Cameron fully understood his wishes in the matter. It is clear from this that Dicey's daughters had never been freed, and in this way Bennehan seemed to be asking, discreetly, that they be liberated then along with their descendants, who included Ben Umstead and his family.

That Duncan Cameron so construed the language is clear from a letter of his to Paul.[67] He wrote that he was then (1848) contemplating buying Harriet's son William from Dr. Webb with the intention of sending her and her children out of the country. Cameron's discretion in this matter as in all matters, as well as as the particularly sensitive nature of manumission at that time, is manifest in his added injunction to Paul, "say nothing to any one whatsoever." Apparently he never carried out his intention; the Stagville slave list of 1857 includes Harriet, her husband Lewis, also an Umstead slave, and their children Ovid, Amy, and Peggy.[68]

Duncan Cameron had been president of the Colonization Society of the state in 1834 and presumably contributed to the cause over the years.[69] A state chapter had been formed in 1819 to manage and encourage the liberation of slaves and their resettlement in Liberia. An urgent letter from the society's general agent in 1839 asked Cameron, as executor, for money to send to Liberia 125 emancipated slaves of John Rex, who also left money to establish a hospital in Raleigh. The bank's funds had been shut off and the society needed the money immediately, for the slaves were already on their way to Norfolk to board ship.[70] Presumably he continued to support the cause. In 1848 he was directly involved with the society when he made the arrangements for the liberation and transportation to Liberia of certain of Thomas Bennehan's slaves.

Duncan Cameron's own will did not free any of his slaves. The case of the Umstead slaves, however, was still on his conscience. Item eight of his will states, "I give, devise, and bequeath to my son Paul C. Cameron and his heirs, Ben Umstead and his wife and all their children now born or to be born hereafter, being the same slaves devised to me by my late friend Thos. D. Bennehan decd with the like injunction as is contained in his devise to myself."[71] Ben Umstead and all his children were still on the 1857 slave list.

Though Thomas Bennehan, Duncan Cameron, and Paul Cameron seem never to have fulfilled their obligations to most of Dr. Umstead's slaves, all three were instrumental in the freeing of Virgil, his wife Fereby (Phebe), a boy William (called Toast), and his sister Margaret (called Peggy). These were Thomas Bennehan's own slaves whom he wished to liberate for their devoted service to him. He stipulated in his will that they be freed and transported to a free state or to Liberia, whichever Virgil preferred. After his manumission Virgil was to receive $500.[72] Perhaps Thomas Bennehan was afraid Paul and Duncan Cameron would fail to act on this instruction, and to preclude that possibility he devised his plantations of Stagville and Little River to Paul Cameron *on the condition* that he free the four slaves.

Virgil's was a very special case. He was the son of Mary (his father unknown) who was the daughter of Phil and Esther, slaves whom Mary Amis had brought with her when she married Richard Bennehan. Fereby (Phebe), Virgil's wife, was an Umstead slave, as were William and Margaret. All were mulattoes. Virgil probably had early displayed his intelligence and dependability. In 1836 Thomas Bennehan wrote of him to Paul, "I can very badly spare him from home, particularly of a night."[73] Virgil became for Bennehan more than a trusted house servant; he was a kind of general manager in charge of slave rations and the keys to the smoke house, and even substituted as housekeeper when Charlotte Rice was away from home. A friend of Bennehan's stopped at Stagville while Bennehan was away, and after his visit wrote him a note to say, "Virgil does the honors of your house with much propriety to your old friends."[74]

In addition to his other tasks the greatest service he performed was that of doctor to the slaves. How he acquired the special knowledge required for this function is unknown. Perhaps he picked up over the years from the Bennehans and Paul Cameron enough experience to prescribe the standard medicines any master or mistress could dispense. Perhaps he had more specialized training from Dr. Umstead or another of the white family's doctors. Many references to him in this capacity are found in Paul Cameron's letters: "Virgil has all his sick at Stagville and is as in times gone by attentive and kind to them. . . . Virgil tells me that day-before-yesterday whilst on a visit to the plantations in Wake he found 15 persons sufficiently sick to give each a portion of calomel and ipecac. . . . In Uncles family Virgil is up again and about the house and yard, and in the mornings and evenings rides over the road to see such as need his aid."[75]

After Bennehan's death in 1847, Virgil apparently appealed to Duncan Cameron to make the decision for him whether or not to go to Liberia. Paul referred to his father's responsibility in the matter when he wrote him: "I don't know a more useful man in his condition in life — and his destiny and residence will be made and controlled entirely by your advice."[76] Cameron decided on Liberia and made the arrangements with the Colonization Society. Paul escorted the four Negroes to Baltimore in April 1848 and saw them equipped and ready for their passage on the *Liberia Packet* which sailed April 11th. The *African Repository*, the Colonization Society's publication, contains the passenger list for that sailing; the final four names of the 138 emigrants were Virgil Bannehan *(sic)*, 37; his wife Phebe, 40; William his nephew, 22; and Peggy his niece, 19; all named Bannehan and all mulattoes.[77] Two letters came back from Virgil to the Camerons: one, now missing, written after he boarded ship with a heart too full to say more than farewell to his friends;[78] the second letter arrived months later, containing a long description of Liberia, the land and the inhabitants, persons he had met and dined with, and what the prospects were for him in that country. "I find practice anuf in this place but no pay mony in Africa is out of the question. Every Boddy wants Drs But non can pay Them. I have at this time 5 Pashints and the five is not worth $5."[79]

Twice in the letter Virgil mentioned his indecision about remaining in Africa. "This is a very fin country for sum people but I am afrad it will not sut me." And it did not suit him. The Baltimore County Census of 1850 shows that all four Bennehans had returned to the United States.[80] In the census Virgil listed himself as a speculator and William as a mariner. Paul Cameron received one more letter from Virgil saying he had settled his family in Baltimore and was leaving soon for the gold region of California to be absent two years.[81] A letter from Phebe still in Baltimore was received by her daughter (probably by a former marriage) Miss Anna Bell at Judge Cameron's in Raleigh in 1852. Phebe did not mention Virgil though she did report that William was working on a steamboat and that Margaret was well. Phebe herself had been very sick but had had a good doctor and was then well.[82] She hoped to go to Philadelphia on a visit.

Virgil had been kept very busy on the Bennehan-Cameron plantations, for the health of the black family, like that of the white, often gave cause for concern. For the master is was an economic as well as an emotional interest. In 1835, after a season of more than usual sickness, Paul wrote to his father, "I fear that the negroes have suffered much from the want of proper attention and kindness under the late distemper — No love of lucre shall ever induce me to be cruel, or even to make or permit to be made any great exposure of their persons at inclement seasons — It is besides miserable economy!"[83]

In the early days of Stagville and Fairntosh, sickness seems to have been less frequent and less severe. When the population multiplied, however, the possibility of contagion and illness multiplied too. At first smallpox was the most dreaded scourge, but near the turn of the century a safe inoculation came into use in Virginia, and Richard Bennehan's commission merchant in Petersburg, Ebenezer Stott, wrote to him, "We have heard that some of our Doctors intend this Spring inoculating with the *Cow* pock which is said effectually to secure the patient against the *small* Pox, with the advantage of being entirely free from danger — It is already introduced at several places in this State, & will probably soon be generally used as a substitute for the other — It is also said not to be contagious, of course the patients may go through it at their own house, & so avoid the inconvenience of a public Hospital."[84]

The older method of using the small pox matter itself had involved serious risk and seems not to have been resorted to for inoculation of slaves. Bennehan quickly took advantage of the new method; Dr. John Shore of Richmond sent him some matter which Bennehan reported he used successfully on his slaves, he and his son Thomas already having tried it out successfully on themselves.[85] From that time on smallpox ceased to be any problem. There were other diseases to take its place, however, against which they were helpless. Typhus and typhoid visited them at intervals; bilious and intermittent fevers came seasonally, and as the century grew older malaria proliferated alarmingly. Measles, whooping cough, and diphtheria ran through the black families from time to time killing many children; and there were always the chronic diseases of worn-out bodies. More slowly and insidiously ran the mysterious consumption, a disease which killed a number of Duncan Cameron's children as well as slaves. Young adults were the most susceptible to it. In 1837, for example, a year in which Paul Cameron kept a record of slave deaths and their causes, of twenty-eight slave deaths eight, or almost one-third, died of tuberculosis.[86]

In certain years the slaves, and the white family too, endured particularly severe epidemics of fever, and as the slave force grew, the burden of nursing and doctoring became heavier and heavier. It was Paul Cameron who bore the brunt of it with help from his uncle and Virgil; he made the rounds of the sick every day to dose them, evaluate their progress, see them through the crises, and if possible to snatch them from the jaws of death. "I must confess that I am nearly worn down with the troubles of the past six weeks and am not a little disheartened at the result of our labours in your black family," he wrote to his father during one of the bad years, 1836.[87]

Treatment of the slaves' illnesses went beyond Paul's attentions, however; for a doctor was called in at the beginning of an epidemic to diagnose the illness and prescribe a cure, or more commonly a palliative; most treatment doctors could give was irrelevant if not downright harmful. Medical practitioners in the eighteenth and nineteenth centuries, besides the copious use of drugs, resorted almost entirely to bleeding and blistering, measures which weakened the patient or aggravated his suffering. Emetics, purgatives, opiates, and barks formed the materia medica and could be dispensed by anyone, along with home remedies from herbs and the tonics, whiskey and brandy. The Bennehans and Camerons had a number of doctors they called in for themselves and their slaves, and the doctor often stayed many days at a time until the worst of an epidemic was over.

Individual cases of organic or acute disease were often sent to Dr. Webb in Hillsborough, where they stayed until treatment was complete or where an operation was performed and their recuperation supervised. On at least one occasion Richard Bennehan took an old slave, Soloman, with him to the springs, where he seemed to derive so much benefit that he was left behind in the charge of a friend when Bennehan returned home.[88]

Childbirth, too, was medically supervised, but entirely by midwives. Mrs. Margaret Cothran attended the Person County slaves for many years, and her bills, submitted by her husband William, are found throughout the family papers.[89]

When the slaves numbered in the hundreds, the medical bills became very large, and in the 1840s Paul Cameron decided to manage the slaves' fevers himself. "I have called no one to see them," he wrote to his father, "And by Gods help, I will have less to do with Drs than heretofore, unless they assure me of better success and shorter bills."[90] By then blistering and bleeding were going out of fashion. As early as 1815 Rebecca Cameron had been able to write to Duncan that Dr. Umstead had been there ten days treating the blacks for pleurisy and had not bled a single case. In 1848, Paul had found that his system worked: "cases of chills & fever we shall have & with the quinine & opium easily managed by our overseers — the best practice ever in use in our family."[91]

Though ignorant of the pathology of disease, the Camerons were not unaware of the contributory factors of housing and hygiene. Certainly crowded, unclean living conditions accounted for some of the rise in illness in general over the years; lice were the vector for typhus, one of the regular fevers. The reason for the increase in malaria can only be guessed at; the clearing of more and more bottomland, much of it at time under water, extended the mosquito breeding grounds. Perhaps a period of greater than usual rainfall raised the water level in watercourses and made more of the bottomland marshy. Certain it is that malaria increased markedly in the 1850s. Though Paul was not aware of the connection, he commented on

Richard Bennehan (1743–1825). Portrait attributed to John W. Jarvis. Photograph by Walter E. Shackelford.

Above: Bennehan House, Stagville, 1933. Courtesy Duke University Archives. *Below:* Bennehan House, Stagville (1787–1799). Photograph by Duncan Heron.

Above: Duncan Cameron (1777–1853). Engraving of Wm. G. Browne portrait in Sam A. Ashe, ed., *Biographical History of North Carolina,* 1905. *Below:* Kitchen and Dairy (1814), Fairntosh. Courtesy N.C. Division of Archives and History.

Above: Salem Chapel (1825–1826), Fairntosh. Photograph by Kenneth McFarland. *Below:* Fairntosh Plantation house (1810–1827), south view. Photograph by Kenneth McFarland.

Above: Outbuildings, Fairntosh, left to right kitchen, dairy (not visible), smoke house, commissary, slave house. Photograph by Kenneth McFarland. *Below:* Fairntosh Plantation house (1810–1827). Photograph by Kenneth McFarland.

Left: Slave gravestone, Little River Plantation: "Sacred to the memory of Phillip Meaks who departed this life on the 22th [*sic*] June 1837 aged 74 years." Photograph by Kenneth McFarland.
Below: Slave house, Shop Hill (c. 1851). Wing at right is later addition. Courtesy Stagville Center.

Above: Paul C. Cameron (1808–1891). Engraving from Sam. A. Ashe, ed., *Biographical History of North Carolina*, 1905. *Below:* Barn at Horton Grove (1860). Courtesy N.C. Division of Archives and History. Photograph by Joann Sieburg-Baker.

Above: Bennehan Cameron (1854–1925). Engraving from Sam. A. Ashe, ed., *Biographical History of North Carolina*, 1905. *Below:* Fairntosh Plantation house (1928) before restoration. Courtesy N.C. Division of Archives and History.

the infestations of mosquitoes in those years and described how his wife with a servant or two went round at night the last thing before going to bed to kill the mosquitoes clustered on the walls despite the doors and windows having been shut since dark. "Never since I have known this place have I seen the like of mosquitoes."[92]

Paul sensed, however, that there might be a connection between the mill ponds and the health of the blacks. In a letter to Bennehan, quoted above, advising him against repairing the mill dams he wrote, "I was fully convinced that it would [be] a hard sum to work to say to what extent the Mill pond water poisend the land, & shortened the product & destroyed the health of the neighborhood. The Harris Hill and Little River Grave yard [slave graveyards] can make the best response."[93]

In the early days, housing for slaves on the Bennehan-Cameron plantations was probably no better than that supplied on any other plantation and certainly no worse. Still there could be wide variations in the way the quarters were maintained: whether they were kept dry and in repair, how many persons each one sheltered, and how frequently they were cleaned. A letter from Duncan Cameron's brother Dr. Thomas Nash Cameron deals with housing in relation to the problem of disease.

> It really gives me much concern to hear that, you loose [sic] so many of your negroes, and I have reflected much on what might be the most effectual mode of remedying the evil — The plan most likely to effect it I am satisfied, is to have new houses built for your Negroes, in situations high and dry, and to have the old houses destroyed by fire — Your Physician may make his fortune out of you by prescribing for your sick; but until *the cause* is removed, you will continue to have disease in your family assuming different forms and symptoms as it is influenced by the changes in the seasons — In the winter, genuine Typhus, in the spring Bilious pleurisies, and in the summer and fall bilious fevers which quickly degenerate into the low nervous type of fever —
>
> I think where a number of blacks live on the same plantation, their houses should be changed every five or seven years. They are naturally dirty in their habits, and in that time they accumulate filth enough about them to create disease; independent of this, the materials of which their houses, generally speaking, are constructed, very soon go to decay. Hence, it is that they are always breathing an impure atmosphere."[94]

Ten years later Paul was echoing his uncle's opinion when he commented, "In and about their cabbins are to be found all the predisposing causes to typhus fever."[95] A few years later he reported, "The negroes have been located in their new quarters (excellent cabbins)."[96] It is clear that the Camerons took the advice seriously and continued to improve the slave quarters whenever they could. The really superior houses standing today at Horton Grove and Shop Hill show how far they went in these efforts. Nothing like these slave quarters can be found anywhere else: houses of four rooms each, on two floors, the rooms almost seventeen feet square, separated by passages on each floor, the solid walls filled with brick nogging for insulation, situated on high ground and shaded by oaks. These are the culmination of Duncan Cameron's endeavors to improve the blacks' living conditions. Earlier examples of what they built for this use can be found in the double cabin still standing at Eno Quarter, and in a single cabin behind the main house at Fairntosh.

Whether there was overcrowding is difficult to say, but judged by today's standards there probably was. The 1860 census gives the only known figures for the number of slave houses.[97] Paul Cameron is credited with thirty houses, his brother Thomas with ten houses, his sister Mildred with fifteen to house a total of 592 slaves, an average of between ten and eleven slaves per house. The figures, however, do not tell the whole story; double cabins could house two families; the Horton Grove and Shop Hill houses could shelter four families each. From other documents it is clear that other buildings on the plantations were used to quarter slaves: the old shop, the old store, and the kitchens as well.[98] Some of the house servants slept in the main houses. Perhaps all these structures were included in the count for the census, but that seems unlikely. If the census figures do not include these other structures, then the density per house for the Cameron slaves was considerably less than the census would indicate. A clearer picture is obtained from the Alabama and Mississippi figures, for there there were fewer miscellaneous buildings to supplement the slave houses. The 1860 census for the Alabama plantation shows that 116 slaves were housed in 25 slave houses, on the average a little more than four and a half per house; the Mississippi figures are 83 slaves in 16 houses, just over five per house. These densities are much lower than the Carolina figures would indicate, suggesting that the number of slave houses in the Carolina census does not reflect the true housing situation.[99]

The Camerons tried to instill in their slaves the importance of cleanliness and hygiene. "To day is a day for general cleaning up of all our negro quarters — make all matters clean & [remove] all the trash of the yards," Paul wrote to his father.[100] In another letter Anne Cameron reminded her husband to tell the house servants "that in their own persons I shall expect neatness and cleanliness."[101]

Almost nothing is known about the food which the Cameron slaves ate, but it is reasonable to conclude that it was the standard fare provided for slaves all over the South — meat (invariably pork), corn meal, a sweetener such as molasses or syrup, potatoes and other vegetables when in season. They could catch fish and some game like opossum and rabbits. The fruit was probably minimal, mostly apples and pears. Their clothing, too, was undoubtedly of the standard variety, cotton for summer and perhaps some wool woven in with the cotton for winter wear. All was woven on the plantations either by the slaves or by weavers who visited the plantations for the purpose. Some idea of how the Camerons clothed their slaves may be gathered from a contract for hiring out his slaves drawn up by Duncan Cameron in 1806.[102] The men were to have a coat and overalls of "negro" cotton or substantial homespun fit for winter wear, two shirts and a pair of shoes, a pair of summer overalls, a coarse woolen hat, and a blanket. The women were to have jackets and petticoats of the same kind of cloth, two shifts, a summer petticoat, shoes, and a blanket. The children were to be well clothed summer and winter though their clothing was not itemized. The last stipulation was less standard; many accounts of northern visitors to southern plantations comment on the scantily, scarcely decently clad slave children.

An undated memo in the Cameron Papers from Joseph Woods concerns the weaver who was to come make the clothing. "We will send you the worp to dye Red imeadidtely. The Green for the worp must be died pale blue first. Then use the barks which maks a pretty green, we suppose 1 1/2 oz. of Indigo & 3 of mader."[103] An effort seems to have been made to make the cloth attractive. Another paper indicated that wool hats were not the only head covering used. Caps were on the list, 48 to be ordered of seal skin.[104]

Furnishing the shoes each year was an enormous undertaking. Enough sole and top leather had to be amassed first, sole leather from Petersburg, top leather from the home tanning operation. Then the shoemakers among the slaves had to set to work to make the shoes. The names of some of these men are known: Ben, Lewis Toe, Robbin, Streton, and Walker. The size of the undertaking is indicated in a memo from Paul to his father: "We shall need for all hands some 2400 lbs. of heavy soal leather to shoe family — now about 890 in number."[105] Doc Edward's narrative of his memories of slavery days tells something about the shoemaking process. "We had a shop," he said, "whare our shoes was made. De cobbler would make our shoes wid wooden soles. After de soles was cut dey would be taken down to de blacksmith an' he would put a thin rim or iron aroun' de soles to keep dem from splitting. Dese soles was made from maple an' ash wood."[106]

To see that the people were shod became a sacred duty to Paul. "I know, next to doing my duty, to my beloved father, yourselves and our brother, I cannot better follow the example of our venerated Mother, than in doing my duty, to her faithful old slaves, and their descendants. Do you remember a cold & frosty morning, during her illness, when she said to me 'Paul my son the people ought to be shod' this is ever in my ears, when-ever I see any ones shoes in bad order; and in my ears it will be, so long as I am a master."[107]

The spiritual health of their black family was of concern to the Camerons, too. Duncan Cameron built the chapel on his plantation for their use as well as for that of the white members of the community. The annual Episcopal *Journals* give the best evidence of the chapel's use. One of the first reports states that twenty-six children were baptized at Salem, only one of whom was white.[108] The report of 1828 states the the blacks had instruction on the Saturday preceding the regular Sunday service.[109] In 1843 the Reverend William M. Green, under whose supervision the chapel had been since its beginning, reported that services were still being held once a month at Salem, that a class for black catechumens was held, but that the number of slaves then on the Cameron plantation was so large that the exclusive labors of a missionary were called for.[110] Apparently the call went unheeded; the Camerons hired no missionary, although Josiah Collins, Jr., an acquaintance of the Camerons who had built a chapel on his Lake Phelps plantation, employed a missionary to minister to his own slaves.[111] In 1857 the Reverend George Patterson was that missionary, a man who soon after became a fast friend of the Camerons possibly through the marriage of Paul Cameron's daughter Anne with Josiah's grandson, George Pumpelly Collins.[112] Patterson, who had then joined the theological department of the University of the South at Sewanee, consecrated the new chancel at Salem in 1884 after Paul had made his improvements there.[113]

The concern the Camerons felt to safeguard their economic investment and to perform their Christian duty to others of God's children had another dimension; long association of master and slave led to accommodation on both sides and even to strong affection that transcended the social bounds and color bar. Particularly was this true of the white women and their house servants, for the mistress of the house spent all her waking hours with her young children or in the kitchen or the garden supervising the work and running the household. The children's nurses were never apart from them, and their mother could look on these responsible and affectionate slaves as extensions of herself relying on them to give the children the same anxious attention and love as she would give them herself. In a description (already quoted) of the children written to entertain his father, Paul Cameron gives a picture of this close association. "Maggie & her maid & I may say her shaddow pass the day on a 'seesaw' in the yard. . . . The little boy in the arms of his faithful nurse delights himself out of doors under the shade of a wide hat."[114]

A particular poignancy existed in the relationship of child and nurse, for their fates were often bound up together. In 1844 Paul and Anne lost their oldest child, Jean; a year and a half later the nurse also died. Of her illness Anne wrote to Paul, "I am grieved to hear poor Minerva is still such a sufferer (if she yet lives) Say to her she is constantly in my thoughts, and has my warmest prayers for support and comfort, all here unite with us in our anxiety on her account as she has, by her faithfulness attached herself to all; May God have mercy on her (and I can but hope she will be welcomed and ushered into Heaven by our own dear little lamb, whom I doubt not, will recognize her faithful nurse and friend.)"[115]

Many years later Anne and Paul again lost a child and two nurses. Christiana, a nurse, died just about the same time as their daughter Mary Amis at Judge Ruffin's home on Haw River. "Our nurse Christiana, breathed her last on yesterday about 11 o'clock and her husband returns home to day with a letter to our brother, it was thought prudent to inter Christiana at dark last night."[116] A year later when the family was again visiting the Ruffins the second nurse died. She had been ailing for two years with consumption and had had a hemorrhage from her lungs as early as 1854. Still she went on caring for the children. At last, "yesterday two weeks ago we lost our faithful friend & nurse Moriah. I had her remains taken down home — A sad loss to us all — I had a great regard for her — ever faithful & affectionate to my little ones."[117]

How the slaves felt towards the Bennehans and Camerons is harder to discover. By the nature of the relationship the whites were likely to hear only flattery and the warmer sentiments of their slaves. Feelings of anger and hostility were necessarily suppressed. Still a few examples of their servants' seeming devotion to them are not without value. Jim Ray was a most trusted slave, even an overseer on one of the Person County plantations which was always designated Jim's Place in the records. He may have been the slave Jim whom Duncan Cameron brought with him from Virginia when he first came to Orange County. On one of Paul's visits to Jim's Place after Duncan Cameron's move with his family to Raleigh, Jim said to Paul, "Master Paul I am a ruined man my 'mistis' is gone too far from me; and my Old Master has forgotten that he owns so black a negro as Jim."[118]

Another slave who knew how to oil the wheels of human relations was John Sears, an important servant in the Raleigh household. Writing to Duncan Cameron who was then in Philadelphia with his invalid daughter Mildred, he said, "We are all of us anxious to see Miss Mildred again & pray to God that she may return in health. Although she thought we were tired of toting her tell her, I would rather be toting her all my life, — though life is short, than be without her company so long."[119]

Because of the long years of apparently affectionate association between them, a particular bitterness of the Civil War to the Camerons was what they saw as the defection of their slaves. A few went off and those who remained refused at first to work or return to their duties. They broke into the smoke houses, killed the stock and ate it, and consumed the many months' supply of rations already distributed to them.[120] The sudden freedom after so many generations of slavery brought work to a halt. To the Camerons the freedmen seemed unable to regulate their own lives. The summer of 1865 found them still enjoying their new freedom. "Just now not one is at work a sort of Carnival — all at the Marble yard & on the River banks," Paul wrote to Thomas Ruffin.[121]

It was no doubt with some self-pity that Paul wrote to his sisters, "I am glad to hear Annie [Davis] is still with you. I hope you may not be deprived of her services — We have been without a female servant, but a day or two ago, Uncle Ovid from Stagville came up & brought his family & Mima — He is the only one that has expressed any wish to come to us at all."[122] Ovid had been an Umstead slave purchased by Thomas Bennehan in 1831. The 1870 census discloses that his name was Ovid Jurdon, then 65 and black, but his wife and children were mulattoes.[123] Paul hired him for the Burnside house along with all his family. A receipt for their wages shows what they received: Ovid, $96, his wife Ellen, $56, and his children much less for periods of service ranging from Ovid's sixteen months to his daughter Dicey's four.[124]

It was undoubtedly Ovid Jurdon who was described in another slave narrative, that of Abner Jordan, born at Stagville in the 1850s. He said that his father's name was Obed and his mother Ellen and that there were thirteen children in the family. "My pappy wus de blacksmith an' foreman for Marse Paul, an' he blew de horn for de other niggahs to come in from de fiel' at night. . . . My pappy an' his family stayed wid Marse Paul five years after de surrender den we moved to Hillsboro an' I's always lived 'roun' dese parts."[125]

Actually, another freedman stayed with the family. In 1868 Paul told his sister Margaret that only one black was left at Fairntosh, "and strange to say he will be the first negro born to our father as his slave — old Whiskey George!"[126] Long after George's death, Bennehan Cameron in a speech to the boys at his old school in Oxford told of coming to school pulled by an old horse (which Colonel Wheeler's Cavalry had not taken) driven by George, "an old negro, . . . the first slave born the property of my grandfather in 1790, who was a very trusted man in slavery days, as he was also in the days of the Freedmen's Bureau. He had all his life charge of the road wagons to Petersburg, before the days of railroads, & then to Henderson after completion of the old Raleigh & Gaston R.R. So that he knew every body along the Road, & every body knew him. And his accounts of the incidents in his life, while traveling over the road was very interesting, as it then had become a sealed chapter."[127]

George's history is fuller even than this account indicates, and some of Bennehan's facts are wrong. Duncan Cameron was still a school boy in 1790, and George was born long after 1790; he was not on Duncan Cameron's 1804 list of slaves. And after 1858 he could no longer be wagoner because of an accident that befell him that year.

While Paul was in Alabama in the winter of 1858, one of his children became very ill. Anne sent George off driving a sulkey with a horse tied to the side to fetch a doctor. The sulkey was for the doctor, the horse to bring George back. But as they were passing the corner of Stagville, a shaft broke and then the reins. The horses bolted and George jumped from the sulkey breaking his leg so badly that it could not be set and had to be amputated. Anne and her daughter wrote their versions of the story to Paul. Anne was struck by his misfortune: "Poor fellow! Poor fellow! He bore the operation manfully, and was the most grateful and thankful creature you ever saw. . . . Poor George! Poor George! I feel exactly as if he had died; I cannot get over it; and to think, too, it was done in the service of my sick child. His claims on us are strong and peculiar."[128] Morphine and chloroform got him through the operation and he began to look to the future with optimism, talking of his cork leg and how he would drive the family carriage.[129] His sobriquet "Whiskey George" seems to have been acquired years before, for it appears on a slave list of 1844.

After the Civil War he registered his marriage and in the cohabitation records he appears as George Cameron and his wife as Winney Cameron. They had been living together as man and wife since 1826.[130] George continued to live out his life at Fairntosh. When young Duncan Cameron was also living there managing the plantation, he reported George's death. "I know you and all will be sorry to learn of the death of poor old 'Whiskey'. He was taken on Monday last & died Wednesday morning. I had him decently buried. I will miss him more than any one even his wife."[131] The old bond between mistress and slave survived everything, and on his deathbed George bequeathed to Anne Cameron a little Negro girl, probably a granddaughter, who was sent in to Burnside to enter her service.[132]

The Camerons were touched by other expressions of loyalty and affection in their old slaves. When young Duncan was sick, the old slave Joe Nichols, a carpenter, showed up at Burnside and offered to sit up at night with Duncan.[133]

Paul Cameron would have been touched, too, by Doc Edwards's feelings for him and Stagville. In his narrative he said, "When de Yankees come dey didn' do so much harm, only dey tole us we was free niggers. But I always feel like I belong to Marse Paul, an' I still live at Stagville on de ole plantation. I has a little garden an' does what I can to earn a little somethin'. De law done fixed it so dat now I will get a little pension, an' I'll stay right on in dat little house 'til de good Lawd calls me home, den I will see Marse Paul once more."[134]

Paul Cameron's view of blacks was a common one in his day: he saw them as members of an inferior race. In an undated copy of an address to the University of North Carolina [Summer] Normal School, Paul Cameron wrote, "If the race were blotted out today it would not leave behind a city, a monument, an art or an invention to show that it ever existed."[135] But in his individual dealings with them he was kindly disposed. At his death Serena Turner Jeffries, a long-time servant in the Raleigh household wrote, "it has ended & nothing but kindness has it been."[136]

The passage of years brought about a natural fading from memory of both whites and blacks of the harsher moments of their long association, in some leaving a residue of only the happier times. A nostalgia for the past and friends long gone was an emotion some whites and blacks shared, so that it was with warm feeling on both sides that Bennehan Cameron was sent and received in 1914 letters from an ex-slave Victoria Williams. She wrote from Missouri where she was working for the summer though her home was in Atlanta, Georgia. She reminded him that her father was Samuel Williams who had taken his family away right after the war. She asked whether any of the old servants were around on any of the plantations. "I know there has been quite a change made in the old home but I remember the old Stagvill place the old plantation and I am going to ramble all over the place when I do get there again."[137] In the second letter she thanked Bennehan for answering her first letter, "and letting me know about each member of the family that I love and honor so much it bring me back to the old days."[138] Her sincerity and affectionate memory would have been very gratifying to Paul if he had lived to read it: he had striven long and conscientiously to be a good master. Her parting promise was equally conciliatory. "If my life is spared, God willing I will be with you and cook your Christmas dinner for you on X-mas day, and Mrs. Annie Collins on new years day, I look forward to this home coming as a day of rejoicing for me."

Victoria Williams, George Cameron, Joe Nichols, Doc Edwards, and Serena Jeffries are only five voices from a body of hundreds and cannot be counted as representative of the entire group. The records do not reveal the majority verdict. The Camerons' benign management notwithstanding, it is clear that slavery in any form incorporated hard toil, injustice, and cruelty. It may also be said that even within such a system affectionate ties were forged that survived for some as the dominant memory of a time long past and a place called home.

11. "When All Went Down in Night"

The imminence of the Civil War and the move of the Cameron family to Hillsborough were purely coincidental. The causes that lay behind their move, as has already been shown, were two: concern for the children's education and health.[1] Any foreboding of the conflict to come seems to have been absent from their motivation, preoccupied as they were with their own problems. In fact, in 1860 Paul Cameron went to Alabama with the intention of purchasing another plantation there, and he actually bought more land in Mississippi in 1861.[2] Perhaps he saw the political turmoil as just another in a series of threats such as those they had weathered in 1832 and 1849-50.

The summer sojourns in Hillsborough of 1856 and the years following had given Paul Cameron ample occasion to observe the handful of schools for both boys and girls in the town and perhaps to enroll one or two of the older children in the summer terms that then formed part of the school year. In fact it was the accessibility and quality of these schools that changed the Cameron family from summer visitors to permanent residents.[3] Though the schools were probably the main determinant in their move, there were undoubtedly other enticements. The loneliness of plantation life, which cut them off from daily association with any but members of the family and the many slaves, was relieved by relations, friends, and neighbors whom the town provided. The convenience of the daily mails, the stores, and the railroad filled other needs. The doctor, the lawyer, the banker, and the minister were all at their beck and call. The church lay actually only a stroll away through the garden. Life was pleasanter and easier at Burnside, and these benefits, added to the solutions the town supplied for the problems of health and schooling, accelerated the Camerons' accommodation to town life. Even without the Civil War, they would probably have remained permanently in the town.[4]

The war that came upon them in 1861 changed the course of their lives and completely altered the world they had known. The daily events of these years and their reactions to them are poorly documented in the family papers. Years afterwards, Bennehan Cameron explained the reason for this to the state historian, R. D. W. Connor, who had appealed to him for family papers; in the closing days of the war Bennehan and his mother had burned many papers pertaining to the war years to destroy evidence that might have implicated Paul Cameron in the Confederate cause.[5]

In his plea for pardon, however, Paul Cameron stated his political views and the degree of his involvement in the southern struggle for independence.[6] He had at all times, he declared to President Andrew Johnson, hoped for the preservation of the Union and had strongly supported the Peace Conference of February 1861 in which his father-in-law had played a prominent part. He admitted that he had committed himself to the cause of the southern states when the peace effort failed and after the action of other southern states left North Carolina no other option than secession. He had contributed clothing to the volunteers of Orange County and had exhorted them in a few public speeches. To the needy and the destitute, who included the soldiers, their wives, and families, he had made large donations. He had held no position in the Confederate government, had participated in no military actions, and had stayed at home and engaged in farming. The products of his farms "were freely used by the Confederate government most generally under impressment or circumstances equivalent to impressment," and the surplus was sold from time to time at regular prices. He admitted to having owned 650 slaves whom he then (1865) regarded and treated as liberated. He acknowledged that his income exceeded $20,000 a year (the cutoff for inclusion in the general amnesty). He rejoiced that the war was over and he accepted the terms of peace. He had taken the oath of allegiance on 29 May 1865 and meant to abide by its terms.

Letters that Paul wrote to Thomas Ruffin during the war and surviving Cameron papers substantiate Paul's declaration. For most of the war years, because the fighting did not come to central North Carolina until the closing days, life went on very much as usual on the plantations. Samuel Piper at Fairntosh and Philip Southerland at Stagville, competent, trustworthy, and experienced, kept all matters running smoothly: the slaves at their labor, the animals and tools in trim, the crops planted and harvested, the produce sent to market, the fields cleaned and the fences mended, the firewood cut, the food and clothing distributed, the ditches cleared, and the buildings repaired. Some of the slaves were conscripted for work on fortifications.[7] Otherwise the Camerons felt the physical impact of war only slightly. Paul Cameron began laying out his Hillsborough tract in gardens and ordered from Parsons Nursery in Flushing, New York, quantities of flowers, shrubs, and trees.[8] Their variety and number gave Burnside a beauty that is remembered to this day in the survival there of the name Cameron Park. It was at this time, too, that Thomas Ruffin made his gift of an orchard to young Duncan Cameron. Only in the closing days of the war did the Camerons' lives and the plantations become vulnerable to the conflict raging around them. Perhaps to protect the plantations, perhaps for their own protection, Anne Cameron and her younger children moved back to Fairntosh in the spring of 1865 and remained till the war ended. A slave narrative collected in the 1930s from an ex-slave, Cy Hart, gives an eyewitness account of what happened at that time:[9]

> One day some of Wheeler's men come an' dey tried to take what dey wanted, but Marse Paul had de silver money an' other things hid. Dey wanted us niggers to tell dem where everythin' wus, but we said we didn' know nuthin'. Marse Paul wus hid in de woods wid de horses an' some of de other stock.
>
> Den Wheeler's men saw de Yankees comin' an' dey run away. De Yankees chased dem to de bridge an' dey done some fightin' an' one or two of Wheeler's men wus killed an' de rest got away.
>
> Den de captain of de Yankees come to Mammy's cabin an' axed her whar de meat house an' flour an' sech at. She tole him dat Pappy had de keys to go an' ax him. "Ax him nothin'," de captain said. He called some of his men an' dey broke down de door to de meat house. Den dey trowed out plenty of dose hams an' dey tole Mammy to cook dem somethin' to eat and plenty of it. Mammy fixed plenty of dat ham an' made lots of bread an' fixed dem coffee. How dey did eat! Dey was jus' as nice as dey could be to Mammy an' when dey wus through, dey tole Mammy dat she could have de rest, an' de captain gave her some money an' he tole her dat she wus free, dat we didn' belong to Marse Paul no longer.

Family letters, too, tell of the visit by Wheeler's cavalry and the theft of horses and mules by federal foraging parties who did not spare the children's pony.[10] The most serious damage on the plantation was done not by the armies of the North and South, however, but by the slaves themselves. They had been given a five months' supply of provisions, when the end of the war was imminent, to tide them over a period of confusion that was bound to come. Instead of allowing themselves the usual weekly ration, they had feasted on the unaccustomed plenty and devoured the whole supply in short order.[11] At the war's end they refused to work even after contracts had been drawn up to grant them a share of the crops. All but six or seven remained on the plantations, killing and eating the livestock, breaking into and plundering the smoke houses, refusing to supply the white family with milk or butter, keeping the overseer out of the field and threatening his life. As Paul described it to Thomas Ruffin, "At Fairntosh and Stagville all are going to the devil or dogs as fast as they can — wont work — and destroying stock — out houses, enclosures! No reliance can be placed in any contract."[12]

Paul's request to the military authorities for a guard to restore order was granted. After a visit by Anne Cameron to Fairntosh Paul described to Ruffin what she had found. "She comes back sick of the conduct of the negroes — she says without hesitation — drive all off — get white tenants on any terms — have peace if you have no money. A Yankee officer refused to let them have a 3rd of the crop at Stagville farm by reason of their bad conduct, and sent them off with a 4th, and ordered some to leave the place for plundering. He was sent up from Raleigh and was at Fairntosh with my wife and [she] says he is a well disposed man."[13]

Paul's first impulse with the war over and the slaves freed was to sell all his land. He would be willing to take what he could for it, he told Ruffin, and move to "some new field of industry and hope. But I see no chance to make a sale and my brother and sisters' affairs I must not give up nor can they go with me."[14] Finding no buyers, he accepted the situation and adapted to it. Following the example the military authorities had already supplied, Paul Cameron had his lawyer, John W. Norwood, draw up a contract to be used with his former slaves.[15] As written it granted to the workers shelter on the plantations, firewood, garden plots, farm animals and tools, one fourth of the wheat and sweet potatoes grown, one third of the molasses, and general supplies for the first few months until a harvest could be made in return for ten hours of labor every day but Sunday. In the following year their share was to increase to one-half. This sample contract seems to have been modified, for contracts actually signed in the following year show the workers' share of the crop as one-third.[16]

Two other systems were improvised to manage the land and keep it in production. Paul Cameron was able to rent for cash or crops some of his farms to men who supplied their own tools, animals, and labor. Joe Piper, a son of Samuel, rented Snow Hill for a few years on this plan, and Joseph Woods rented the Leathers Plantation.[17] Rents varied with the amount and quality of the land. Woods paid $600 a year for the Leathers place whereas one portion of Snow Hill rented for $150, and the fork field on Eno, another portion, rented for $250. The group of men who rented Stagville, which included Philip Southerland, agreed to work fifty men and twenty-five mules with their own equipment and pay Paul Cameron one-third of the crops.[18] They were obligated, of course, to keep in repair all buildings and fences (ten rails high).

The third system kept the land in the owner's hands but worked it with hired labor. For example, Paul Cameron hired Jasper Jones, an ex-slave, for $120 a year and the use of a house for his family.[19] Irksome as these new systems were, they relieved Paul of any direct daily burden of land management and kept a modicum of order on all the farms, which probably paid for themselves if they yielded no profit. It was a way for him to mark time until the South could work out a new economic and social order, and his sons could mature enough to shoulder the burden.

These accommodations to change that Paul achieved were not easily arrived at despite the surface poise he seemed to maintain. The mortification, anger, and sense of injustice he felt; the sorrow, poverty, and death suffered by so many around him; and the insensitive federal imposition of regulations, restrictions, and changes — all these tormented him inwardly.

The humiliation of the oath of amnesty and the plea for pardon (as was stated earlier, he was excluded from the general amnesty because of his wealth) bothered him most of all. His daughter Rebecca wrote to her aunts of her father's taking the oath. "He has to-day passed through a great trial, and has taken a most important step. You will understand what I mean."[20]

The wealth which has traditionally identified Paul as the richest man in the state both before and after the war is easily analyzed.[21] It was not the fruits of speculation or exploitation of others' adversity which often underlie fortunes made at times of social upheaval. The truth evidently is that his fortune was so large before the war that even the loss of slaves, the steep decline of agricultural production, and the rampant inflation and worthlessness of Confederate currency could not materially damage its preeminence. Times were hard and the Camerons' life changed dramatically, but their resources were sufficient to enable them to weather the years of deepest depression until gradual economic recovery and natural growth of their remaining investments could replenish their coffers.

The largest Cameron investment was, of course, the vast plantation lands, which remained unharmed. In 1859 Paul had estimated the value of his real estate at $218,000.[22] Unlike many other planters, he was able to hold on to all of it, relying on other kinds of investment to tide him over the worst years. The land values eventually recovered and increased though for many years land seemed more a liability than an asset. The value of his stocks and bonds, which he had estimated at almost $100,000 in 1859, continued to increase as well. North Carolina State bonds, Wake County, North Carolina, and City of Petersburg, Virginia, bonds along with various railroad bonds proved sound investments in the long run. The loss in farm production, the volume and profit of which had depended so heavily on slave labor, was offset by the savings in food, clothing, and doctors' bills which the end of slavery occasioned. The $443,000 invested in the slaves was obviously a huge loss on paper but in practical terms meant less. Everything grown beyond the supplies for his own family was pure gain. In the desperate year of 1863 Paul Cameron's income was roughly $25,000, no mean sum for those days.[23] It was a tremendous reduction from pre-war years, but there was still ample margin for safety.

The long period from 1860 through the war and reconstruction years until the military authorities finally withdrew from the South in 1877 (though autonomy was restored to the people of North Carolina at the end of the 1860s) can be viewed as a unit in the Camerons' lives as well. During it the Cameron children received their schooling and the two sons grew old enough to assume some of their father's responsibilities.

In their earliest years the younger children were sent to the new Nash and Kollock School, which opened in 1859 in the buildings their Cameron grandfather had built in 1801, or to the school run by the Misses Heartt. As they grew older, the girls were sent to Saint Mary's School in Raleigh, where they lived with their aunts, Margaret Mordecai and Mildred Cameron, and their uncles, George Mordecai and Thomas Cameron, in the house Duncan Cameron had built in 1836. They were happy in their schools and friendships and presented no problems to their anxious father.

The schooling of young Duncan Cameron, however, was another matter, and whatever educational experiments were tried on him always failed. He, too, was sent first to the Nash and Kollock School and then to a succession of classical schools: the Bingham School at Oaks, Dr. Wilson's school at Melville, H. G. Hill's school in Hillsborough, and finally the Hillsborough Military and Polytechnic Academy.[24] Unhappy, homesick, bored, and generally disinclined to study, Duncan ran away from each in turn. After fleeing from Dr. Wilson's School in March 1865, he fell in with a group of soldiers he met on the railroad on their way to Bentonville. He went with them and was on the periphery but within firing distance of the battle there.[25] Paul's alarm and anger at this foolhardiness were underlain by secret pride which surfaced in these words of young Duncan's epitaph which Paul wrote, "A true Confederate Soldier at Fourteen."[26]

On another occasion Duncan ran to the Pipers at Fairntosh, and several times after the war to the Mississippi plantation where his sister Annie and her family were living.[27] During his final schooldays, a short-lived engagement to a commanding officer's daughter and a large accumulation of debts at the local stores for soda and cigars finally convinced Paul Cameron that Duncan's schooldays were over and further education was futile.[28]

Unlike his brother, Bennehan Cameron caused his parents little trouble in these years. After primary schooling in Hillsborough he, too, was sent off to boarding school. He went to the Hughes Academy in Cedar Grove and then to the Horner Classical Academy in Oxford, North Carolina.[29] Minor infractions of rules resulted in his suspension on one or two occasions, but mostly he stuck to his studies and performed his assignments creditably. He took a summer term at the Eastman National Business College at Poughkeepsie, New York, before entering the Virginia Military Institute in Lexington where he remained until he took his degree in 1875.[30]

Both sons were chronically short of funds and complained to their father of their meager allowances. "How do I get into debt," Bennehan had the courage to write his father, "because you never give me any pocket money."[31] Whether their own improvidence or their father's penuriousness was the cause of this tension is now difficult to decide. Possibly one reinforced the other.

Release from school did not transform the sons into the hoped-for props in their father's declining days. Duncan spent ten years trying his hand at various employment. He spent altogether three years at different times in Mississippi helping his brother-in-law George Collins on the plantation there.[32] In desperation at the boy's idleness, Paul Cameron bought Duncan in 1872 a one-third interest in a tobacco manufacturing partnership with James Webb and W. S. Roulhac at a cost of $6,500.[33] Duncan wearied of this, too, for business was slow, and he was incapable of tending shop and doing nothing. Once more he ran, again to Mississippi, where he got a job on a Mississippi River boat as a "mud clerk," a job he had attempted in his earlier days there and from which his father had rescued him and brought him home.[34] This time a fight with another youth, who attacked him with a knife and against whom he retaliated with a pistol, effectively ended this career.[35] After his wounds were beginning to heal, his mother brought him home once more, somewhat chastened but unreformed. His next effort, farming on shares at Fairntosh, again with George Collins, proved equally unsuccessful until a few years after his marriage at the end of 1877 he began to channel his energy and interest to prolonged endeavor. He married Mary B. Short, only daughter of Colonel Henry Short, whose substantial wealth included a short line railroad, and who probably assisted the young couple financially.[36] At any rate, Duncan's pleas for money ceased and he began to farm in earnest.

Bennehan was still doing his father's bidding by studying law with his uncle, William K. Ruffin. He was admitted to the bar in 1877 but, like his father, seems to have felt no strong inclination to practice.[37]

Two of Paul Cameron's children, Rebecca and Anne, had already finished their education when the family moved to Hillsborough in 1859. They were of marriageable age and suitors soon appeared. Anne married George Pumpelly Collins, a son of Josiah Collins III, and therefore of impeccable lineage.[38] As a product of southern plantation culture, however, he was totally unprepared for the changes about to take place. His service as an officer in the Confederate army only aggravated his unsuitability for gainful employment by damaging his health.

Immediately after the war Paul Cameron sent him to inspect the Mississippi plantation and set it going on a new footing. The overseer, Vick, was dead, his widow was suing Paul for back wages and other damages, and the Negroes were gone.[39] Paul had arranged for their transportation to the Alabama plantation for safekeeping when Mississippi became a theater of war. For almost ten years, except for almost annual trips home, George and Anne Collins and their growing family lived in Mississippi struggling to make the plantation productive. The first year there George Collins, obviously untutored in elementary farming, neglected to raise hogs and corn, an error that cost him dearly the following year.[40] Of some of his troubles he wrote, "with free negroes, buffaloe gnats & high water it is almost enough to run a man crazy."[41] Despite $10,000 poured into the effort, George Collins had to admit defeat and brought his family back to North Carolina in 1874.[42]

Paul Cameron next offered them Fairntosh on shares. George Collins had learned a great deal in Mississippi and probably would have been content to go on indefinitely at Fairntosh if Duncan's marriage had not ended his tenancy.[43] Paul next fixed up the McNair property just outside the town limits of Hillsborough for the Collinses, enlarging and improving the house for their occupancy. There they moved in 1879.[44] The house and large acreage on which it stands remain in the family to this day, the only parcel of Cameron land to do so.

George Collins worked hard to make a living, clerking in various stores in Durham, Hillsborough, and Raleigh.[45] He found it as difficult to meet his father-in-law's expectations as Paul's sons did. Paul wrote of the family, "I take great interest in poor Anne — she is a noble woman — she has a fine family of children — smart — amiable — good looking — her husband in very poor health — at Raleigh — smoking & chewing tobacco — without mental or physical energy. I shall hope little from him."[46]

Rebecca Bennehan Cameron worried her parents in a different way. She fell in love with her cousin Robert Walker Anderson and was determined to marry him despite their objections.[47] Her mother objected on the grounds of their kinship. Her aunts in Raleigh loyally took her part, and Rebecca and Walker were married in 1863.[48] Walker Anderson, the grandson of Duncan Cameron's sister Mary, was studying for the ministry when the Civil War began.[49] He enlisted in the Confederate forces and a year after his marriage to Rebecca was killed in the Battle of the Wilderness in May 1864.[50] In December Rebecca gave birth to their son, a large boy born dead.[51]

Rebecca next married John W. Graham, a neighbor and son of former Governor William A. Graham.[52] His lineage, too, was impeccable, and he had, moreover, the profession of law to support him. For the first seven years of their marriage they lived at Burnside, but in 1875 they moved into the fine, new house John Graham built on his father's property adjoining Burnside.[53] Paul found something about Graham to object to, too. "I have never lived with so silent a man & hope he will do better in his own house."[54] Through Paul's declining years, the proximity of the Grahams and their growing family gave him daily pleasure. Rebecca was his favorite child.[55]

The end of 1877 might have been a hopeful time for Paul Cameron. The war was over and the northern soldiers had finally withdrawn entirely from the South. All his children had come safely through childhood and had received their education. All the plantations were being farmed in one way or another, despite the loss of the slaves. Paul remained outwardly the large, corpulent man, handsome and kindly-looking, commanding in presence, powerful in action. Unfettered in mind or tongue or pen, his sense of humor had never failed him. In 1871, writing to Bennehan away at school he said, "Occasionally, but very rarely, I see some young gent in a buggy driving out with a lady by his side — & sometimes from the piazza I recognize by his peculiar mustash & goatee your brother Duncan whose identity it is impossible to mistake both by that remarkable appearance on his face, and also by the length of the ears of the *animal* he drives — I hope you will not let the northern belles with whom you have the good fortune to become acquainted know that the Southern chivalry are reduced so low as *that* — but he enjoys himself hugely & says the young ladies do too, jackass or no jackass — and that he is not to be laughed out of his enjoyment by my jokes."[56] Paul added in a more serious vein, "By the way, Duncan has grown to be a *large* man and is much improved in every respect (save only in those mustachios) — He is steady, and I should judge, very industrious when at home, and promises to make a very useful man." Now in 1877 Duncan was married and the promise seemed about to be fulfilled.

Only outwardly Paul remained the same. Inwardly he bore immedicable wounds, for the world he had loved was gone. Years later writing to his sisters of this period he revealed what it had meant to him and what it would always mean — "when all went down in night."[57]

12. "One Long Dark Night"

The gloom never lifted for Paul Cameron. To his sick wife he wrote in 1867, "God bless you & make you well & if possible happy — as for me my life is one long dark night."[1] He continued to use the metaphor throughout his remaining years. A combination of circumstances conspired to cause his melancholy. The new social and economic order to which he was forced to adapt, the responsiblity of the land (not just his own large holdings but those inherited from his brother and sisters), increasing financial drains over a long period of economic depression, his children's apparent inability to manage their lives without his help, the anxiety and grief over successive family illnesses and deaths, and his own infirmities, all joined to create for him a sense of coming doom: the break-up of the plantations, the loss of the fortune, the end of the family. He realized too, that he would never escape any of them. "This dark night will last me to the end," he wrote.[2]

His former slaves were free but Paul Cameron was still tied to the land. In days past the land had been his pride and glory even while it had been a heavy responsibility, and his strength had become its strength, and its flowering had coincided with that of the Cameron family. The symbiotic relationship nourished them both. Paul had been the planter par excellence. In a tribute to him after his death the faculty of the University of North Carolina described him accurately as "a splendid embodiment of the Southern planter, an almost ideal symbol of the southern life and character of the olden times. . . . Few men have enjoyed so fine a combination of mental, physical, and moral power.[3]

It is useful in understanding Paul Cameron to see him in terms of the essential planter, for his attitudes and instincts and his place in the world were all determined by that mold. His views of blacks and women, for example, were perfectly predictable. The Negro he saw as a member of an inherently inferior race and women as inherently barred by their sex from certain activities. Of the proper place of women he said in a lecture to a class at the summer Normal School of the university, "Woman is utterly out of her sphere when she seeks to control the ballot or the jury box or to handle the cartridge box."[4] His impulsive and warm responses to causes that challenged his chivalric code and his equally warm temper spurred him to action, good and bad alike.

But his character was not circumscribed by the pattern. In political and business matters he thought and acted independently. Driven by an overriding sense of duty he put into whatever he undertook his last ounce of strength. In writing of his duty toward his children when they were still young, he remarked with characteristic insight, "I look on the bright faces of my dear children all as happy and intelligent as I have any right to expect — and if my life be spared shall be made useful members of the community in which they shall live — I have much to do — and shall attempt to do it — with all my heart mind & soul."[5] His clearsightedness and good sense showed him his duty, but they also showed him how to adapt, survive, and prevail. When the old world was swept away, planters typically became an extinct species, but not Paul. He himself evolved along new lines, and he did his best to equip his children for the change. He wrote to the schoolboy Duncan in 1865, "We are to have a great revolution in society & social life — and those who do not go to work & make a manly effort to sustain themselves & families will go down. . . . [Y]ou will have to labour to live either by your head or your hands!"[6] Even to his daughters at Saint Mary's School in Raleigh he preached the same message: "I would advise you both to be smart and to be able to make a living for yourselves either as teachers or as Dancing Masters — for I shall dry up & not be able to take care of you."[7] The fear that he would not be able to take care of them became an obsession.

When Reconstruction ended in 1877, Paul Cameron was almost seventy years old and feeling the weight of his responsibilities. His largest responsibility, the land, was left more or less intact after the war was over, but it suffered from neglect, the buildings most of all. Rotten sills, leaking roofs, sagging porches, peeling paint made visible the fundamental changes that had come over everything. The daily appraising and loving eye of the master had long turned to other affairs. James Hunter Horner, the noted schoolmaster and son of Paul's old partner and superintendent, after a view of the plantations in the 1870s wrote to Paul about them.

> In going up I passed by Staggsville; and really after looking at your rich and extensive bottoms on the river studded with shocks of wheat or dark with a luxuriant growth of corn extending as far almost as the eye can reach, the hill farms, afterwards I saw on my way, presented a very shabby appearance! . . . In passing by the Staggsville farm, I was reminded of Lossing's description of it in his Field Book of the Revolution which I saw at your house. It is indeed a magnificent estate even in its present somewhat dilapidated condition — and how truly must it have appeared so when the author of that book saw it — I presume it had reached its highest state of improvement just prior to our late war. It must then have presented to the eye of the farmer a grand and goodly prospect. I have heard you speak in glowing terms of the Valley of Virginia — but do any of the Valley farms surpass your river farms in Orange and Wake?[8]

Land, Paul knew, was still good for investment if not for planting. He sold the Alabama plantation to his former slaves and invested in orange groves in Florida.[9] He bought town property in Hillsborough, commercial and residential.[10] He expanded his boundaries at Burnside by buying up adjacent lots when he could.[11] As the result of a lawsuit brought against the university trustees by his sister, he bought at auction close to 100,000 acres of North Carolina mountain land that the university had owned.[12] To manage these transactions and others that he undertook, Paul needed an agent. Bennehan was a natural choice to supply the vigor that he lacked and to become his errand boy, for Bennehan was unmarried and undecided on a career. Therefore it was Bennehan who went to Florida to spy out a good buy and to purchase land there, as it was Bennehan who went to the mountains to discover where that immense tract lay, and went to Chapel Hill to buy at auction land the trustees were divesting the university of — an act Cornelia Spencer saw as traitorous to the spirit and generosity of its early benefactors. An eloquent letter of hers brought Paul to the rescue; he bought up numbers of tracts both in and out of the village from which he chose two acres to give Mrs. Spencer in recognition of her long devotion and service to the university which they both loved so well.[13]

During his twenty-six years as a loyal trustee Paul served the institution in other ways. He was chairman of the building committee and in charge of restoring the buildings and readying them for the reopening of the university in 1875.[14] Bennehan was his deputy in this matter as well, as he was in the much larger undertaking of the construction of Memorial Hall.[15] Paul supplied $8,000 from his own funds in order to complete this building, a debt his heirs accepted repayment for (then amounting to $10,000) in the form of ten scholarships in Paul Cameron's memory.[16] It had been Paul's job not only to oversee the long and underfunded construction but finally to give the dedicatory address, one of his last public functions. An honorary degree conferred on him in 1889 was a small return for his many services to the university.[17]

Other educational institutions received his attention, too. Education, he recognized, was the white man's means to achieve economic independence and self-sufficiency; it would be increasingly vital in the changed world of the postwar era. When the buildings of the defunct Hillsborough Military Academy were up for auction in 1872 and were in danger (as he saw it) of being bought for use as a school for Negro girls, Paul bought the whole school and the forty-two acres it occupied for $5,000.[18] Finding someone to lease or buy it from him proved a constant problem. In 1874 James Hunter Horner and R. H. Graves rented it and established a school they called the Hillsborough Military and Polytechnic Academy. Graves's death two years later and Horner's mental breakdown forced its closing. Two of their teachers, D. H. Hamilton and Hugh Morson, Jr., attempted to continue their own school there in 1876 but were unsuccessful.[19]

Saint Mary's School in Raleigh had been from the start a family preserve and recipient of Cameron charity. In 1833 Duncan Cameron had supervised the building there of a school for boys under the auspices of the Episcopal Church. The Reverend Aldert Smedes from New York had been appointed to run it. When it failed in 1841, Duncan bought the land and school buildings and established a new school for girls again under church supervision and with the same principal.[20] This time it succeeded admirably and the school continued to expand and flourish. Margaret Cameron Mordecai, who inherited it from her father, decided many years later to donate an art building, and the job of supervising its building fell to Paul. Bennehan was put in charge of overseeing the work. The very next year after its completion a fire completely destroyed the building, and Bennehan began the work all over again. In an attempt to preclude further accidents, this time he installed a central heating system.[21]

The construction experience Paul had first gained in building Burnside in 1834, followed by the railroad sections in the 1850s, was repeatedly put to use in his later life. It was a business he thoroughly understood and enjoyed. The McNair house in Hillsborough, renovated for his daughter Anne Collins, the Warren mansion in Edenton, renovated for his daughter Pauline, the alterations to the Fairntosh chapel, and the alterations to Burnside — everything his hand touched showed the master builder he was.

It was Burnside that received his personal attention in the postwar years. The gardens, orchards, and park he planted there were his daily concern. Practical matters were not neglected either. Keeping the land planted and productive to feed his livestock was a major concern, "to take my cows & horses out of my pocket," as he phrased it.[22] There he also raised hogs, poultry, cattle, corn, oats, rye, and clover. On the little Burnside estate the Camerons lived as comfortably as at Fairntosh.

New sources of wealth required his attention, too. From his father he had inherited bank and railroad stock, but it was his conviction that investment in industry would provide a growing profit in the years to come. He first invested in the Great Falls Manufacturing Company at Rockingham, North Carolina, and next in Rocky Mount Mills, both cotton factories.[23] The Battle family had owned the latter since its establishment in 1818 but were forced to incorporate in 1874 to refinance the business. At that time Paul Cameron lent them money which when repaid in stock shares in 1883 made him the largest stockholder and a director of the company.[24] Besides these mills he acquired stock in the Pee Dee Manufacturing Company, the Raleigh Cotton Mills, the King Manufacturing Company, and the Sibley Manufacturing Company. In the last year of his life he became a director of the Clarendon Coal Field Company, a new field of investment for him.[25]

A push for railroads as the answer to the Piedmont's economic problems had been a lifelong effort. His directorships of various railroads were a natural consequence: the North Carolina Railroad, of which he was also president a short while, the Raleigh and Gaston Railroad, and the Chatham Railroad.

Despite these apparently successful adaptations to the changed times, his children and their problems depressed him in his declining years. Margaret, the third daughter to marry, became the wife of Robert Bruce Peebles in 1875, a lawyer of Northampton County, North Carolina.[26] Maggie's health, never robust, gave her parents almost uninterrupted concern after 1881. She suffered an intestinal complaint which evolved in a series of crises for each of which she would enter a private hospital in Richmond operated by Dr. Hunter McGuire. Treatment would relieve her and she would eventually return home. As the years wore on, her stays in the hospital became longer and her recovery less complete. Her mother often accompanied and nursed her at these times, thereby depriving Paul of her company which he sorely needed. Maggie had one child, Anne, and died in 1896 at the age of forty-eight.[27]

Pauline, the next daughter, presented a different kind of problem. Paul's feelings about her were always ambivalent; he called her "an uncertain bird."[28] Though his namesake and a beautiful and charming woman, he thought her lazy and unresourceful. She wrote him long, emotional letters, usually invoking his aid, for which he reproached her. In 1879 she became William Blount Shepard's second wife.[29] Of an illustrious Edenton family, like his cousin George Collins, he was unprepared to do battle in the business world. Paul financed a series of enterprises involving the local economy, such as farming, fishing, and shingle-making, but either hard times or mismanagement doomed each one.[30] In 1889 Paul received one final plea for help and wrote in despair to his absent wife, "Go as I will & do as I shall I find stumps & stones in all my roads & I am ready to cry out I will surrender. Give up. I hardly know what to do or where to turn — I feel like the man of old who was destroyed [by] his own hounds: I mean not in my case dogs — but my children. I will enclose a letter received this morning — can you tell me what I should do — for I am so deeply anxious, I do not know what to do. I can see no end to it but *ruin to us all*. In the last year I have advanced him all of $10,000 — now he wants $8,000."[31]

Margaret Mordecai, who was exceedingly generous to everyone and particularly to Paul's children, helped Pauline by presenting her with the fine house in Edenton Pauline had set her heart on. It fell to Paul, however, to make and finance the renovations, which turned out to be extensive and expensive.[32] Pauline, true to her nature, wished everything to be in the most elegant style. When she asked for stained glass in parts of the windows, Paul balked. He called it poor taste to aim at anything so grand in a poor little town like Edenton. "It is not my taste — simple — plain neat & substantial."[33] But Pauline got her glass.

Her health, too, like that of all Paul's daughters except Anne, gave cause for concern. Paul recounted in disgust and puzzlement (he could never understand weakness of any sort) how Maggie and Pauline had reacted to the fire alarm's sounding in Hillsborough one morning. "Pauline fainted & made to vomit! — Maggie only vomited — Where did all this come from! Not from me I am sure."[34] Their easily excitable natures might have suggested a neurotic basis if their early deaths had not confirmed physical weakness. Pauline died at thirty-eight. She, too, had an only child, another Anne, who grew up to marry her Aunt Rebecca's son, William A. Graham.

Pauline's younger sister Mildred, loyally remained with her parents, relieving her mother of the household management until 1896 when she married her brother-in-law, William Blount Shepard, Pauline's widower. She died in 1904, the third wife to predecease him.[35] Her life seems to parallel that of her Aunt Margaret of the previous generation. Mildred, too, outlived many sisters, became the prop for her father's declining years, was an interested and capable manager of domestic concerns, and married late in life. Unlike her aunt, she died while still in her forties.[36]

Of Paul Cameron's seven children who survived childhood, only two outlived their forties, Anne and Bennehan. Paul must have felt the death of young Duncan most of all. After his early indecision and indiscretion Duncan had finally settled down and promised to become Paul's ideal, a useful citizen. His determination to live and farm at Fairntosh was aided by his own daily labor there and by his hiring of William Daniel Turrentine, a fortunate choice, to direct the large enterprise. A semblance of the old order reappeared in the fields and structures. Everything was spruced up by paint and repaired. The mills were kept up and continued to grind. At first alone, and then with his brother Bennehan, Duncan reestablished and ran a country store at Stagville in a new building across the road from the old stand.[37] He entered politics with the encouragement of his neighbors, mostly those resident on the plantations, and won election as a county commissioner for the recently formed County of Durham, though he failed in an attempt at the state senate.[38] Duncan became a director of the North Carolina Railroad and in many ways seemed ready to fill his father's shoes at last. He and his wife became the parents of three little girls, Mary Warren, Pauline, and Rebecca who died in childhood. Though times were still hard and Duncan labored in the fields with many fewer helpers and more machinery than in prewar days, he found time to go to the races, an enthusiasm he shared with Bennehan, and to visit his in-laws, the Shorts, at Lake Waccamaw.[39] But Paul's hopes were not to be fulfilled for him. A large man like his father, in 1885 Duncan went from his usual 232 pounds in weight to 197 and intended to try to reduce his weight still further to 175 pounds, probably as a remedy for the illness which had begun to manifest itself. He grew still worse. A true diagnosis eluded his doctors until the fall of 1886. After a first diagnosis of hydrocele, then kidney stones, for which he was operated on by Dr. McGuire, and next enlargement of the spleen, Dr. McGuire at last recognized an inoperable tumor from which Duncan died in November 1886.[40] Over his grave Paul erected a tall obelisk like the one he had ordered for the first Duncan. On it he had inscribed:

> A Useful Citizen
> A true Confederate at Fourteen;
> Devoted to Agriculture;
> Affectionate, Generous, and Brave by Nature
> Beloved by his Neighbors and Friends;
> With heroic Fortitude
> He endured the Suffering which fell to his Lot
> and with a firm Faith in Christ
> passed into Rest.[41]

In Paul's memory, Duncan had become all that he had wished him to be.

The final element in Paul Cameron's gloom was his own failing health and strength. For a man with his enormous vitality and will power, who had been for half a century the mainstay of a large family and who had endured countless sorrows through the illness and death of those near him — his parents, an uncle, six sisters, a brother, seven children — his own decline became intolerable. First deafness with its consequent isolation and loneliness, varicose veins and dimming sight, which limited his mobility, and finally heart disease which increased his sedentary tendency — these depressed him further.[42]

In all these trials, however,, he had his wife, the "oldest and best friend" as he frequently told her. Their long letters to each other throughout the almost sixty years of their marriage tell of a perfect confidence and mutual respect which survived everything. Anne Ruffin Cameron did not have Paul's love of words or gift for self-expression, but her letters were always completely frank and uninhibited even as they were usually businesslike and factual. Her main interest was from first to last her household and children, but her duty was to her husband. Despite much ill health, a strong constitution and a strong will enabled her to perform whatever obligations were laid upon her. In one letter Paul said of her, "My wife helps me nurse the sick — and keeps her own head up and the head of everything in the garden in despite of the dry weather."[43] Their long absences from each other when Margaret Mordecai's illnesses kept Paul in Raleigh or Maggie's hospitalization demanded her mother's presence in Richmond were very hard for Paul. During one of them in 1889 he wrote her that he was having trouble sleeping. If she were there, he wrote, and he could feel her arm over him he would sleep better.[44] He then reminded her of an old family anecdote. "A very cold night & I thought of old Dr. Mitchel['s] declaration to my uncle Bennehan when they were sleeping in the same room at Dr. Webbs in Hillsborough, when Mr. B. was snug & warm in bed & Dr. M. could not make himself comfortable after putting everything on his bed that could be had. 'Ah Mr. B. you are [an] old Batchelor & dont feel the want of a wife — but my wife is good to me for a dozen blankets.' I had bed clothing enough but last night I needed my wife to make me warm — a great deal of truth & good sense in the observation."[45]

His letters to her never failed to sound a similar note. During the war when she was temporarily at Fairntosh to oversee the lard rendering he wrote, "I confess that what ever I may say or do that looks otherwise that I do not wish to be at any time a mile from you."[46] At still another time he wrote her, "No man either in prosperity or adversity ever was blessed with a more prudent or judicious a wife or a more tender sharer of a husband's joys & sorrows. I thank you for all your long life of kindness & devotion to me."[47]

On 6 January 1891, after years of heavy responsibilities, emotional and financial drains on his resources, and increasing infirmities, his long dark night came to an end; he died of pneumonia after a short illness.[48] Bennehan's diary, usually only a bare list of daily events, on this day gives a glimpse of what his father's death meant to him:

> By one o'clock we suspected the end was at hand; & sent for Dr. Strudwick. Father passed away quietly at 4:10 A.M. shortly after the sweetest recognition of me & tenderest caress.[49]

The newspaper accounts of the funeral include no mention of the exslaves' role in the proceedings which forms so important a part of the narrative and memories of one ex-slave, Cy Hart. He said in 1937:

> I lived with Marse Paul 'til he died an' he done selected eight of us niggers to tote his coffin to de chapel, an buryin' groun'. He said, "I want dese niggers to carry my body to de chapel an' de grave when I die." We did. It wus a load I would have been glad had der been two or four more to help tote Marse Paul for he sho wus heavy. After everythin' wus ready we lifted him up an' toted him to de chapel an' we sat on de floor, on each side of de coffin, while de preacher preached de funeral sermon. We didn' make any fuss while sittin' dere on de floor, but we sho wus full of grief to see our dear old Marse Paul lying dere dead.[50]

13. Bennehan Cameron at Stagville and Fairntosh

At Paul Cameron's death the plantation complex came to an end. Divided among his heirs and the moieties used variously or sold, the land lost its coherence. Only Stagville and Fairntosh, still united as Bennehan's inheritance, continued for another generation under the Cameron name. Paul Cameron's holograph will, like his letters, bears the strong stamp of his personality. As he disposed of his vast estate item by item, in plain English free of legal jargon, he explained his decisions, supplied the history of a specific tract, or expressed his hopes about the future.[1] In leaving to Bennehan the two plantations and the Bennehan square in Raleigh he wrote, "This square and the lands that made up the farms of Stagville & Fairntosh in the County of Durham will I hope long be held & owned by the heirs of Richard Bennehan & Duncan Cameron to which they were strongly attached."

In order to write his will Paul Cameron had needed to ascertain the full extent of his land holdings and for that purpose had hired a surveyor, D. G. McDuffie, to sort out his deeds, survey the ground, and draw up a map showing the location and boundaries of all the Bennehan and Cameron lands.[2] The survey had become necessary because the death of Margaret Mordecai, the residual legatee of her brother Thomas and sister Mildred, had brought their shares of the Bennehan and Cameron estates into Paul Cameron's ownership.[3] For the first time all the family lands were vested in one owner. Although Margaret Mordecai had died in 1886, Paul Cameron as her administrator left the estate unsettled at his own death five years later.[4] He did include all her real estate in his own will, however, for the survey had made its size and location patent and a fair distribution possible. Paul Cameron's will and McDuffie's map together delineate the extent of the estate which the joining of the Bennehan and Cameron families and fortunes had achieved. Ironically, it is only at the moment of its partition in this will that its true immensity is grasped. The amassing of land and riches culminated in Paul Cameron; at his death they splintered.

The Raleigh *News and Observer* obituary estimated his character and wealth correctly:

> He was indeed a thoroughgoing agriculturist, uniting theory and practice with unusual skill and was always energetic in the pursuit of agricultural science. . . . He inherited large wealth from his father, which by prudence and sagacity, he greatly augmented, investing in lands, and in cotton mills and

bank stock chiefly, and his estate is understood to be valued at more than a million dollars.

He was a man of pronounced views and great intelligence, and was possessed of a strong will and unusual firmness, and was careful to do what he deemed justice to other men.

In person he was stalwart, and of a robust frame, and of distinguished appearance, with a fine carriage, carrying his advanced years with unusual vigor.[5]

A later notice of the funeral listed the honorary and active pallbearers.[6] Among the former, which included Governor Daniel Fowle, Lieutenant-Governor T. M. Holt, and other men distinguished in the legal, medical, and teaching professions, was Philip Southerland, the old overseer at Stagville.

At Stagville Bennehan Cameron first took possession of his inheritance. In the 1880s his father had handed over the plantation to him not to own but to make what he could of it, just as he had put Fairntosh into young Duncan's hands. His two sons represented in their names, he told his sister, the plantations he would eventually leave them.[7] How Bennehan was to use his future inheritance was decided during the decade preceding Paul Cameron's death.

In 1882 Paul received a letter from Bennehan, then in Baltimore with his Aunt Maggie, telling of the fine estates to be bought in that vicinity. Paul replied, "You are in possession of a dear old place called Stagville [which] under a broad cast system with well fed herds of cattle & flocks of sheep can be made equal to anything on the western shore of Maryland except the 'Carroll Manor.'"[8] Stockfarming was the direction Bennehan had already taken at Stagville, probably on the advice of his father. Paul later amplified his statement. "I have often said — that with mule power I would introduce a system of broadcast that should be saved by machenery as much as needed — and the remainder should fatten the animal[s] and the land."[9]

Bennehan began to assemble the best stock he could buy. A Jersey cow, his first purchase, proved to be the best producer of milk and butter ever seen on the plantation.[10] Heartened by this success he next invested in two Holstein cattle, but these expensive animals died; Bennehan had lost his jewels, his father lamented.[11] His boundless energy like his father's and restless nature like his grandfather's made it impossible for him then and afterwards to remain in one place any length of time or concentrate on any one goal. Moving about from Stagville to Raleigh or Hillsborough or Durham or places farther afield, like his brother he sought pleasure in society, foreshadowing the course his life was to take when independence from his father's yoke and authority would permit it. Paul Cameron with his strict and dutiful view of life was uncomprehending. "I live," he wrote his sister, "with a runabout rolicking set & tell them all that they had better stay at home & attend to their business: raise chicken ducks turkeys & house pigs."[12]

During the 1880s until his brother's death, Bennehan lived at Stagville, which felt again the improving hand of a resident master. He built in the ground behind the house the cistern which is found there today, to supply good drinking water, the well water at Stagville not being potable.[13] He brought out of storage the old furniture and invited his Graham and Collins nieces and nephews to visit him. Annie Collins, one of his nieces, wrote home in an undated letter, "You don't know how nicely Uncle Ben is fixed in his house, all of the old Stagville furniture put back in its place & makes the house so nice & comfortable. Then too he has such a nice servant who takes excellent care of his house and everything in general; she is both a nice cook & wash woman. He likes to have things as near as possible like they used to be."[14] After young Duncan's death, he moved in 1887 to Fairntosh and continued to direct the improvement of both houses.

His venture into animal husbandry picked up momentum in 1886 when James Smith, a Scottish farmer who had been living in Illinois, came to Stagville to manage the stockfarm and the dairy and to help Bennehan with his purchase of livestock.[15] Smith stayed almost three years, during which time Bennehan bought at a cost of almost $1,000 more cattle and goats and added twelve horses from Aurora, Illinois.[16] The reason for Smith's leaving is not known; perhaps his services were too costly for Bennehan or perhaps Smith found better employment in Minneapolis where he went on leaving Stagville in January 1889.[17]

Bennehan's farming experiment was costly and greatly worried his father. "Poor fellow he cant stay long at home. . . . To me it is a hopeless prospect, nothing will be accomplished — & five thousand a year will not pay expenses — & I paying all the taxes all the time," Paul Cameron wrote to his wife.[18] Nevertheless Bennehan persevered; he bought $2,000 worth of hogs in Ohio, an extravagance which provoked his father to exclaim that hogs could be grown and fattened in North Carolina as well as in Ohio.[19] In 1889, in another letter to his wife he complained, "For his use I sent an order to Chicago for 30,000 lbs of salted sides costing $2,000: he has never made anything — & I fear never will — & sometimes makes me fear he will cripple me in his attempts at farming."[20] A few weeks before he had threatened, "If he dont do better I will take the bridle off & let him go, he shall not harass me."[21]

But Paul Cameron was not paying all his son's expenses. Bennehan had borrowed over $10,000 in the time-honored manner of heirs-in-waiting. The banks had allowed him to use as security the stock and equipment he purchased with the funds he borrowed, but a time came, in 1889, when they refused to extend him any further credit because the title to the land was not in his name, and he had no other collateral.[22] It is easy to understand the frustration Bennehan felt as a man in his thirties with no property of his own and no salary for his labor, completely dependent on his father for all that he needed. But Paul Cameron viewed Bennehan's position from the angle of his own experience. Paul had married and raised a large family while living in a house owned by his father, managing his father's lands and slaves, taking nothing from the profits but his own and his family's subsistence, and always increasing the produce and value of the land through careful attention to the best farming principles. The contrast in their respective relations with their fathers struck him forcibly. He wrote to his wife, "I will seek to do my duty to all as long as I am here — but feeling that at the same time I am but poorly rewarded by some who owe me reverence affection & duty. I know that I have tolerated in idleness inefficiency & deception what my own father would never have submitted to in his domestic life."[23]

Bennehan, having been refused by the banks, appealed to his father for more capital. He reminded him that instead of going to Colorado in 1881, where he had glimpsed a business opportunity, he had agreed to undertake the management of his father's and his Aunt Maggie's estates. He felt he had thereby forfeited a fortune. Bennehan could not help revealing the underlying emotion he felt. "Sometimes I am afraid you take but little interest in me or my doings — certainly no pride."[24] A few years before, Paul, for his part, had expressed to his wife the exact inverse of this feeling about Bennehan; "I know nothing of his objects plans & purposes — he does not need, certainly does not wish my advice."[25]

Communication between them, however, did not entirely break down despite their misunderstandings and incompatability, and Bennehan's letters to his father in August 1889 also tell of the record-breaking floods caused by freshets in the rivers and, again, of bridges swept away and milldams destroyed.[26] Paul advised against any mill repairs as unprofitable labor. He also told Bennehan that it had come to his attention that the wall around Stagville graveyard was in need of repair, and he ordered Bennehan to get a good mason to do a good job. The trouble was, he explained, that Thomas Bennehan had "allowed the mason *to build the wall* on top of the ground" instead of beginning on the hard clay.[27] The firm and massive wall there today seems to be the original wall, still not footed in the clay, but patched and mortared.

In principle Paul Cameron approved of stockfarming at Stagville but not of the way Bennehan went about it. He could not instill in him his own unflagging industry and single-minded purposefulness. His misgivings are evident in one of his last letters to Bennehan:

> The changed husbandry of grass & clover for small & superior crops of cotton & tobacco may bring you all the money that a careful man may need & fine herds of cattle & flocks of sheep may occupy all the land & bring larger & better results in the improved condition of the land & its products of food with reliable markets — at Durham, at Chapel Hill, Raleigh, Goldsboro — & at

Wilmington all on one line of R R. If I was only back to 30 I would make a development that would make me a name as an improver & as long as I am here I shall seek to do all that I say if that plan is executed with intelligence & the high born purpose to succeed & excell.[28]

Apparently some kind of rapprochement had been reached and the requested money probably supplied, but Bennehan was being warned to keep his hand to the plow. "Work makes the man," Paul Cameron was fond of saying, "idleness the drone & cypher."[29] However, Paul Cameron's power to control events — and Bennehan, was expiring. With his father's death in 1891 Bennehan slipped his reins and at the age of thirty-six became his own man at last.

Superficially Bennehan's life seems a replay of his father's; there are so many similarities. Born into a family and tradition well defined, Bennehan would naturally exercise his new influence and power in already established channels. He had been a dutiful schoolboy, had graduated from college and studied law, had been admitted to the bar, and still like his father had chosen not to practice but to take over the management of the family lands. He had done his father's bidding and run his errands. He, too, took pride in his heritage and understood all the importance of historical perspective. He was, after all, the third Cameron to be master of Fairntosh. He, too, devoted himself to agriculture, railroads, banks, industry. He, too, tried politics and government. Consciously or not, he followed in his father's footsteps.

Beneath the surface, however, Bennehan Cameron was an entirely different man from his father. Moreover, times were different and the place was dramatically changed. To begin with, the little town of Durham to the southwest of Fairntosh, no more than a stop on the railroad before the Civil War, was experiencing enormous growth because of its tobacco industry. The discovery of bright leaf tobacco by the invading soldiery had been responsible for the change. The soldiers had scattered to their homes at the war's end but had taken with them the memory of that tobacco. They became a ready-made market for Durham's "American gold." Overnight, small tobacco manufactories were established to supply the demand. With the industry grew the supporting functions of banking and transportation; these offered to men with money new fields for investment. Paul Cameron had already invested in the new Morehead Banking Company in Durham, of which Bennehan soon became a director; Bennehan also helped to organize the First National Bank there. He fostered the building of railroads: the Lynchburg and Durham, the Oxford and Clarksville, the Durham and Northern, and the Dickerson branch line. He became director of the Raleigh and Augusta Air Line Railroad which from 1911 to 1913 he served as president.[30]

Durham also needed highways to connect it to other parts of the nation and to make it what its boosters envisioned, the hub of the South. Bennehan became an ardent advocate of the good roads movement and a leader in the promotion of the Quebec-Miami International Highway and organizer and vice-president of the Southern National Highway. As president of the Bankhead National Highway in 1924 he worked tirelessly to have the road past Stagville and Fairntosh incorporated in the route for the highway which would connect Oxford and Durham. For all his success in other such efforts, ironically in this one he failed: the highway commission, on which he had once served, favored the Creedmoor to Durham route, and the road past Stagville and Fairntosh (#1004) was never paved or improved in Bennehan's lifetime.[31]

Two terms in the state legislature as a representative (1914, 1916) and one as a senator (1918) gave Bennehan opportunity to achieve purposes congenial to his temperament. He worked to get state and federal aid for the building and maintenance of roads. For farmers and their concerns, he worked for weather bureau reports, for rural delivery of mail and parcel post, for deep waterways for cheap transportation of produce, and for a tax on colored oleomargarine. He lent his support to the building of the Panama Canal. As might have been expected, again like his father, he campaigned against the proposed amendment to the constitution on women's suffrage, falling back on the principle of states' rights to support his stand and to cloak his deep-seated objection to the intent of the bill. Every state, he argued, should be allowed to decide the matter for itself.[32]

To membership and leadership in agricultural societies he gave his time and energy as well. He was vice-president of the Southern Cotton Growers Protective Association, vice-president and president of the Farmers' National Congress, president of the North Carolina State Agriculture Society, and a member of the State Dairyman's Association.

Vacancies on various boards left by his father's death seemed almost a part of Bennehan's inheritance; his appointment to them was virtually automatic. Banks, cotton mills, railroads, and the state university felt in Bennehan the father's continuing presence. In his public character, therefore, he projected much the same image as his father; the face was familiar.

That so much of his life was public, however, in contrast to his father's largely private life, demonstrates a difference between them and the times in which they lived. Organizations of every sort had multiplied with the population and with the complexity of life. A nation of farms was well on the way to becoming a nation of towns. Gregarious by nature, Bennehan eagerly joined and supported organizations whose causes he believed in.

With so much to occupy his time, he spent very little of it at Fairntosh, particularly after his mother's death in 1897, when the house in Raleigh came into his possession.[33] He chose to make it his principal home where

Serena Jeffries, who had been so long a servant to the Mordecais, continued to manage the household. What drew him frequently to Fairntosh was his interest in the horses.

Although the emphasis on stockfarming begun at Stagville in the 1880s continued for a time to be an important operation, after Paul Cameron's death Bennehan felt free at last to indulge his real passion, race horses. From childhood he had shown this predilection, alluded to as early as 1860 in a letter of his father to Thomas Ruffin which described the fine new stables at Stagville as "Bennehan's affair." In his father's lifetime he had acquired the stallions Choctaw and Ferdinand, and for them and his other new prize stock he embarked at Stagville and Fairntosh on a building program, lasting at least a decade, to provide them the best in barns, stables, and silos.[34] The farm diaries kept during the years 1887, 1888, and 1889 by James Smith and W. P. Durham at Stagville and George Collins at Fairntosh give a day-by-day record of that work. The middle barn, big stable, and long barn and their construction and repairs figure in the daily accounts. Surmounted by a graceful cupola, the huge barn that stands today at Fairntosh was built in the 1890s as part of these improvements.[35] In the cupola, tradition says, Bennehan would sit with a child on his lap and watch the race horses on the track below. Some of the other barns built at this time were shortly afterwards destroyed by a fire that broke out at Fairntosh in August 1897. Five barns in whole or part were burned but the horses were unharmed.[36]

The letterhead on Bennehan's stationery in 1894 suggests the range of breeds of the stock he was raising and the breadth of the operation he was attempting.[37]

Office of B. Cameron

> Plantations: Fairntosh, Stagville, Eno, Little River, Harris
> Stock Farm, Dairy, Grist Mill, Saw Mill, Cotton Gin
> Hambletonian Horses, Thoroughbred Horses, Cleveland
> Bay Horses, Percheron Horses, Jersey Cattle, Berkshire
> Hogs, Sheep and Poultry
> Telegraph and Express Office
> Fairntosh, North Carolina
> (Lynchburg & Durham R.R.)

Besides William Daniel Turrentine, the overseer at Fairntosh whom young Duncan had engaged in 1879, there were other assistants. W. P. Durham was overseer at Stagville until he died in 1895; W. P. Clements worked as a kind of secretary as well as bookkeeper during the 1890s; and W. F. Black became Durham's replacement around the turn of the century, even possibly earlier. [38] Except for the letters from Turrentine, which continued as long as he stayed at Fairntosh (he died in 1924 but had been in ill health for some time before), there is almost no continuous and coherent information about the running of the plantations. Even these letters are comparatively few. Nothing like the weekly letters of Paul Cameron during his long years at Fairntosh illuminates the period of Bennehan's ownership. Many pertinent records, however, do remain: calendars of the breeding of mares, lists of births of colts and fillies, sporadic store and crop accounts of the tenants, and invoices for purchases and sales. The names of his prize horses — Steel Eyes, Croatan, Pamlico, Eno, Wilful Hilda, Rhoda J., Del Rio, Powhatan, Regulator, and Choctaw — recur in his correspondence. Bennehan's business and pleasure coincided on the racetrack where his horses by their performance could advertise his stables as well as gratify their owner's love of sport.

Choctaw, Bennehan's particular pride, earned a place in history, not equestrian but martial. Bennehan offered him to General Fitzhugh Lee for his personal use in the Spanish-American War. Lee accepted the offer, and Choctaw was shipped to the army in Florida in 1898. He soon after carried the conquering general through the streets of Havana before retiring with honor to Fairntosh in 1901.[39]

Bennehan's offer to Lee was entirely in character. He had long flirted with military life in his own quasi-military career. It had started in his student days at the Virginia Military Institute, continued after graduation with his reorganization of the Orange Guards whose captain he became, and matured with his appointment as assistant to the staff of the state Inspector General, his cousin Francis Cameron.[40] With the rank of captain he served governors Vance, Jarvis, and Scales; after his promotion to colonel and the adjutant-general's staff, he served governors Fowle, Holt, and Carr. Like many men of his time who had been too young to enlist in the Civil War, Bennehan viewed that lost cause nostalgically and its participants with envy. He found a substitute in state ceremony for the role fate had denied him.

Bennehan was able to play the hero, however, more than once in civilian life. He was a passenger on the train that wrecked near Statesville, North Carolina, in the summer of 1891 when it jumped the track at Bostian's Bridge over Third Creek plunging the cars into the creek below.[41] Through presence of mind and brute strength he was able to extricate himself from his berth and to rescue some of those still alive and trapped in the cars that had not submerged. He afterwards walked barefoot in the darkness of night to Statesville to give the alarm and telegraph his own safety to his mother. Congratulations on his preservation and tributes to his coolheaded courage flowed in. In a characteristic family gesture, the next year he donated a memorial window to the church at Statesville.[42]

Later train wrecks — six in all — threatened his life, but he always escaped injury. The number of these occurrences is not so much an index of the hazards of travel by train in those days as of Bennehan's restlessness. He was always on the move, "rolicking" as his father had termed it, hardly ever in one place more than a few days at a time. Some forty years of his personal diary detail his peregrinations.

This foot-loose mode of life was not due to a lack of a home and family. At the time of his father's death his attentions and affection were already centered on Sally Taliaferro Mayo, a daughter of Colonel Peter Mayo of Richmond, Virginia. They were married on 28 October 1891.[43] Probably his long bachelorhood (he was already thirty-seven years old) was due to his lack of money, not to lack of interest, for he had always been a ladies' man. His father's death enabled him at last to marry. Bennehan and Sally first made their home at Fairntosh, but town life was more congenial to both and the Raleigh house more comfortable than Fairntosh. Therefore, when the Raleigh house came into their possession, they made it their principal residence. Bennehan continued to visit Fairntosh regularly to keep an eye on his horses, but for his wife and children Fairntosh became only a vacation house. In this role, it was neglected; it failed to acquire the modern conveniences of indoor plumbing and central heating that made life in the Raleigh house more comfortable. Its appeal diminished year by year as it grew more antiquated; moreover, Sally Mayo Cameron and her children did not have the memories of its past and long association with it and its family that kept it always foremost in Bennehan's affections. Of Fairntosh and Stagville he had once acknowledged to his father, "I have an abiding love for these old places & all of their surroundings."[44]

Bennehan's inveterately restless mode of life had a predictable effect on his marriage. Though they kept constantly in touch through letters and telegrams, his life and Sally's grew more and more independent of each other. Too many directorships, committee appointments, horse races, clubs, societies, organizations, and causes claimed his attention.[45]

Though Bennehan possessed his father's physique and mental energy, he had not inherited his general good health. Even as a young man he began to suffer physical afflictions that required treatment and enforced rest: chronic catarrh (probably allergies in modern terminology), rheumatic gout (possibly arthritis, a common Cameron complaint), enlarged veins (varicose veins and hemorrhoids), and a heart ailment which struck him in his fifties and may have been a contributory cause of his death from pneumonia at the age of seventy-one.[46]

He did not suffer, however, from the chronic sense of duty which had made Paul Cameron assume early in life the responsibilities of son and heir in default of his handicapped brother. As one of the younger children in a large family, Bennehan entirely lacked this sense and had in its stead a capacity for pleasure and self-indulgence his father could never understand. Neither did he suffer from his father's pecuniary inhibitions, which had become an obsession in Paul Cameron's later life; Bennehan freely spent and freely enjoyed the results of his forefathers' labors. Some years before he died a millionaire, Paul Cameron, when staying at Barnum's Hotel in New York with his sisters, fumed at the cost. He wrote to his wife, "I do not like the House and the *price* less — $4 a day!! Will try to make a change — this is no place for poor people."[47] Bennehan suffered the consequences of the incongruity between his father's great wealth and his anxious frugality.

By the perverse economy of nature which makes a main trunk strong by pruning its branches, the Cameron family in each generation lost many of its young members. This fate, to be sure, operated to the good of the plantations by preserving their unity; Stagville and Fairntosh through two generations remained as a whole. Although the same fate did not fail to operate again in Bennehan Cameron's family, it resulted this time in the division of the plantations and their ultimate sale. Sally's and Bennehan's first child was born in the year following their marriage, a boy named Paul Carrington Cameron. The parents' devotion to this child was complete. His birth probably cancelled emotional debts to the past and promised happiness in the future. He lived just over three years. In May 1895 he began to ail with a disease that baffled the best medical knowledge the Camerons could obtain, and in July the deeply anxious parents took him to White Sulphur Springs, where Richmond doctors attended him daily but could not save him. He died in early September. Again Bennehan's diary, in an entry unlike the others which almost without exception are terse, factual jottings bare of any emotion, suggests the depth of his grief: "5.40 o'clock my Darling little Paul Carrington Cameron my only child breathed his last, & entered upon his rest with the angels."[48] On his fourth wedding anniversary in the following month Bennehan wrote, "Anniversary of our wedding day, which we celebrated by placing flowers on the grave of our darling little Paul & then went to Durham & saw Busey's portrait of him — & on to Fairntosh in desolation."[49] Three daughters were afterwards born to Bennehan and Sally, one of whom died in infancy, but no more sons.

Bennehan Cameron resumed his restless course, throwing himself into the countless endeavors which led to his many accomplishments already rehearsed and finding his satisfactions in the world at large. He made his mark on his time and place in the spirit of his forefathers. Pride in his family heritage for Bennehan became membership in the Society of the Cincinnati and the Sons of the American Revolution. He was also intimately involved in the development of the Stone Mountain Monument. As a friend of Gutzon Borglum he took an active role in its progress. Other monuments to history's heroes received his support as well: the monument to Francis Nash at Guilford Courthouse Battleground and the monument at the Bennett Farmhouse near Durham where General Joseph E. Johnston had signed the peace treaty with General William T. Sherman. He also erected a monument of his own to his great-grandfather John Cameron by the gift of a memorial tablet to the old Blandford Church in Petersburg, Virginia.[50] Possibly the crowning moment of his pride of ancestry came two years before his death when the Scottish Society of America met at Fairntosh, and he played host to its special guest and his own distant cousin, Colonel Donald W. Cameron, Laird of Lochiel and twenty-fifth chieftain of Clan Cameron.[51]

A year and a half later when Bennehan Cameron was returning from Dallas, Texas, where he had attended a Confederate reunion, he became ill with what was thought to be influenza. Four days later, on 1 June 1925, he died of pneumonia at his home in Raleigh.[52]

Despite the discipline that made him keep a daily memorandum for almost forty years, and despite his long years of leadership, his large estate, and his legal training, he died intestate. Was it indolence or negligence that kept him from that melancholy task? Or regret for a past that locked away his unfulfilled hopes and indifference to a future that lacked his male heir?

The obituary in the Durham *Morning Herald* reflected his popular image, probably not unlike one he had had of himself.

> Colonel Benehan [sic] Cameron, the beloved type of the typical Southern gentleman, and one of the most characteristic men of North Carolina, sleeps his eternal sleep beside his forebears and kinspeople, in the soil of his native state he loved so well and accomplished so much for, in the beautifully quaint cemetery yard of the venerable St. Matthews Episcopal church, at Hillsboro. . . . Assembled at St. Matthews church, were the citizens of Hillsboro, who knew him in youth and honored him through life, in large numbers, with sympathizing friends from the surrounding country, various parts of the state and other states. Sorrow and the deep sense of the irreparable loss to his family and the state was pronounced among the large gathering of friends to pay him the last evidence of respect, and the love they cherished for him, in the time of this mortal life. . . . It was a singular co-incident, that during the service at the grave a mocking bird, in a tree overlooking the burial rites, sang throughout the solemn moments the sweetest songs of his repertoire. A similar incident took place at the grave of Gen. J. S. Carr, when he was buried, just about one year ago. He and Col. Cameron were the most intimate of friends.
>
> > Now the laborer's task is o'er;
> > Now the battle day is past;
> > Now upon the farther shore
> > Lands the voyager at last.
> > Father, in Thy gracious keeping
> > Leave we now Thy servant sleeping.[53]

To the song of the mockingbird and the strains of the hymn the last Cameron to be master of Stagville and Fairntosh was carried to his grave.

Appendix A
Bennehan-Cameron Plantation Lands

The following list includes land transactions pertaining to the plantation complex in North Carolina and to the cotton plantations in Alabama and Mississippi up to the death of Paul Cameron in 1891. Dozens of other purchases and sales of land by the Bennehans and Camerons have been excluded. They owned land at various times in Virginia, in Halifax County, North Carolina, and in the towns or vicinity of Raleigh, Chapel Hill, and Hillsborough. Duncan Cameron was one of a commission to sell public lands in Raleigh; a number of these transactions are in the Wake County deed books. He was also involved in a number of purchases or sales as a trustee, executor, or middleman buying for a third party.

A few parcels of real estate that they owned have historical interest. After serving in the group that planned Raleigh, Richard Bennehan acquired a whole city block, called the Bennehan Square. Duncan Cameron bought the Governor Thomas Burke estate north of Hillsborough from his widow and a large tract on Haw River belonging to Archibald D. Murphey when it had to be sold for debt. Thomas D. Bennehan became the owner of the Eagle Hotel in Raleigh through default of payments on a loan.

Duncan Cameron became the sole owner in 1841 of the land and buildings of the Episcopal school for boys in Raleigh when that institution could no longer pay its way. In 1842 he leased them to Saint Mary's School on the site. The buildings and one hundred and fifty-nine acres were owned by the Camerons until 1897 when a portion of the land and the school buildings were sold to the Episcopal Diocese of North Carolina by Paul Cameron's heirs.

Some of Paul Cameron's own interesting purchases were the Hillsborough Military Academy buildings and land, five thousand acres of orange groves in Florida, and half ownership in almost one hundred thousand acres of land in Buncombe, Henderson, and Transylvania counties in North Carolina, a portion of which was later in the Vanderbilt estate.

In the following list the names of Thomas D. Bennehan, Duncan Cameron, and Paul C. Cameron are abbreviated respectively as T. D. B., D. C., and P. C. C.

APPENDIX A
Lands of Richard and Thomas D. Bennehan

Source (Orange County unless otherwise specified)	Date	Grantor	Location (Amounts stated in acres)
C.P. #133: v. 1 (deeds are missing for both purchases)	25 May 1776	Tyree Harris	Land on Flat River; 893 on southwest side of Flat River
	before 1778	Tyree Harris	320 on east side of Flat River. Bennehan's tax lists give total of 1213 and sometimes the separate tracts with their locations.
Deed Book 3:166	31 Aug 1786	James Munro	303 on Flat and Eno Rivers
Deed Box 3:53	27 Feb 1787	Judith Stagg	66 on southwest side of Flat River
Deed Book 4:1	31 Mar 1788	Joseph Speed	320 on north side of Flat River
Granville Co. Deed Book O:630	15 Oct 1789	Caleb & Lucy Brassfield	153 at fork of Neuse River and Knap of Reeds Creek
Deed Book 5:648	2 Nov 1796	John Martin	450 on Little River
McDuffie Map of 1890	15 Nov 1796	John Marshall	120 (part of Brick House farm)
Deed Book 5:624	28 Nov 1796	Trustees of UNC	247 on waters of Flat River
McDuffie Map of 1890	18 Jan 1797	Bryon Stonum	106 (part of Brick House farm)
Deed Book 6:41	4 July 1797	James Williams	461 on Little River
Deed Book 7:274	24 Aug 1798	James Baxter	225 (no location; only lifetime interest deeded)
Deed Book 9:24	26 Nov 1799	State of N.C.	35 on waters of Flat River

Deed Book 8:233	28 Nov 1799	Trustees of UNC	116 on waters of Flat River
Deed Book 10:45	3 Feb 1801	William Lingo	76 on waters of Knap of Reeds Creek
Deed Book 10:46	16 Apr 1801	Anthony Ricketts	390 between Flat and Little rivers
Wake Co. Deed Book U:409	16 Nov 1801	Mayton Thompson & Nancy Grant	155 on waters of Fox Grape & Grindstone branches
Deed Book 10:48	23 Dec 1801	John Tilley	222 on waters of Flat River
Wake Co. Deed Book T:201	16 Mar 1802	Jacob Bledsoe	120 on north side of Neuse River, the Ashley place; 462 on north side of Neuse River
	14 Apr 1803	Wm. T. Booker	244 on south side of Neuse River
	10 Sept 1803	Jacob Bledsoe	151 1/2 on north side of Neuse River
	22 Nov 1803	Richard Banks	320 on south side of Neuse River
	26 Dec 1804	Isaac McCallum	291 on both sides of Rocky Branch, south side of Neuse River
Wake Co. Deed Book T:265 (same year transferred to T. D. B. & D. C.)	24 May 1806	John & Wm. Bell	694 1/2 on south side of Neuse River
Deed Book 12:291	26 July 1806	Charles Kennon	100 and mill on Eno River
Wake Co. Deed Book U:275	30 July 1806	R. Bennehan to Charles Kennon	327 on both sides of Panther Creek
Wake Co. Deed Book U:20	18 Dec 1806	Joseph Gales	133 on drains of Rocky Branch purchased with D. C.

Continued on next page

APPENDIX A – Continued
Lands of Richard and Thomas D. Bennehan

Source (Orange County unless otherwise specified)	Date	Grantor	Location (Amounts stated in acres)
Deed Book 13:19	11 Aug 1807	Sam. Dickins, exec. of Robt. Dickins	222 on west side of Flat River
Wake Co. Deed Book V:42	16 Feb 1808	Sam. Oslin	128 3/4 (no location) bought with D. C.
Granville Co. Deed Book T:306	14 Dec 1808	John & Wm. Bell	357 1/2 on Knap of Reeds Creek
Deed Book 14:109	9 Sept 1812	Walter Alves	266 on both sides of main road
Deed Book 14:151	6 Nov 1812	Walter Alves	324 1/2 on both sides of main road, including the Boggan tract
Deed Book 17:117	7 Nov 1814	Wm. & Fielding Leathers	300 on south side of Eno River
Deed Book 14:714	24 June 1815	R. Bennehan to John Fort	301 on Knap of Reeds Creek
Deed Book 23:211	27 Jan 1821	Duncan Cameron	552 on north side of Little River
Wake Co. Deed Book 11:269	10 Aug 1821	Griffin Crooke	238 (no location)
Deed Book 22:11	24 Oct 1823	Wm. Horton	410 1/2 on Flat River (Horton Grove)

C.P. #133	Mar 1824	Thos. Reavis	271 (no location)
Wake Co. Deed Book 7:168	26 Sept 1826	Blount Cooper	165 3/4 on east side of Neuse River
Deed Book 24:2	2 Jan 1827	Hugh Cain	1/30 of 688 on both sides of Little River
Wake Co. Deed Book 9:403	– – 1829	T. D. B. to Alex Penny	1/2 interest in 238 on Ledge of Rocks Creek
Wake Co. Deed Book 11:189	13 Oct 1827	John Singleton	505 1/2 (no location)
Wake Co. Deed Book 9:315	29 Apr 1829	Wm. A. Tharpe	132 on Little Lick Creek
Wake Co. Deed Book 11:13	23 Mar 1830	Wm. A. Tharpe	822 on Panther Creek
Granville Co. Deed Book 4:432	28 Sept 1830	Nathaniel Robards	750 on north side of Neuse River
Wake Co. Deed Book 11:199	1 Jan 1831	Hudson Yearby	75 1/2 (no location)
Wake Co. Deed Book 19:115	– – 1834	T. D. B. to John Pennington	68 on Big Ledge of Rocks Creek

Lands of Duncan Cameron

Granville Co. Deed Book Q:547	5 Feb 1802	John B. Pulliam	293 mouth of Cedar Creek

Continued on next page

Appendix A — Continued
Lands of Duncan Cameron

Source (Orange County unless otherwise specified)	Date	Grantor	Location (Amounts stated in acres)
C.P. #133	Apr 1802	Richard Simpson	(no acreage or location given)
Granville Co. Deed Book R:37	3 June 1802	John Marshall & John Ligonire	585 on Knap of Reeds Creek
Granville Co. Deed Book R:67	5 Nov 1802	John Peace	1087 3/4 on waters of Tabbs Creek
Wake Co. Deed Book R:283	13 Dec 1802	Wm. Bibb	240 on waters of Horse Creek
Deed Book 14:35	4 Apr 1803	Richard Bennehan	1200 on Knap of Reeds Creek, Neuse River (Brick House Farm)
Granville Co. Deed R:347	22 July 1803	John Marshall & John Ligonire	694 on Little Ledge of Rocks Creek
Granville Co. Deed Book S:136	18 July 1805	John & Wm. Bell	585 on Knap of Reeds Creek adj. his own and John Green's lands
Deed Book 12:108	13 Nov 1805	John Pryor Smith	348 on Eno River at mouth of Little River
Wake Co. Deed Book T:201	10 Mar 1806	Richard Bennehan (a deed of gift to to D. C. & T. D. B.	462 on Neuse River, north side 120 on north side of Neuse River 151 1/2 on north side of Neuse River 291 on south side of Neuse River

Land Transactions Concerning the Plantations / 151

Deed Book 12:166	29 Aug 1806	Willie P. & Wm. P. Mangum	244 on south side of Neuse River; 320 on south side of Neuse River; 694 1/2 adj. first tract
Wake Co. Deed Book U:20	18 Dec 1806	Joseph Gales	640 on Flat River and 320 on Dials Creek (deed of trust; not transferred)
Wake Co. Deed Book V:42	17 Feb 1808	Sam. Oslin	133 on drains of Rocky Branch purchased with T. D. B.
C.P. #133	14 Dec 1808	John & Wm. Bell	128 3/4 purchased with T. D. B.
Deed Book 13:268	29 Dec. 1808	Sterling Harris	357 1/2 in Granville Co. at mouth of Knap of Reeds Creek
Wake Co. Deed Book V:44	21 Feb 1809	Wm. Sears	1/7 of 350 on Eno River
Person Co. Deed Book D:140	7 Apr 1809	Osborn Jeffreys, Sen.	100 (no location)
Person Co. Deed Book D:205	12 May 1810	Woodson Hubbard	2300 on forks of Flat River
Deed Book 13:324	18 July 1810	Richard Bennehan	170 1/2 (no location)
Deed Book 14:36	27 Dec 1811	James & Delilah Hopkins	300, part of two tracts formerly Monro's & Martin's (Fairntosh)
Person Co. Deed Book D:333	15 Sept 1812	Osborn Jeffreys, Jr.	1/7 of 350 on Eno River
			738 1/2 on both sides of Flat River

Continued on next page

Appendix A — Continued
Lands of Duncan Cameron

Source (Orange County unless otherwise specified)	Date	Grantor	Location (Amounts stated in acres)
Deed Book 14:360	31 Oct 1812	Robt. & Mary Newton	1/7 of 350 on Eno River
C.P. #133: 12 Dec 1835	30 Apr 1813	Sam Yarbrough	181 on both sides of south fork of Flat River adj. Thos. Sneed & Moses Chambers
Deed Book 14:335	1 Mar 1814	John Alston	547 3/4 on south side of Neuse River
Person Co. Deed Book D:403	31 May 1814	Spivey McKissack	314 3/4 on both sides of Tapleys Creek
C.P. #133	19 Sept 1815	D. C. to John Mayton	155 on waters of Fox Grape & Grindstone branches
Deed Book 15:381	10 Mar 1816	John Arnold & Fielding Leathers	203 on south side of Eno River opposite mouth of Flat River
Deed Book 15:382	5 June 1816	Hugh Cain	6 acres and 13 poles adj. tract D. C. bought of John Pryor Smith
Deed Book 16:188	8 Feb 1817	Hugh Woods	1/7 of John Cain's estate; 173 of Eno plantation; 117 1/2 of Benj. Forrest place; 222 of Widow Manning's place
Deed Book 16:187	24 Feb 1817	Mary Woods	1/7 of John Cain's estate (same tracts as above)

Deed Book 16:190	12 Mar 1817	D. C. to Wm. Cain, Jr.	All D. C.'s right in the estate of John Cain purchased of Hugh and Mary Woods and Young Dortch and his wife Nancy (the last is not in deed books but occurred 23 Feb 1817)
Person Co. Deed Book E:16	23 June 1817	David Jeffreys	320 1/2 on both sides of north fork of Flat River
Deed Book 16:68	2 Sept 1817	Richmond Harris's heirs	330 in fork of Eno and Flat Rivers
Person Co. Deed Book E:27	14 Nov 1817	David Jeffreys	105 (no description)
Deed Book 16:345	3 Mar 1818	Edward Harris	1/7 of 1/2 of 353 on Eno River
Person Co. Deed Book E:176	13 Sept 1819	Francis Epperson	37 8/10 plus 1 on north side of south prong of Flat River
Person Co. Deed Book F:44	7 – 1820	David Jeffreys	290 1/2 (no location); 234 2/3 on Tapleys Creek and Flat River
Wake Co. Deed Book 5:21	13 Oct 1820	James Kimbrough	434 on both sides of Ellerbee Creek
Deed Book 19:278	25 Jan 1821	James Alves, exec. of Walter Alves	3929 on Eno and Little rivers, Snow Hill plantation
Deed Book 23:211	27 Jan 1821	D. C. to T. D. B.	552 on east bank of Little River
Deed Book 19:282	1 Mar 1821	Willie Harris	1/2 of his father's land and 1/7 of his brother Nathaniel's 1/2 of 350

Continued on next page

Appendix A — Continued
Lands of Duncan Cameron

Source (Orange County unless otherwise specified)	Date	Grantor	Location (Amounts stated in acres)
Wake Co. Deed Book 5:280	5 May 1821	Bennehans & Cameron to Dudley Phipps	85 on Panther Creek
Deed Book 19:290	2 Oct 1821	James Briggs	200 adj. Thos. Reavis and Sam Southerland tracts
C.P. #133	1 Dec 1821	Sam. Southerland	lands on north side of Ellerbee Creek in exchange for D. C.'s tract on south
C.P. #133	17 May 1822	Sam. Southerland	same exchange as above in reverse
Deed Book 20:134	17 Oct 1822	Heirless Harris	1/7 of 1/2 of 352
Person Co. Deed Book G:1	3 Nov 1823	Lewis Daniel	389 on south fork of Flat River
Person Co. Deed Book G:178	6 Nov 1824	James Clack	991 on east side of Tapleys Creek
C.P. #133	3 Aug 1826	T. D. B.	271, the Reavis tract; 294 3/4, the Leathers tract; 100, the Chas. Kennon tract (mill not included)
Wake Co. Deed Book 7:15	20 Mar 1826	D. C. to Daniel Call	422 3/4 on both sides of Ellerbee Creek, partly in Orange Co.
Deed Book 27:101	20 Dec 1826	D. C. to Sam.	88 in exchange for two small tracts at mouth

Deed Book 24:2	2 Jan 1827	Southerland	of Long Branch where it enters Ellerbee Creek
Deed Book 24:2	2 Jan 1827	Hugh Cain, Hugh Cain, Jr.'s heir	1/5 of 1/6 of 688; two tracts on both sides of Little River
Deed Book 24:1	9 Aug 1827	Hugh Cain, Jr.'s heirs	D. C. bought seven shares each 1/5 of 1/6 of 680 acres
Person Co. Deed Book K:106	3 May 1828	Francis Epperson	139 on west side of Fishing Run of Flat River
Deed Book 26:229	10 Dec 1830	D. C. to Fielding Leathers	69 1/7 on south side of Eno River adj. Fish Dam Road
Deed Book 24:313	– – 1831	Margaret Cain Few, heir of Hugh Cain, Jr.	120 3/4 on west side of Little River
Deed Book 25:10	26 Nov 1831	Hugh Cain Jr.'s heirs	95 3/4 on Little River
Deed Book 25:13	29 Nov 1831	William Cain, heir of Hugh Cain, Jr.	95 3/10 on Little River
Deed Book 25:242	27 Nov 1832	Allen Cain's heirs	two tracts of 95 3/10 each
Wake Co. Deed Book 11:100	8 Mar 1833	David W. Stone	750 on Neuse River
Deed Book 25:494	17 Mar 1833	D. C. to Ripps Scoggins	90 3/4 on waters of Ellerbee Creek called Lovin's Place
Deed Book 26:322	7 Nov 1834	James Cain's heirs, Adam & Nancy Douglas	120 3/4 (no location)

Continued on next page

Appendix A – Continued
Lands of Duncan Cameron

Source (Orange County unless otherwise specified)	Date	Grantor	Location (Amounts stated in acres)
Deed Book 26:323	7 Nov 1834	James Cain's heir, Elizabeth Cain	120 3/4 on Cain Branch
Deed Book 26:267	25 Aug 1835	James Alves, exec. of of Walter Alves	60 on north side of Eno River
Wake Co. Deed Book 12:250	2 Sept 1835	Sam. Nichols	200 adj. Richland Creek
C.P. #133	12 Dec 1835	D. C. to Moses Chambers	181 on both sides of south fork of Flat River
Deed Book 27:160	30 Apr 1836	John Brown	15 on north side of Eno River
Deed Book 35:111	10 July 1837	D. C. to Fielding Leathers	69 1/7 adj. John Tilley and Fish Dam Rd.
Wake Co. Deed Book 13:386	15 June 1839	D. C. to John H. Bryan	1/2 of 200 on Richland Creek
C.P. #133	6 Apr 1844	Leonard Laws	180 on East side of Flat River adj. Brick House farm
C.P. #133	27 Nov 1844	Wm. Armistead	1680 in Green Co., Ala.

Lands of Paul C. Cameron

C.P. #133	1 Jan 1831	T. D. B. deed of gift	357 1/2 in Granville Co. adj. late John Green and Neuse River
Deed Book 28:100	1 Aug 1834	T. D. B. deed of gift	222 on Flat River purchased from John Tilley in 1801
Person Co. Deed Book O:294	24 Dec 1834	D. C. deed of gift	2000 on both sides of south fork of Flat River (excepting the mills)
Person Co. Deed Book P:421	21 Dec 1841	Wm. McKissack	900 on Flat River on Richland Creek near Robt. Pain's mill
C.P. #133	1 Mar 1851	will of D. C.	lands in Ala. already conveyed to P. C. C. through a deed of gift
Person Co. Deed Book S:151	19 Dec 1851	P. C. C. to J. J. Rodgers	925 on both sides of the north fork of Flat River near Robt. Daniel's mill
C.P. #133	24 Mar 1857 14 July 1857 13 Mar 1861	Samuel Tate	2240 in Tunica Co., Miss.
Will of P. C. C. B. Cameron #3623	28 Feb 1890 17 Nov 1873		
Person Co. Deed Book CC:318	27 Apr 1870	P. C. C. & Anne Cameron to Ruffin Rhew & Henry H. Garrett	1109 1/2 on east bank of Richland Creek

Continued on next page

Appendix A — Continued
Lands of Paul C. Cameron

Source (Orange County unless otherwise specified)	Date	Grantor	Location (Amounts stated in acres)
Person Co. Deed Book U:516	17 Aug 1871	P. C. C. & wife to Granville Andrews	99 + (no location)
Person Co. Deed Book U:382	14 Nov 1874	P. C. C. & wife to Jas. H. & Peleg Rogers	261 + on waters of Flat River
B. Cameron #3623	15 Feb 1875	P. C. C. to former slaves beginning 1872	1600 in Ala.; 160 still to be sold
Person Co. Deed Book U:461	17 Aug 1875	P. C. C. to Nancy Sneed	323 on north fork of Flat River
Deed Book 45:216	29 Sept 1877	P. C. C. to Alvis K. Umstead	100 on waters of Flat River adj. Robt. Harris
Person Co. Deed Book W:478	4 Sept 1879	P. C. C. to Harrison Ashley	127 + (no location)
Person Co. Deed Book W:479	4 Sept 1879	P. C. C. to Jas W. Ashley	203 (no location)
Person Co. Deed Book Y:490	10 Apr 1882	P. C. C. to Public School Committee	1 (for a school)

Person Co. Deed Book Y:267	10 May 1882	P. C. C. to Virginia Saunders	25 (no location)
Person Co. Deed Book GG:529	3 June 1882	P. C. C. to Andrew J. Bowling	100 (no location)
Person Co. Deed Book GG:511	1 Aug 1888	P. C. C. to Chas. G. Nichols	133 (a plat shows location)
Person Co. Deed Book KK:336	7 Dec 1889	P. C. C. to Virginia Saunders	agreement to sell 50 (no location)

Appendix B
Slaves Acquired by Purchase or Gift

Date	Slaves	From	To	Price
1764	Ned, about 26; Esther, about 36; Humphrey, under 10; Phebe, under 11; Bett, under 10 (These ages are figured from Bennehan's 1778 tax list.)	Will of Thomas Amis	Mary Amis	
1777	Arthur, Phebe, and their daughter Lucy Beck and her daughter Bett	Ralph McNair Alex Telfair	Richard Bennehan Richard Bennehan	£250 £250
1798–1804	Yellow Daniel, upwards of 50; Frank, upwards of 50; Black Daniel, 44; Jim, 38; Davie, 29; George, 21; Luke, 18; Jim Dickinson, 10; Anderson, 9; Allen, 9; Cyrus, 7; Charles, 4; Nanny, upwards of 60; Esther Dickinson, 30; Rilley, 30; Mary, 27; Sukey, 25; Aggie, 19; Amie, 19; Mariah, 11; Jamima, 7; Lillah, 7; Molly, 5; Harriot, 4; Nelly, 3; Viney, 1 (These ages are given in 1803.)	Thomas Amis, Jr.	Rebecca Bennehan	
1798–1804	Will; George; Dinah (grown); Sall; Donum, 15; Sam, 11; Paymore, 9; Phebee, 9; Clarisy, 7; Joe, 6; Paymor, 5; Jim Frog, 2; Peggy, 2	Thomas Amis, Jr.	In possession of Richard Bennehan	

Bennehan & Cameron Slaves / 161

			Duncan Cameron (D. C.)
ca. 1800	Jim	Rev. John Cameron	
1802	Moses	Rev. John Cameron	D. C. £230 ($460)
	Paumey		£215 ($430)
ca. 1802	Abraham		D. C.
1804	Hannah and her children Jenny and Davy	Robert Bell	D. C. £207
1805	Absalom, about 10	John K. Carson	D. C.
1807	Hampton, Betty and two children: Maria and Wm.	John Ross	D. C.
1810	Peter	Wm. P. Mangum	D. C. $350
1810	Squire, about 19	Ashley Dunnagan	D. C. $450
1810	Dick, about 17 or 18	John Marshall	D. C. $450
1811	Ben		D. C.
1811	Rhoda and her three children: Sam, Milley, Humphrey	Wm. Bennehan's estate	D. C. $700
1812	Amey, and her child	Walter Alves	Thos. D. Bennehan (T. D. B.) in exchange for Dempsey
1812	Tapp and Jenny	Ashley Dunnagan	D. C. $600
1814	Peter, about 33	Thomas Reavis	D. C. $400
1817	Two unnamed girls		D. C. $505
1817	Cherry, 23 and son Green, 2	Andrew Gray	D. C. $550
1818	Sally, Melissa, Patty, Caroline	John R. Archer	D. C. $1650

Continued on next page

Appendix B — *Continued*
Slaves Acquired by Purchase or Gift

Date	Slaves	From	To	Price
1818	Fanny, a little girl; Hannah and her children	W. R. Johnson	D. C.	
1818	Hannah's husband Joe hired in 1819	W. R. Johnson	D. C.	$80 per annum
1818	Phillip Coxe; Jenny; Sam; Hannah; Lucy; Anthony; Lizzy; William; Nancy; Henry; Archer; Rainy, Henry (weavers)	Wm. B. Giles	D. C.	$6755
1818	Rosetta, Fanny, Caroline	Ann Graham	D. C.	$1200
1818	Charles and LaMarque (These slaves had been in Bennehan's possession for many years.)	Thomas G. Amis	T. D. B.	T. D. B. paid T. G. Amis's estate $100 and $500 respectively for them in 1818 after their evaluation by James Webb and Hugh Cain. Both slaves had physical infirmities.

1819	Jemmy Green	J. Y. Tubb	D. C.
1821	Dave, 17 and Mime, 14	James Walker	T. D. B.
1821	Faithey and her three children: Fanny, John, and Beckey	James Clack	D. C.	$700
1822	Mariah, Edmund, Simon, Sally, Barbara, Minerva, Eliza, Delphia, Lydia, Peggy, Ephraim, Mary, Bob, Susan, Lewis, Amos, Caroline, Alexander, Nancy, Christianna, Jasper, Becca, Mariah, Anna, Zilpha, Owen, William	Dr. John Umstead	D. C.	$7000
1822	Isbel and her children Ned, Peter, Grace, Commodore	Wm. Leathers	D. C.	$1150
1823	Patsy, about 8	John Farrar	T. D. B.	$175
1824	Margaritt, about 16	Dr. James Webb	T. D. B.	$300
1824	Betty,[1] about 8 or 9	John Farrar	T. D. B.	$150
1824	Little Amy,[2] about 20, and her son Abner, about 4	Thos. Reavis	T. D. B.	$267.50
1824	Daniel, about 27	J. J. Carrington	D. C.	$375
1824	Dilcy, and daughter Sillars; Hannah; Walter, a boy.	Elizabeth Laws	T. D. B.
1824	Jincy and her child Malinda	Richard Young	D. C.	$350
1824	19 negro slaves, among them Charlotte, 37 or 38 and her son Jerry, 8 or 9	Thos. H. Taylor	D. C.	$3875

Continued on next page

Appendix B – *Continued*
Slaves Acquired by Purchase or Gift

Date	Slaves	From	To	Price
1825	Nelson, a boy	John T. Clement	T. D. B.	$216
1825	Judy, 19; and her child Matthew, 18 mos.	James Ray	T. D. B.	$300
1825	Fanney, 19, and her child Ailsy, about 18 mos.	James Ray	T. D. B.	$450
1826	Sepia (a male), 47	James Ray & Alcy Dunnagan	T. D. B.	$300
1826	On the dissolution of D. C.'s and T. D. B.'s partnership they bought slaves from each other: Elsy; Holly; Sina; Alfred; Bett, 16; Kitty, 14; Nat, 12; Tempe, 10; Polly, 8; Nancy, 11; William, 4; Frank, 2; Edy, an infant. (Some of these are children of Cressie, deceased.)	Duncan Cameron	T. D. B.	$5950
	Jack, 14; Dudley, 12; Gilly, 10; Lethe, 6; Anthony, 8; Reddin, 4; Daniel, an infant (children of Nimmy, deceased)	Duncan Cameron	T. D. B.	
	Jack; Peter; Devin; Milly; Sam; Cato, 14 Lucy, 10; Milly (previously jointly owned)	Duncan Cameron	T. D. B.	
	Donam, 48; Isham, 21; Peter, 14; Nelson, 11; Chaney, 7; Polly, 2; Willson, 2, a child	Thos. D. Bennehan	D. C.	$2600

	of Olly; Luke, 9, an infant of Nancy; Peggy, 36; Nancy, 31; Dinah, 13; Olly, 21	J. J. Carrington	T. D. B.	
1827	Pompey; Stanford; one unnamed slave	J. J. Carrington	D. C.	$830
1828	York; his wife Fanny; their children Monroe, Horton, Mary, Zachariah	Thos. Brownrig	T. D. B.	$765
1828	Aggy, about 30	Nancy Laws	T. D. B.	$200
1828	Alfred, 10; Isaac, 8 (sons of York)	John Campbell, deceased	T. D. B.	$360
1829	Phillip, a boy	Thos. Mitchell	T. D. B.	$350
1829	Cynthia, Dandridge, Isack, John, Nelly, Mary, Dicey, William, Margaret, Ferrabee (Phebe), Ben, Guy, Henderson, another (undecipherable name)	Dr. John Umstead, deceased	T. D. B.	$3150
1831	Robin, Phebe, Violet, Moreau, Betty, Cornelius, Amy, Peggy	Dr. John Umstead, deceased	T. D. B.	$1575
1831	Henry, about 13	Frances Laws	T. D. B.	$300
1832	Mary, Esther, Harry (mulattoes)	Hugh Cain, deceased	T. D. B.	$942
1842	Stephen, about 50	James Weddell	T. D. B.	$150

Duncan Cameron in taking deeds of trust on property and slaves may have acquired title to other slaves not listed here Slaves named in such deeds have not been included here if they did not show up on later slave lists of Duncan Cameron. Not all such slaves were individually named, and it is impossible to know whether they became members of this Bennehan-Cameron slave family.

Continued on next page

166 / Appendix B

[1] This slave was bought at an auction held at the Stagville Store.

[2] Sam Yarbrough, Thos. Bennehan's partner, was the actual purchaser of these slaves.

Certain slaves came to Duncan Cameron from his father's estate soon after 1815, but the number is uncertain. Gabriel and McKensa are names found in Duncan Cameron's slave lists. According to a bill of sale, he sold Ossian for $400 in 1818. Of the others nothing definite can be said. The Rev. John Cameron's slaves were as follows:

Robin	Charlotte	Lucinda
Henry	Matilda	Mary
Gabriel	Maria	Patty
Ossian	McKensa	Rhoderick

Appendix C
Tentative List of Overseers at Stagville and Other Plantations

Approximate Dates	Name of Overseer	Stagville	Elsewhere	Location Not Specified
1781	Hezekiah Ferrell			X
1782–1784	Thomas Head	X		
1786	Hezekiah Ferrell			X
1797–1825	Wm. Leathers, Jr.			X
1804	Drury Smth		Brick House	
1805	Hugh Woods		Little River	
1806	Shim Cooke		Brick House	
1808–1809	John Ferguson		Little River on Eno	
1812	Hugh Woods			X
1816	John Wilkins (blacksmith at Stagville) (he had been in Bennehan's employ many years)		Brick House	
1816	Fred Gates	X		
1818	Arthur Bobbitt			X
1824–1845	Fendal Southerland	X		

Continued on next page

Appendix C — Continued
Tentative List of Overseers at Stagville and Other Plantations

Approximate Dates	Name of Overseer	Stagville	Elsewhere	Location Not Specified
1830	William Leathers		Eno	
	Andrew Williams			X
	Alford Carrington			X
1837	Richard Holman			X
1837–1858	James Cothran	Person County		
1839–1843	William Piper		Fairntosh	
1839–1849	Mark Tate		Fish Dam	
1842–1867	Samuel Piper		Snow Hill, Fairntosh	
1842–1848	William Nichols (he may have been the Nichols at Fairntosh earlier [1835] who had almost killed a slave)		Person County	
1844	Walker		Snow Hill	
1844	William Piper			X
1846	Philip Southerland (hired and fired)	X		
1846–1847	Williams Harris	X		
1848	William Piper		Wake County	
1848	Phill Laws			X

1848	Williams Harris	X	
1849	Williams Harris		
1849	Isham Parrish	X	Wake County lands of Margaret Cameron
1850–1888	Philip Southerland		
1850	Philip Tate	X	Fish Dam
1851–	Arthur Bobbitt		Peak Place and Fish Dam
1858	Arthur Bobbitt		Brick House
1860	Nathaniel Walker	Person County	
1865	H. Card		Person County
1866	Calvin Clark		Person County
1866–1870	Joe G. Piper (renter)		Snow Hill
1866	Joseph Woods (renter)		Brick House
1867	Joseph Woods (renter)		Leathers Place
1874–1878	George Collins		Fairntosh
1878	Duncan Cameron II		Fairntosh
1881–1884	Bennehan Cameron (directing Southerland)	X	
1887	James Smith (renter) (the Scotch Farmer)	X	
1887	W. P. Durham		Fairntosh

Continued on next page

APPENDIX C — Continued
Tentative List of Overseers at Stagville and Other Plantations

Approximate Dates	Name of Overseer	Stagville	Elsewhere	Location Not Specified
1889	W. P. Durham	X		
1889–1924	W. D. Turrentine	X	Fairntosh	
1899–1901	J. B. Kirkland		Fairntosh	
1901–	W. F. Black	X	Fairntosh	
ca. 1920s	Aubrey Turrentine	X	Fairntosh	
late 1920s	Clarence Tilley	X	Fairntosh	
1928–1932	Vestal Taylor	X	Fairntosh	
?	Norman Moore	X	Fairntosh	
?	J. A. Harris	X	Fairntosh	
?	Alton Sutton	X	Fairntosh	
?	Claxton Sutton	X	Fairntosh	
1956–1974	N. E. Gilchrist		Fairntosh	
1953 to present	Allen Needham	X		

Appendix D
Cemeteries

Only one known cemetery exists on the Stagville property today, that of the Bennehan family, on land now owned by the State of North Carolina not far east of the Bennehan house. Probably set off at the time of Mary Amis Bennehan's death in 1812, it lies at the edge of the level ridge in a grove of oaks surrounded by a massive red sandstone wall of well-dressed stones in gradually diminishing size from bottom to top. An iron gate closes the one entrance in the wall on the south side.

The large size of the cemetery certainly reflects the hope of Richard Bennehan that his daughter and her family would also be buried there. Nevertheless there are only three graves, that of Mary Amis Bennehan, Richard Bennehan, and Thomas Dudley Bennehan. The grave markers are large stone slabs resting on rectangular brick supports forming table graves.

Slaves cemeteries would certainly be expected at Stagville, considering the size of the "black family," but none have been located and none are remembered.

The Horton family had a cemetery on the land now called Horton Grove, but this has not been found either. Bennehan Cameron believed that it contained four graves; one of them he was certain was that of Mrs. Horton, another, possibly her husband's. He indicated that the graveyard was on land that he owned, but he did not give its location. (B. Cameron: Family Data Series, 5 July 1904)

The oldest slave cemetery now known is on the Little River Plantation, now part of Fairntosh Plantation, on a hill over the old Norfolk and Western Railroad tracks. It covers a very large area and may contain several hundred graves. The inscribed stones are mainly post–Civil War and later, for it continued to be a black cemetery through the first half of this century.

Another slave cemetery called Harris Hill is situated on a knoll over the Eno River east of Red Mill Road. Now badly overgrown and almost impenetrable, its extent cannot be determined, but it is probably as large as Little River cemetery.

Appendix D
Stagville Cemetery

Sacred to the memory of
Richard Bennehan, Esq.
who departed this life
Dec. 31. 1825
Aged 78 years and 9 months[1]

Sacred to the Memory of
Mrs. Mary Bennehan
who departed this life
on the 17th December
1812
age 51 years[2]

In Memory of
Thomas D. Bennehan Esq.
only son of
Richard and Mary Bennehan
He was born in Orange County
and departed this life in Raleigh
on 24th June A.D. 1847
in the sixty-sixth year of his age

---

[1]According to his birthdate recorded in North Farnham Parish, Richmond County, Virginia, he would have been eighty-two years old at the time of his death.

[2]In Richard Bennehan's unfinished account of his life, he gives his wife's age at death as in her 56th year.

Continued on next page

Appendix D — *Continued*
Fairntosh Cemetery

Anne Owen Nash Cameron	15 June 1753–25 Aug. 1825[1]
William Ewan Cameron	(no dates on stone; ca. 1792–1827)
Andrew Williams	(no marker of any kind; d. 1837)
Jean Syme Cameron	18 Aug. 1815–8 Aug. 1837 (interred here 30 Nov. 1837)
Mary Ann Cameron	10 Jan. 1804–22 July 1839
Rebecca Bennehan Cameron	17 May 1810[2]–15 Sept. 1839
Ann Owen Cameron	20 Dec. 1817–22 Mar. 1840
Jean Cameron	26 Oct. 1836–12 Oct. 1842
Rebecca Bennehan Cameron	28 Sept. 1778–6 Nov. 1843
Duncan Cameron	17 Apr. 1846–16 Nov. 1848
Duncan Cameron	15 Dec. 1777–6 Jan. 1853[3]
Mary Amis Cameron	26 Apr. 1844–20 Aug. 1855

[1]This deathdate is incorrect. C.P. #133: 10 Aug. 1825 makes it clear that Duncan Cameron's mother died in Hillsborough 9 Aug. 1825.

[2]This birthdate is incorrect. Rebecca was born in 1813. The Cameron Papers make this very clear but the exact date is not mentioned; possibly the May date on the stone is correct.

[3]Duncan Cameron's deathdate is also incorrect. A check of newspapers as well as of the family papers and parish record will disclose that he died on the 3rd of January and was buried on the 4th.

Continued on next page

Appendix D — *Continued*
Little River Cemetery

Rosa Brand[on]
was born
Sep 8th 1891
She Died Sep ?th 1903

Sue Brockrum
born Dec. 28 1879
died Oct. 2 1922

Elvie Dunegan
born 1872
died 24 Nov. 1929

Isaac Dunegan
born 5 July 1900
died 28 Mar. 1920

John H. Dunnegan
born Nov. 5 1931
Pvt. 1 CL 344 Serv.

Mildred Edwards Dunnegan
born Feb. 15 1883
died July 11 1939

Abram Edward
was born
May the 14th
and died ? 12 1906

Allen Edwards
   born
Jan. 7 1871
   died
Feb. 22 1929

Esther
Dide 16 May 1841

Nellie
wife of
Rev. Sidney Harris
Born April 8 1896
died Jan. 14 1934

Jennie Harts
   died
Dec 11 1907
   age 45
"Her Farewell end was Peace"

Kate Hart
died Feb. 28 1937
age about 50's

Paul Harts
   Born
Mar 25 1900
   Died
Oct 10 1928
He is not dead but sleepeth

Willis Hart
died Mar 30 1946
aged 80

Mrs. Janie Holeman
1881–1951

George Holman
died Apr. 27 1956
aged 75 years

Joe Annie Jones
Died J. 22, 1925

Isaac Jones
Died July 31, 1912

Jasper Jones
Born March 20, 1874
Died July 2, 1944

Continued on next page

Appendix D – *Continued*
Little River Cemetery

Louis Justice
Died Apr. 1 1928
   age 60 years
Gone but not forgotten

Lettey
DIDE NOVE
EMBER 24
1848   Aged 43

Ardelia Lewis
born Nov. 18 1927
died Jan. 29 1934
granddaughter of
Fannie Anderson

Mary
a slave
died Jan 30
1860

Lether Magnum – wife of
Nick Jones
   1857–1935

Tempie Markham
died Jan. 15 1933

Sacred to the memory of
Phillip Meaks who
departed this Life on
the 22th [*sic*] June 1837
aged 74 years

Nelly
died 15 June 1836
aged 69 years

Barbara Jean Peaks
born Jan. 19 1885
died Aug. 26 1939

John A. Peaks

Sallie Peaks
Born Mar 1830
She died June 28, 1901

Manda Satterfield
died August 12, 1913

Luke Sowell
died Aug. 19, 1933

Sandy Peaks
born Jan. 22 1864
died Jul. 10 1950

Nellie Ruth
wife of
Jake Sowell
Born Dec. 10 1905
Died Mar. 28 1927

Mrs. Ora Sowell
Dec 13, 1946   43 years

   Husband
Henry Walker
born Feb. 17 1888
died Jan. 21 1928

Jerry Webb
Died Mar. 29, 1928
Age 67 years

Continued on next page

APPENDIX D — *Continued*

Harris Hill Cemetery

Betsy An Adams, wife of Wilie Adams
    died March 23, 1927,
        78 Yrs

Burton Dunegan
    died 1944

Ovena Haliburton, daughter of
Hiram and Angerline Haliburton
    b. Jan. 25, 1903
    d. June 5, 1924
        and
Myrtle Haliburton, sister of Ovena
    b. Nov. 19, 1900
    d. July 11, 1924

Sedly Webb
    b. Dec. 4, 1888
    d. Aug. 15, 1936

Three gravestones of small children who died around 1900 — unnamed.*

---

*The inscriptions from the Harris Hill cemetery were gathered by Kenneth McFarland, site manager of Stagville.

Appendix E
Paul Cameron's Agricultural Schedule for the 1850 and 1860 Federal Censuses

	1850	1860
Acres improved	2,000	2,605
Acres unimproved	2,400	4,070
Cash value of farm	$25,000	$72,000
Value of farm implements and machinery	$1,500	$9,000
Horses	35	50
Asses & mules	22	45
Milch cows	40	60
Other cattle	150	160
Sheep	205	450
Swine	600	600
Value of livestock	$5,408	$15,000
Wheat (bushels)	3,000	8,000
Rye (bushels)	4,000	800
Indian corn (bushels)	6,000	14,000
Oats (bushels)	2,000	2,000
Tobacco (pounds)		30,000
Ginned cotton (400-lb. bales)	65	400
Wool (pounds)	500	800
Beans & peas (bushels)	1,500	2,000
Irish potatoes (bushels)	40	200
Sweet potatoes (bushels)	500	800
Butter (pounds)	300	800
Hay (tons)	100	60
Flax (pounds)	400	1,000
Flaxseed (bushels)	60	60
Value of homemade manufactures	$1,200	$1,000
Value of animals slaughtered	$2,000	$4,500
Honey (pounds)		200

Continued on next page

Appendix E — *Continued*
Agricultural Schedules of Thomas and Mildred Cameron for the 1850 and 1860 Federal Censuses
(Their farms were under Paul Cameron's management.)

	Thomas Cameron 1850	Thomas Cameron 1860	Mildred Cameron 1860
Acres improved	5,000	1,200	1,500
Acres unimproved	3,000	1,800	1,500
Cash value of farm	$50,000	$30,000	$30,000
Value of farm implements & machinery	2,000	600	600
Horses	45	15	15
Asses & mules	40		14
Milch cows	80	20	40
Working oxen	24	6	12
Other cattle	350	60	80
Sheep	700	80	112
Swine	700	150	200
Value of livestock	$10,000	$3,000	$4,900
Wheat (bushels)	3,500	2,000	1,300
Rye (bushels)	700	150	300
Indian corn (bushels)	10,000	700	5,000
Oats (bushels)	5,000	400	600
Tobacco (pounds)		2,000	5,000
Ginned cotton (400-lb. bales)	75	80	200
Wool (pounds)	800	200	300
Butter (pounds)	800		
Flax (pounds)	500		
Flaxseed (bushels)	70		
Beans & peas (bushels)		400	400
Sweet potatoes (bushels)		400	200
Hay (tons)		6	10
Value of home-made manufactures	$2,500	$260	$300
Value of animals slaughtered	$2,500	$800	$800

Continued on next page

Appendix E — *Continued*
Duncan Cameron's Agricultural Schedule for the 1880 Federal Census

Acres tilled	300
Acres permanent meadows	25
Woodland	300
Other unimproved land, old fields, etc.	100
Value of farm	$4,000
Value of farm implements	$500
Value of livestock	$600
Cost of building and repairing in 1879	$100
Cost of fertilizers	$100
Wages paid	$450
Weeks of white labor	51
Weeks of colored labor	200
Value of farm products	$4,000
Acres mown grass	6
Tons of hay	6
Horses	7
Mules	6
Oxen	3
Milch cows	3
Other cattle	12
Calves	
Dropped	2
Sold living	2
Slaughtered	3
Died	5
Butter made (lbs.)	400

Continued on next page

Appendix E — *Continued*
Duncan Cameron's Agricultural Schedule for the 1880 Federal Census

Sheep	8
Dropped	4
Slaughtered	2
Died	2
Fleeces clipped (25 lbs.)	7
Swine	30
Poultry	15
Eggs (doz.)	140
Acres in Indian corn	
yield: 1,000 bus.	50
Acres in oats	
yield: 500 bus.	75
Acres in wheat	
yield: 500 bus.	75
Acres in cotton	
yield: 7 bales	10
Acres in potatoes	
yield: 100 bus.	1
Acres of apple trees	
(400 bearing trees)	25
Bushels of apples	
$200 value sold	500
Cords of wood cut	
$50 value	40

Appendix F
Stock and Tool List for Person Co., N.C. (1844) and Green Co., Ala. (1846)

	North Point	Mill Plantation	Jim Ray's	Alabama
horses	6		3	4
mules	2	8	7	25
cattle	32	30	59	12
hogs	60	80	147	160
single plows	6	6	13	22
double plows	3	3	6	10
single bull-tongues				10
harrows	4	2		
coulters	2	2	2	
mattocks	4	6	7	10
cutting knives				7
weeding hoes	8	10	15	7 doz.
hilling hoes	3	3	11	
cane hoes				10
axes	6	8	10	16 (6 in a box)
frows			3	
wedges	2		5	
trace chains				34 pairs
scythes	4	4	8	8
cradles	2	4	8	8

Continued on next page

APPENDIX F — Continued
Stock and Tool List of Five Orange County, N.C. Plantations (1841)

	Fairntosh	Snow Hill	Eno	Bobbitt's	Brick House
plow gear		6 prs.	8 prs.	12 prs.	
crosscut saw		1		1	
wagon		1	1	1	3
cart		1	1	1	
horses	17	4			
colts	8		6		8
cattle	33	39	52	22	44
calves	16	7	8	5	4
hogs	166 + 21	175	66	140	100
pigs	44	54	42	40	
ewes & lambs	101		65		
mules	5	10	15	12	
wagon gear		1		1	1
gear	12 prs.	14 prs.	15 prs.	10 prs.	8 prs.
cart	1	1	1	1	1
log chains	3	1	2	1	2
axes	8	8	8	6	8
scythes & cradles	12	8	5	5	5
M. blades	4			2	
I. wedges	2	3	5	5	3
cutting box	1	1	1	1	1
spades	2	4	4	2	

Lists of Plantation Tools & Livestock / 183

Item				
wheat fans	2			
carpenters tools	1 set			
smiths tools	1 set			
pad locks	8		3	
steelyards	1		1 pr.	
stable forks		4		2
shovels		1		
drawing knives	1	1		1
pitch forks		1		1
two-horse plows		6	4	
one-horse plows	5	21	10	2
weeding hoes	14	35	25	9
hilling hoes	16	7	4	19
mattocks	5	6	7	5
c. harrows	5	5	5	4
w. harrows	4	2		2
bulltongues	1	5	4	1
coulters	2	2	1	2
handsaw	2		1	1
grindstone	1		1	1
sprouting hoes		2	2	2
auger		1	1	3

A comparison of this list with lists of other years shows that animals and tools were moved around, and the numbers of each item at a particular plantation varied from year to year.

Plow gear and *trace chains* were probably meant to describe the same item: harness for the mules to pull the plows or other machinery.

Appendix G

Mill Information from the Census Records

1860   Products of Industry   p. 2   Orange County, N.C. (F 2. 113 P)
Paul C. Cameron   Stagville Mills
   $3,000 capital invested
   17,000 bushels of wheat ground
   $17,000 value of wheat ground
   3,400 barrels of flour annual product
   number of hands employed   2
   wages $30 per month

1870   Industry Schedule 4   Orange County, N.C. (no page numbers)
Paul C. Cameron   Merchant mill   all custom grinding
(F 2. 118 P)
   $4,000 capital investment
   25 horse power
   employing one male over 16
   earning $200 a year
   two wheels
   diameter 18 feet
   width 3 feet
   one pair burrs
   one pair stones
   4,000 bushels of wheat ground
   $4,000 value of wheat ground
   800 barrels of flour
   $5,600 value of flour
   3,000 bushels of corn ground
   $3,000 value of corn ground
   $3,000 value of meal

1880   Special Schedule of Manufactures: Nos. 7 and 8: Flour and Grist Mills — Cheese Butter & Condensed Milk Factories (F. 2. 135P)
   Lebanon Township, Orange County, N.C. [New Mill]
   Paul C. Cameron
      $3,000 capital investment
      employing 1 hand, male over 16

Continued on next page

Appendix G — *Continued*
Mill Information from the Census Records

12 hours May to Nov.
8 hours Nov. to May
9 months in operation on full time

1 month on 3/4 time
2 months on 1/2 time
2 runs of stones
grinds 100 bushels per day capacity
both custom and market milling
no elevator
on Eno into Neuse
12 feet height of water fall
2 wheels
turbine
18 horse power
3,000 bushels of wheat ground
$3,000 value of wheat ground
2,000 bushels of other grain
$1,000 value of other grain
$150 mill supplies
$4,150 total value of products
600 barrels of wheat flour
96,000 lbs of corn meal
61,000 lbs of feed
$6,048 value of all products

1880   Special Schedule of Manufactures: Nos. 5 & 6   Lumber Mills and Saw Mills — Mangum Township, Orange County, N.C.   Brick Yards and Tile Works (F. 2. 135 P)

    Duncan Cameron   Saw Mill
    $2,000 capital investment
    employing 3 hands   males over 16
    runs 10 hours per day May to Nov.
    runs 8 hours per day Nov. to May
    wages $1 per day per skilled labourer
    wages $.75 per day per unskilled labourer

Continued on next page

Appendix G — *Continued*
Mill Information from the Census Records

$125 total paid in wages
6 months full time operation
6 months idle
1 circular saw
value of logs cut $550
value of mill supplies $25
total value of all $575
number of feet of lumber   90
value of products $900   wood procured from woods near mill
do half of own logging
on Little River
height of fall   12 feet
one turbine
4 feet in breadth
8 revolutions per minute
30 horse power

1880   Special Schedule of Manufactures: Nos. 5 & 6   Lumber Mills and Saw Mills — Brick Yards and Tile Works
Lebanon Township, Orange County, N.C. (F. 2. 135 P)

    P. C. Cameron   Saw Mill
$800 capital investment
employing 3 hands   males over 16
runs 10 hours May to Nov.
runs 10 hours Nov. to May
average day's wages $.75
total amount paid in year $300
3 months full time operation
2 months half time
7 months idle
1 circular saw
value of logs cut $780
value of mill supplies $25
total value of all materials $805
number of feet of lumber   156
number of thousand shingles   25

Notes

Abbreviations

B. Cameron	Bennehan Cameron Papers
C.P.	Cameron Family Papers
DAH	Division of Archives and History
GCD	Granville County Deeds
G. W. Mordecai	George W. Mordecai Papers
NCLG	North Carolina Land Grants
OCD	Orange County Deeds
OCW	Orange County Wills
Ruffin Papers	Thomas Ruffin Papers
SHC	Southern Historical Collection
Slave Narratives	Federal Writers' Project, Slave Narratives, North Carolina, vol. 11.

All interviews were with the author.
Orange County, North Carolina, is meant where a census reference contains no place name.

Chapter 1. NEW TERRAIN

[1] Richard Bennehan's birth is given as 15 April 1743 in *The Register of North Farnham Parish 1663–1814 and Lunenburg Parish 1783–1800, Richmond County, Virginia* ed. by George H. S. King (Fredericksburg, Va., 1966), 14. His tombstone, which records his age at death in December 1825 as seventy-eight years nine months, is therefore incorrect.

[2] C.P.: A loose paper in vol. 4 is a copy of the contract between Johnston and Bennehan specifying their obligations and rights.

[3] William F. Wilson and P. Albert Carpenter III, *Region J Geology: A Guide for North Carolina Mineral Resource Development and Land Use Planning* (Raleigh, 1975), 9–13; Robert M. Kirby, *Soil Survey of Durham County, North Carolina* (Washington, D.C., 1976), 6–34 and sheet no. 11.

[4] Harry R. Merrens, *Colonial North Carolina in the Eighteenth Century: A Study in Historical Geography* (Chapel Hill, 1964), 54, quoted from the *Connecticut Courant*, 30 Nov. 1767.

[5] John S. Davenport, "Early Settlers in the North Carolina Piedmont, 1749–1763," *North Carolina Genealogical Society Journal* 4, no. 2 (1978): 74–86.

[6] NCLG, vol. 19, p. 458, Secretary of State's office, Raleigh; Walter Alves Papers, Oct. 1806, SHC.

[7] C.P.: John Kent to Richard Bennehan, 30 June 1787.

8. Jackson Turner Main, *The Social Structure of Revolutionary America* (Princeton, 1965). Main discusses the landholding class and its size, estimating that in the Northern Neck of Virginia as much as 70 percent of the land was held by a small number of wealthy men (p. 45) and that the same amount of land remained in the same families (p. 179), preventing upward social mobility. After a region became a settled community and was no longer a frontier, opportunity to rise markedly declined (pp. 180, 196).

9. Richmond County, Virginia, Wills and Inventories 1709–1717, p. 281, Will of Dominick Bennehan, 16 Apr. 1716; Richmond County Wills, Book 5, p. 643, Will of Dudly Bennehan, 12 Mar. 1749, Richmond County Court House, Warsaw, Virginia.

10. C.P.: 20 Mar. 1762.

11. James G. Scott and Edward A. Wyatt IV, *Petersburg's Story: A History* (Petersburg, 1960), 3–50.

12. Scott and Wyatt, *Petersburg's Story*, 21, 42, 151.

13. C.P.: 11 Nov. 1768; vol. 16, Nov. 1784.

14. C.P.: vol. 1, 12, 14, for example.

15. C.P.: vol. 3; 1779 Tax List of Orange County, North Carolina (L.P. 30. 1), DAH.

16. C.P.: vol. 156; May 1771, Aug. 1778.

17. C.P.: 15 Feb. 1776.

18. The Raleigh *News and Observer*, 7 Jan. 1891. This obituary wrongly identifies Rebecca Bennehan Cameron's father and Paul C. Cameron's grandfather as Col. *Thomas* Bennehan. See also C.P.: 16 July 1803.

19. C.P.: 4 June 1781.

20. C.P.: vol. 1, p. 45; Northampton County, North Carolina, Will of Thomas Amis, 28 Mar. 1764 (C.R. 71.801.1.), DAH. No record survives of their marriage.

21. No deeds survive for Bennehan's purchase of these tracts. C.P.: vol. 1 shows that Richard Bennehan paid Tyree Harris £1,600 on 25 May 1776 for land on Flat River, acreage not stated. C.P.: 1784, Bennehan's tax list, gives the acreage and location of each tract.

22. C.P.: 6 Dec. 1855.

23. C.P.: Vol. 2.

24. Holdings of anywhere from 500 to 1,000 acres of land and ownership of twenty or more slave are figures used by historians to define the planter. See Guion G. Johnson, *Ante-Bellum North Carolina: A Social History* (Chapel Hill, 1937), 59n; Main, *Revolutionary America*, 54, 276.

25. C.P.: Aug. 1778; Hugh T. Lefler and Paul Wager, *Orange County 1752–1952* (Chapel Hill, 1953), 16.

26. Lefler and Wager, *Orange County*, 16.

27. Social classes, their make-up and size, are discussed in Johnson, *Ante-Bellum North Carolina*, 16–17, 55–56, 58–60; Main, *Revolutionary America*, 54–66, 113, 276.

28. Don Higginbotham, ed., *The Papers of James Iredell* (Raleigh, 1976) 2: 8, James Iredell to Hannah Iredell, 12 Mar. 1778.

Chapter 2. THE BUILDING OF STAGVILLE

1. *See* Public Record Office, American Loyalist Claims, Series II, AO 13/100, N.C. Archives for estrangement that occurred between Amelia and the Bennehans. OCD,

Book 3, p. 53, Orange County Courthouse, Hillsborough.

[2]NCLG, Book 19, pp. 455-460; GCD, Book A, p. 169, Book B., p. 95, County Court House, Oxford, North Carolina; Registration of Deeds, Orange County, County Court, June 1752-August 1793 (C.R. 073. 408.1), DAH.

[3]Minutes of the Court of Pleas and Quarter Sessions, Orange County, North Carolina (C.R. 073. 301.2) June Term 1758, DAH. He renewed the license in subsequent years.

[4]C.P.: vol. 18, p. 2.

[5]Interview with Paul T. Hall.

[6]C.P.: vol. 18, pp. 1-2.

[7]U.S. Post Office Department, "Records of Appointments of Postmasters," DAH; C.P.: 11 Nov. 1852.

[8]C.P.: 14 Aug. 1790.

[9]C.P.: Undated papers, Building and Gardening.

[10]C.P.: Dec. 1816. Though undated, this list can be assigned a date close to 1816 because in that year a direct tax was levied on real and personal property by the United States government, the purpose stated on this list, and because the figures it contains for land and slaves are only slightly larger than those on a list dated 1815.

[11]Hardscrabble, the house built by Palmer for William Cain, stands beautifully restored and only slightly altered on Saint Mary's Road in Durham County.

[12]C.P.: 11 Dec. 1845.

[13]Rebecca's birthdate was recorded in the Duncan Cameron family Bible kept at Salem Chapel where Duncan Cameron the son of Paul Cameron copied it and the other family information it contained. (C.P.: 28 Sept. 1878.) Thomas Bennehan's birthdate is not found in any surviving record. His tombstone records only his approximate age at death.

[14]C.P.: Apr. 1815.

[15]C.P.: June 1798. The dollar equivalents are given in the bill.

[16]C.P.: 25 Sept. 1881.

[17]C.P.: 8 May 1799.

[18]C.P.: Aug. 1779.

[19]C.P.: Mar. 1824.

[20]C.P.: vol. 10B.

[21]Elizabeth Amis Cameron Blanchard and Manly Wade Wellman, *The Life and Times of Sir Archie: The Story of America's Greatest Thoroughbred 1805-1833* (Chapel Hill, 1958); C.P.: 17 Oct. 1797; vol. 49, Oct. 1799 contains accounts of Richard Bennehan showing expenses incurred at the races in Hillsborough.

[22]C.P.: 14 Aug. 1847.

[23]C.P.: vol. 72, 25 July, 27 Sept. 1802; vol. 75, 5 May 1804; 16 June 1810.

[24]C.P.: 24 Mar. 1807.

[25]C.P.: 30 July 1806; U.S. Post Office Department, "Records of Appointments of Postmasters," DAH.

[26]Their names occur in the papers over many years. Green began to work for Bennehan, probably as a store clerk, as early as 1795. C.P.: Richard Bennehan to Thomas D. Bennehan, [1795]; vol. 75, 5 May 1804; 21 Jan. 1806; 2 Mar. 1807; 21 Feb. 1814; Jan. 1820; 28 Oct. 1846; OCW, Book E, p. 507.

[27]C.P.: 2 Nov. 1806; vol. 88 contains his estate settlement.

[28]C.P.: 26 Feb., 23 May 1810, 17 May 1824, 24 July 1830.

[29]Kemp P. Battle, *History of the University of North Carolina from Its Beginning to the Death of President Swain 1798-1868* (Raleigh, 1907) 1: 787.

[30]Blackwell P. Robinson, *William R. Davie* (Chapel Hill, 1957), 225-276.

[31]C.P.: 13 July 1796, 6 Apr. 1802; Robert D. W. Connor, Louis R. Wilson, and

Hugh T. Lefler, *A Documentary History of the University of North Carolina 1776-1799* (Chapel Hill, 1953), 2: 389; Battle, *History of the University*, 1: 830. This history credits Thomas Bennehan with the gift of the oyster shells. John H. Wheeler, *Reminiscences and Memoirs of North Carolina and Eminent North Carolinians* (Columbus, Oh., 1884), 346.

[32]Conner, Wilson, and Lefler, *History of the University*, 2: 457-58.
[33]Kemp P. Battle, *The Early History of Raleigh, A Centennial Address* (Raleigh, 1893), 19.
[34]Battle, *Early History of Raleigh*, 33; C.P.: 17 Jan. 1891 (Will of Paul C. Cameron).
[35]David L. Swain Papers, Paul C. Cameron to David L. Swain, 9 May 1853, Private Collections, DAH; B. Cameron Papers: W. Henry Hoyt to Bennehan Cameron, 10 Aug. 1909, SHC.
[36]C.P.: 19 Dec. 1810, 12 Jan. 1811.
[37]C.P.: 7 Oct. 1796; Undated papers, Thomas G. Amis to Thomas D. Bennehan.
[38]C.P.: 3 Mar. 1807; Undated papers, Thomas G. Amis to Thomas D. Bennehan.
[39]Estates Records, Northampton County, North Carolina, Estate of Thomas Gale Amis, 1824 (C.R. 071. 508. 2), DAH.
[40]C.P.: 17 Jan., 21 Jan. 1793.
[41]C.P.: 8 May 1803.
[42]C.P.: 23 Aug. 1803
[43]C.P.: 21 Apr. 1811.
[44]C.P.: 10 May 1811.
[45]C.P.: 25 Sept. 1883.
[46]C.P.: 30 Nov. 1807.
[47]C.P.: 10 July 1806.
[48]Battle, *History of the University*, 1: 823; C.P.: 19 Dec. 1812.
[49]C.P.: 2 May 1824, 6 Aug. 1829.
[50]C.P.: 9 Dec. 1845.
[51]C.P.: Undated papers, Miscellaneous papers, a receipt from A. Lafore, Hair Dresser & Wig Maker, 13 May 1845.
[52]C.P.: 23 June 1834.
[53]C.P.: 6 Oct. 1835.
[54]C.P.: 27 Oct. 1842.
[55]C.P.: 24 Jan. 1843.
[56]C.P.: 13 May 1845; 26 Sept. 1846.
[57]C.P.: 5 Jan. 1826.
[58]C.P.: 6 June 1780; G. W. Mordecai: 21 Apr. 1859, SHC. This letter states that Charlotte Rice was the daughter of Thomas and Mary Ann Rice of Granville County, and that she was born on 1 Sept. 1769 and died on 4 Jan. 1859.
[59]C.P.: Will of Thomas D. Bennehan, 28 Apr. 1845.
[60]C.P.: 7 May 1838, 29 Nov. 1855, 5 May 1857.
[61]C.P.: 25 Sept. 1883.

Chapter 3. THE CAMERON CONNECTION

[1]Alice Read Rouse, *The Reads and their Relatives* (Cincinnati, 1930), 80-91; Catherine L. Knorr, comp., *Marriage Bonds and Ministers' Returns of Charlotte County, Virginia, 1764-1815* (1951), 13. Cameron first served in Charlotte County, Va., next in Saint James's Parish, Mecklenburg Co. (1774-1784), Bristol Parish

(1784–1793), a short while in Nottoway Parish, and finally in Cumberland Parish, Lunenburg Co. where he died.

[2]Rouse, *The Reads*, 80–90; Wirt Johnson Carrington, *A History of Halifax County* (Richmond, Va., 1924), 32.

[3]Bishop Meade, *Old Churches, Ministers and Families of Virginia* (Philadelphia, 1857), 1: 485; Rouse, *The Reads*, 90.

[4]Rouse, *The Reads*, 90; C.P.: 3 May 1820.

[5]Meade, *Old Churches*, 1: 485; Katherine B. Elliott, *Early Settlers of Mecklenburg County, Virginia* (South Hill, Va., 1965), 157. All the following information about the Reverend John Cameron is taken from these sources and from Rouse, *The Reads*, except where cited.

[6]Scott and Wyatt, *Petersburg's Story*, 116.

[7]Meade, *Old Churches*, 1: 485–86, 2: 23.

[8]C.P.: 28 Sept. 1878.

[9]Main, *Revolutionary America*, 101: "the law was the most profitable of all professions."

[10]Carrington, *Halifax County*, 136; C.P.: 5 Sept. 1812.

[11]C.P.: 1 Jan. 1812. Paul Carrington Cameron was first referred to by the family as "little Dick," presumably after his Bennehan grandfather (C.P.: 31 Oct. 1808), but he was christened along with his brother by their Cameron grandfather in May 1809 at which time he received the name Paul Carrington Cameron (C.P.: 27 May 1809).

[12]David L. Swain Papers, Paul C. Cameron to David L. Swain, 9 May 1853, Private Collections, DAH.

[13]C.P.: 17 June, 8 July 1798.

[14]C.P.: 24 Mar., 22 May 1799.

[15]C.P.: vol. 55. 1799–1801.

[16]OCD, Book 9, p. 249.

[17]C.P.: Jan., 14 May 1802.

[18]C.P.: 22 July 1801.

[19]C.P.: 2 June, 3 July 1803.

[20]C.P.: 29 Nov. 1802.

[21]C.P.: 22 July 1801, 10 Jan. 1803, 29 Nov. 1802, 24 Mar. 1807.

[22]C.P.: 10 Jan. 1803, 17 May 1802; vol. 55, 14 Apr., 2 July 1802; 4 Feb. 1802.

[23]C.P.: Jan., 14 May 1802.

[24]OCD, Book 11. p. 110; Book 12, p. 74.

[25]C.P.: vol. 55, 14 Feb. 1807, 24 Mar. 1807; also the latter date in the main file.

[26]No deed for this transaction survives. See C.P.: 3 Feb. 1807; Undated papers, Nash family, folder 2.

[27]C.P.: 7 July 1800, 27 Feb. 1801, 10 July 1804, 26 Apr. 1805. Cameron had bought the Brick House plantation from R. Bennehan at the time of his marriage.

[28]C.P.: 2 Jan. 1804.

[29]C.P.: 18 Feb. 1802.

[30]C.P.: 21 May 1802.

[31]C.P.: 30 Oct., 14 Nov. 1803, 28 Jan. 1805.

[32]C.P.: 24 Oct. 1799.

[33]C.P.: 21 Sept. 1802.

[34]C.P.: 23 Dec. 1802.

[35]He was again a representative from Orange County in 1805, 1806, 1807, 1812, and 1813 (C.P.: 11 Sept. 1802, 21 Dec. 1805, 23 Nov. 1806, 19 Dec. 1807, 18 Aug. 1812, and Lefler and Wager, *Orange County*, 350). He was a senator in 1819, 1822, and 1823 (C.P.: 1 Dec. 1819, 25 Nov. 1822, Jan. 1823, and Lefler and Wager, *Orange County*, 350). He was a candidate for the United States House of Representatives in

1808 and for the state legislature in 1809, in both of which attempts he was defeated (C.P.: June 1808, 28 July 1809).

[36] C.P.: 8 Dec. 1802.
[37] C.P.: 1 Nov. 1802.
[38] C.P.: 29 Nov. 1802.
[39] C.P.: 23 Dec. 1802.
[40] W. H. Hoyt, ed., *The Papers of Archibald D. Murphey* (Raleigh, 1914), 1: 6.
[41] C.P.: 23 Dec. 1802. *See also* Stephen B. Weeks, "The Code in North Carolina," *Magazine of American History* 26 (Dec. 1891): 452-53.
[42] C.P.: 21 Apr. 1803.
[43] C.P.: 23 Dec. 1802.
[44] C.P.: 28 Sept. 1878.
[45] C.P.: 21 Apr. 1803.
[46] C.P.: Jan. 1803.
[47] C.P.: 5 Dec. 1802.

[48] C.P.: 31 July 1800, 26 Dec. 1802. It has been incorrectly stated that Duncan Cameron had but one law student. Besides his relations George and Walker Anderson and John A. Cameron, he taught Gavin Hogg (C.P.: 3 July 1820), William H. Haywood, Jr. (C.P.: 30 Oct. 1827), Willie P. Mangum (Henry T. Shanks, ed., *The Papers of Willie P. Mangum, Raleigh*, 1950, 1: xvii), and Judge Thomas S. Ashe (C.P.: 28 Aug. 1886). He may also have taught Archibald D. Murphey (C.P.: 5 Nov. 1799).

[49] C.P.: 20 Oct. 1804. His father, Daniel Anderson, born in Glasgow, Scotland, was a merchant in Petersburg, Virginia. He and Robert Walker and Archibald Gracie of New York formed the firm of Gracie, Anderson and Co. Gracie built Gracie Mansion, now the residence for mayors of New York. By a first marriage to Maizie Beveridge, daughter of Thomas Beveridge, Daniel Anderson had six sons and two daughters. *See* Elizabeth Willis Anderson Papers, SHC.

[50] C.P.: 24 July 1805.
[51] C.P.: 27, 28 Apr. 1806.
[52] C.P.: 9 Feb., 2 Mar. 1807. The unsold goods were removed to the Fish Dam store in Wake County, owned by Cameron and the Bennehans.
[53] C.P.: 23 May 1803.
[54] WCD, Book T., p. 201, Wake County Court House, Raleigh.
[55] C.P.: vol. 72, 25 July, 27 Sept. 1802.
[56] C.P.: Jan. 1806. This contract contains specifications concerning the partnership quoted in the text.
[57] C.P.: 30 Apr. 1806.
[58] C.P.: 30 June 1807.
[59] C.P.: 10 Sept. 1805.
[60] C.P.: 26 June 1806.
[61] C.P.: 7 Dec. 1806.
[62] C.P.: 24 Aug. 1808.
[63] C.P.: 3 Feb. 1807; Undated papers, Nash family, folder 2.
[64] C.P.: 28 Sept. 1878, 27 May 1809.
[65] C.P.: 12 June 1807.
[66] C.P.: 25 Sept. 1868.

Chapter 4. THE BUILDING OF FAIRNTOSH

[1] OCD, Book 13, p. 324.

2. OCD, Book 5, p. 648, 624.
3. OCW, Book F, p. 375.
4. Wilson and Carpenter, *Region J Geology*, 9–10.
5. Kirby, *Soil Survey of Durham County*. Sheet 11 shows the soils of the Stagville and Fairntosh area.
6. Kirby, *Soil Survey*, 2–3, 11–12, 20–21, 26–27.
7. C.P.: vol. 98, 14 Apr. 1810.
8. C.P.: 16 May 1810, 23 May 1810. William K. Fort and David S. Goodloe were partners, but Fort did the lion's share of the work at Fairntosh. C.P.: 2 Nov. 1811; item no. 51, 1812.
9. C.P.: 23 May 1810.
10. C.P.: 15 June 1810.
11. C.P.: vol. 55, 10 Dec. 1810.
12. C.P.: 31 Jan. 1811.
13. Martin Palmer's letter to Richard Bennehan (C.P.: 14 Aug. 1790) states that he is then enclosing Mr. Cain's house, a house still standing, now completely renovated, on Saint Mary's Road northeast of Hillsborough just inside the Durham County line. The front section of this house is the larger, with Flemish bond brick chimneys and distinctly Georgian paneling. The back section is smaller, with American bond brick chimneys with some glazed headers in one chimney in a diamond design; the wainscot is horizontal, undecorated wide boards and chair rail, but the mantels are ornate, delicate, and later than those in the front.
14. C.P.: vol. 55, 3 May 1811.
15. C.P.: 14 July 1811.
16. C.P.: 21 July 1811.
17. C.P.: 4 Dec. 1812.
18. C.P.: 25 Nov. 1811.
19. C.P.: 11 Apr. 1813.
20. Rouse, *The Reads*, 90.
21. C.P.: 10 Oct. 1811; Rouse, *The Reads*, 90. Lochiel became the name of two other family homes, that of Mary Anderson's son Walker outside Hillsborough and that of John A. Cameron, her brother's estate in Chatham County. C.P.: 13 Dec. 1827, 16 Aug. 1824.
22. C.P.: 28 Jan. 1814.
23. C.P.: 15 Mar. 1814.
24. C.P.: 9 Sept. 1814.
25. C.P.: 27 Dec. 1814; vol. 55, 20 June 1815.
26. C.P.: 7 Jan. 1822, 18 Dec. 1812. John, Elias, and William Fort, who did so much carpentry for Duncan Cameron, were sons of Frederick Fort of Wake County who died in 1819 leaving six sons and four daughters to whom he bequeathed only slaves and money. His lack of real estate suggests that he, too, was an artisan. Wake County Wills, Will of Frederick Fort, 17 Nov. 1815 (C.R. 099.801.21), DAH.
27. C.P.: 1 Sept. 1815.
28. C.P.: 17 Feb. 1816.
29. C.P.: 27 Jan. 1817, 3 May 1820.
30. C.P.: 5 Feb. 1819.
31. C.P.: Dec. 1818.
32. C.P.: vol. 55, 7 Jan. 1820.
33. C.P.: vol. 55, 23 Aug. 1821.
34. C.P.: vol. 55, 27 Dec. 1821.
35. C.P.: 7 Jan. 1822.
36. C.P.: 23 Oct. 1850.

[37] C.P.: 4 Sept. 1834.
[38] C.P.: 21 Jan. 1824.
[39] C.P.: 31 May 1827.
[40] C.P.: Dec. 1826. *Journal of the Proceedings . . . of the Protestant Episcopal Church in the State of North Carolina . . . 1825* (Fayetteville, 1825) 11; ibid. . . . *1826* (Hillsborough, 1826) 17. H. K. Burgwyn and Josiah Collins, Jr., also built chapels on their plantations. *Journal of the Proceedings of the Thirty-eighth Annual Convention of the Protestant Episcopal Church in the State of North Carolina* (Fayetteville, 1854), 16, 18.
[41] C.P.: 5 Aug. 1884.
[42] The window bears the inscription "In memoriam of Duncan Cameron who built this chapel and dedicated to his God and Saviour" and is now installed in Saint Matthews Church, Hillsborough, the gift of Sally Cameron Labouisse, a great-granddaughter of Duncan Cameron.

Besides the window, other chapel treasures are also gone. Bennehan Cameron, Duncan Cameron's grandson, gave the marble baptismal font to Saint Philips Church, Durham, in 1913. (B. Cameron: 15 Sept. 1913. SHC.) A bell that hung in the chapel was requested by Costen J. Harrall, minister of the Mangum Street Methodist Church in Durham. He wrote, "As you no doubt know, I have a large number of persons in my congregation belonging to families that formerly lived on your plantation, including the Carringtons, Rogers, Staggs, and Sutherlands. It seems to me that it would be particularly fitting for the bell from their old home to call them and their children to worship for years to come." (B. Cameron: 3 May 1916.) The bell was given to Mt. Bethel United Methodist Church in Bahama, a community just north of Stagville, where it still hangs. The gift was arranged through William Daniel Turrentine, the overseer at Fairntosh, who was superintendent of the Sunday School in the Bahama church for forty years. (Interview with Mrs. Mildred Mangum Harris, 7 Dec. 1978.)

[43] *Journal of the Episcopal Church, 1828,* p. 9. The chapel was consecrated on 7 Oct. 1827.
[44] C.P.: 3 Sept. 1827.
[45] C.P.: 21 Oct. 1827.
[46] *Journal of the Episcopal Church, 1828,* p. 9.
[47] C.P.: 25 May 1838.
[48] C.P.: 1 Aug. 1833, 23 Jan. 1840, 13 Oct. 1841.
[49] C.P.: 1 Jan. 1828.
[50] C.P.: 22 July 1828.
[51] C.P.: 23 Nov. 1879.
[52] C.P.: 30 Apr. 1853.
[53] B. Cameron: 1973 Additions, 10 Nov. 1837.
[54] Information for the reburial of Jean Cameron is on her gravestone at Fairntosh.
[55] G. W. Mordecai: 13 May 1853. SHC.
[56] C.P.: 23 Mar. 1842, 24 May 1844.
[57] C.P.: 23 Mar. 1842.
[58] C.P.: 4 Apr., 16, 29 Aug. 1844.
[59] C.P.: 23 Mar. 1842.
[60] B. Cameron: 1973 Additions, Undated papers, Paul C. Cameron to Mildred Cameron. William Stronach had come from Scotland to cut stone for the new state capitol.
[61] C.P.: 17 Oct. 1850. The weaving house has more recently been known as the smoke house.

Notes to Pages 33–38 / 195

⁶²C.P.: Dec. 1850.
⁶³C.P.: 24 Mar. 1855.
⁶⁴C.P.: 3 Feb. 1853, Eighth Census, Free Inhabitants, 152.
⁶⁵C.P.: 17 Feb. 1829.

Chapter 5. DUNCAN CAMERON AT FAIRNTOSH

¹A plat of Duncan Cameron's lands in Person County, dated 26 Oct. 1824, shows that he then owned over 6,000 acres. C.P.: Oversized papers. A notation on the map of the later purchases of tracts from Clack and Pain brought the total in Person County eventually to over 8,500 acres.
²C.P.: 12 Sept. 1808, 5 Aug. 1810.
³OCD, Book 19, p. 278.
⁴C.P.: 5 Feb. 1821.
⁵OCD, Book 3, p. 53.
⁶The Penny Bend acres and the large tract west of it have no numbers while numbers 1, 3, 12, 13, 25, 33, 36, 38 are not found on the map.
⁷A comparison of the real estate purchased by the Bennehans and Duncan Cameron, Appendix A, with the tracts listed in the map legend reveals which ones have been omitted.
⁸The Brick House plantation, the 300 acres of Fairntosh, the Red Mill tract but not the mill, and tracts belonging to the Fish Dam plantation.
⁹C.P.: Nov. 1810.
¹⁰C.P.: 12 Aug. 1813, 20 July 1814.
¹¹C.P.: 25 Dec. 1812.
¹²C.P.: 22 May, 19 Oct. 1810, 4 Dec. 1819.
¹³C.P.: 25 Feb. 1813, 16 Feb. 1815, 16 Dec. 1818, 18 Apr. 1819, 12 Apr. 1824, 6 May 1825; WCD, Book 7, p. 153; Orange County Estates Records, Estate of William Cameron, 1838 (C.R. 073. 508. 15), DAH.
¹⁴C.P.: 28 Aug. 1813.
¹⁵C.P.: 9 Feb., 16 Oct. 1816.
¹⁶C.P.: 30 May 1830, 24 May 1832.
¹⁷C.P.: 26 Feb., 30 Nov. 1814.
¹⁸David L. Swain Papers, 9 May 1853, Private Collections, DAH.
¹⁹C.P.: 27 Jan. 1817.
²⁰*Journal of the House of Commons* (1813), *Journal of the Senate* (1822); J. G. de R. Hamilton, ed., *The Papers of Thomas Ruffin* (Raleigh, 1918–20) 1: 183, Duncan Cameron to Thomas Ruffin, 8 Dec. 1816.
²¹Hugh T. Lefler and Albert R. Newsome, *North Carolina: The History of a Southern State* (Chapel Hill, 1954), 304–305.
²²C.P.: 4 July 1811.
²³C.P.: 23 July 1811.
²⁴C.P.: 17 Apr. 1828.
²⁵Kemp P. Battle, *The Early History of Raleigh*, 63; Hamilton, *Ruffin Papers*, 1: 465.
²⁶Hamilton, *Ruffin Papers*, 1: 465.
²⁷Hamilton, *Ruffin Papers*, 1: 470, John M. Dick to Thomas Ruffin, 12 Feb. 1829.
²⁸Hamilton, *Ruffin Papers*, 1: 529; Battle, *Early History of Raleigh*, 63.
²⁹C.P.: 9 Dec. 1829.
³⁰C.P.: 10 Sept. 1805.

[31] C.P.: 8 Jan. 1816.
[32] C.P.: 3 May 1820.
[33] C.P.: 21 July 1833.
[34] Battle, *Early History of Raleigh*, 63.
[35] C.P.: 1 Jan. 1849.
[36] C.P.: 14 May 1836.
[37] C.P.: 26 Nov., 14 Dec. 1812.
[38] C.P.: 4, 5, 8 Sept. 1814, 20 Jan. 1815, 23 Oct. 1818.
[39] C.P.: 2 May 1818.
[40] C.P.: 4 Dec. 1820.
[41] G. W. Mordecai: Thomas Ruffin to G. W. Mordecai, 10 Dec. 1858.
[42] C.P.: 18 Mar. 1836, 18 July 1837.
[43] C.P.: 15 Mar. 1839; G.W. Mordecai: 25 Sept. [1850 or 1851].
[44] C.P.: 2 Sept. 1806.
[45] C.P.: 9 Nov. 1812.
[46] C.P.: 16 Dec. 1813.
[47] C.P.: 31 Dec. 1813.
[48] C.P.: 31 Jan. 1814.
[49] C.P.: 14 July 1814.
[50] C.P.: 5 Oct. 1814.
[51] C.P.: 26 Apr. 1815.
[52] C.P.: 1 Feb. 1816.
[53] C.P.: 10 Apr. 1816; vol. 55, 21 Dec. 1816.
[54] C.P.: 19 Mar. 1817.
[55] C.P.: 5 Sept. 1817.
[56] C.P.: 19 Dec. 1818; vol. 55, 20 Dec. 1820.
[57] C.P.: 5 June 1820.
[58] C.P.: 5 Feb., 20 Apr. 1821, 14 Feb., 20 Nov. 1822.
[59] C.P.: 29 Mar. 1824.
[60] C.P.: 13 May 1824.
[61] C.P.: 6 Feb. 1824.
[62] C.P.: 26 Feb. 1823.
[63] C.P.: 1 July 1823.
[64] C.P.: 20 Jan. 1824.
[65] C.P.: 1 Mar. 1851.
[66] C.P.: 2 Aug. 1830.
[67] Ruffin Papers: 13 Sept. 1837, undated leter from Anne Ruffin Cameron to her father, SHC.
[68] C.P.: 21 June 1827.
[69] C.P.: 21 Oct. 1827.
[70] C.P.: 12 June 1825, 25 July 1825.
[71] C.P.: 27 Sept., 29 Oct. 1825, 16 July 1828.
[72] C.P.: 17 Apr. 1828.
[73] C.P.: 6 Aug. 1829.
[74] C.P.: 6 Feb. 1830.
[75] 15 Mar. 1832, Minutes of the Superior Court, Orange County, North Carolina, Mar. 1821–Sept. 1833 (C.R. 073. 311. 2), DAH.
[76] C.P.: 1 Apr. 1835. All the Cameron women seem to have been more than timid; they were so restrained and inhibited in the presence of strangers that their manner was misinterpreted as hauteur. Two rather immature and not very well-bred youths from Virginia made a walking tour in 1819 from Norfolk to Tennessee and recorded their daily impressions in a diary which both wrote taking turns with the entries.

They were given letters of introduction to Thomas Bennehan and reached Stagville on Nov. 15th:

> When we arrived he was not at the house but we walked in & made ourselves quite at home until he came when he invited us over to Judge Cammerons who married his sister & where his father was then staying. This change we admired as it was getting from a Bachelors to where there were Ladies. The Judge had gone to the Senate But we were introduced to his Brother a very clever Man who married a daughter of Mr. Call's in Richmond; also to his [Thomas Bennehan's] father who is one of the kindest most fatherly old Men I ever saw & the very ditto of Dr. Syntax in his appearance [a character in *Roderick Random* by Tobias Smollett] & our wish to see the ladies was soon gratified by the call to Dinner. But we were much surprised to find them (Mrs. Cammeron the Judge's Mother & his wife & daughter) very stiff formal & unlike the Carolina Ladies very unintelligent as far as we could judge for which we had not much chance as they only spoke when spoken to & they seemed to be so distant we spent the evening in writing & determined to start tomorrow.
> 16 Nov. AT 10 after breakfast we bid his family farewell not much pleased with any but old Mr. Bennehan his son & Judge Cammerons brother.

V. M. Randolph Diary, SHC.
[77]The tombstones at Fairntosh give the death date of Jean Cameron and those of her sisters.
[78]C.P.: 7 Dec. 1839.
[79]C.P.: 16 Jan. 1840.
[80]G. W. Mordecai: 13 May 1856.
[81]C.P.: 26 July 1823.
[82]C.P.: 23 July 1826.
[83]C.P.: 5 July 1826.
[84]C.P.: 3 Dec. 1833.
[85]C.P.: 21 July 1833.
[86]G. W. Mordecai: 13 May 1856.
[87]C.P.: 21 July 1833.
[88]B. Cameron: 1973 Additions, 10 Nov. 1837.

Chapter 6. Paul Cameron at Fairntosh

[1]C.P.: 17 June 1831; Minutes of the Superior Court, Orange County, North Carolina (C.R. 073. 311. 2), DAH; they were married at the Hermitage, Haw River, 20 Dec. 1832. C.P.: 23 Dec. 1882.
[2]Hamilton, *Ruffin Papers*, 2: 108, 1 Jan. 1834.
[3]C.P.: 1 Jan., 8 Mar. 1834.
[4]C.P.: 29 Mar. 1834; Ruffin Papers: 22 Jan. 1834.
[5]C.P.: Dec. 1834, 23 Mar. 1836.
[6]C.P.: Undated papers, Paul C. Cameron, folder 3.
[7]C.P.: 19 Dec. 1835.
[8]C.P.: Tribute of the Faculty of the University of North Carolina to Paul C. Cameron, 15 Jan. 1891.
[9]C.P.: Nov. 1837. Paul's notes jotted on a letter from William E. Anderson; OCD, Book 33, p. 414.

[10] C.P.: 14 May 1836.
[11] Johnson, *Ante-Bellum North Carolina*, 115, 117, 121, 151–180.
[12] Johnson, *Ante-Bellum North Carolina*, 53, 78–79.
[13] Cornelius O. Cathey, *Agricultural Developments in North Carolina 1783–1860* (Chapel Hill, 1956), 195–96.
[14] Cathey, ibid., 45–46.
[15] C.P.: 11 Nov. 1852; Hamilton, *Ruffin Papers*, 2: 48, Henry Stith to Thomas Ruffin, 3 Oct. 1831, tells of poor returns on his store at Haw River that had previously been an excellent investment.
[16] C.P.: 4 Sept. 1842.
[17] Johnson, *Ante-Bellum North Carolina*, 271–72, 307–08.
[18] Ibid., 828–31.
[19] Ruffin Papers: Paul Cameron to Thomas Ruffin, 17 Jan. 1835, James Webb to Thomas Ruffin, 29 Dec. 1836.
[20] C.P.: 1 Jan. 1831; OCD, Book 28, p. 100; PCD, Book O, p. 294.
[21] C.P.: 5 Apr. 1838.
[22] C.P.: 2 May 1833; *Cyclopedia of Eminent and Representative Men of the Carolinas* (Madison, 1892), 2: 92–93.
[23] C.P.: 11 Feb., 25 Nov. 1811, 17 Apr. 1815, 10 Apr. 1816.
[24] C.P.: Mar. 1834, 24 Feb. 1844.
[25] C.P.: 18 Jan. 1845.
[26] C.P.: 30 Jan. 1849.
[27] C.P.: 9 Mar. 1854.
[28] C.P.: 22 Jan. 1854.
[29] C.P.: 12 Apr. 1854.
[30] C.P.: 6 Jan. 1863.
[31] Hamilton, *Ruffin Papers*, 3: 361, 12 Jan. 1864.
[32] C.P.: Undated papers, Duncan Cameron, folder 3.
[33] C.P.: 25 Aug. 1808.
[34] C.P.: 6 Aug. 1813.
[35] C.P.: 19 Oct. 1816.
[36] C.P.: 17 Oct. 1818.
[37] C.P.: Dec. 1823.
[38] C.P.: vol. 55, 24 Mar. 1821; 14 Dec. 1822.
[39] C.P.: 29 May 1830.
[40] C.P.: 30 May 1834.
[41] C.P.: 16 Sept., 5 Oct., 7 Oct. 1835.
[42] C.P.: Undated letter of Paul Cameron to Duncan Cameron, Nov.–Dec. 1835, 3 Dec. 1835.
[43] C.P.: 13 May 1845.
[44] C.P.: 7 July 1848.
[45] C.P.: 5 Nov. 1853.
[46] C.P.: 15 May 1845.
[47] C.P.: 21 June 1848.
[48] C.P.: 23 Nov. 1850.
[49] C.P.: 1 Jan. 1852.
[50] C.P.: 14 Aug. 1847; G. W. Mordecai: 4 Sept. 1855; C.P.: 13 Feb. 1857.
[51] C.P.: 1 May 1851.
[52] C.P.: 3 Oct. 1850.
[53] C.P.: 17 Oct. 1850.
[54] C.P.: 18, 27 Sept. 1850.
[55] C.P.: 25 July 1850.

[56]C.P.: 25 July 1850.
[57]C.P.: 1 May 1851.
[58]Four of these slave houses are standing at Horton Grove, owned by the state as part of the Stagville Center for Preservation Technology. A row of houses exactly like those at Horton Grove once stood at Shop Hill, probably built at the same time. Only two of the latter remain.
[59]G. W. Mordecai: 15, 18 Oct. 1850.
[60]C.P.: 19 Sept. 1850.
[61]B. Cameron: 1973 Additions, Anne R. Cameron to Paul Cameron, 2 Mar. 1860.
[62]Ruffin Papers: 28 Sept. 1860.
[63]C.P.: 1 Mar. 1853.
[64]C.P.: 4 Aug. 1851.
[65]C.P.: Tribute of the Faculty of the University of North Carolina to Paul C. Cameron, 15 Jan. 1891.
[66]C.P.: 25 July 1850.
[67]Hamilton, *Ruffin Papers*, 2: 371, Thomas Ruffin to Joseph Roulhac, 27 Dec. 1852.
[68]Ibid., 379, T. L. Skinner to Thomas Ruffin, 19 Jan. 1853.
[69]Ibid., 368, Thomas Ruffin to Joseph Roulhac, 22 Dec. 1852.
[70]C.P.: Undated papers, Paul C. Cameron, folder 6.
[71]C.P.: 14 Apr. 1853.
[72]Johnson, *Ante-Bellum North Carolina*, 727; C.P.: 9 Nov. 1848.
[73]C.P.: 11 Jan. 1842.
[74]G. W. Mordecai: 4 Sept. 1855; C.P.: 12 Aug., 14 Oct. 1855.
[75]G. W. Mordecai: 11 Oct. 1859, 12 Oct. 1860; Hamilton, *Ruffin Papers*, 4: 338, Will of Thomas Ruffin, 16 Apr. 1865; 2: 505, Paul Cameron to Thomas Ruffin, 8 Feb. 1856.
[76]C.P.: 25 July 1850; G. W. Mordecai: 25 Sept. [1850].
[77]C.P.: 4 Dec. 1851, 6 Dec. 1852.
[78]C.P.: 20 Sept. 1852.
[79]C.P.: 4 Feb. 1850.
[80]C.P.: 3 Feb. 1853, 24 Mar. 1855; Eighth Census, Free Inhabitants, 152, DAH; C.P.: 2 Nov. 1860.
[81]C.P.: 10 July 1824.
[82]C.P.: 5 Mar. 1796.
[83]C.P.: 12 Feb. 1853.
[84]C.P.: 9 Mar. 1853, 14 June 1856.
[85]C.P.: 6 Feb. 1856, 28 Mar., 2 Apr. 1857.
[86]C.P.: 2 Oct. 1857.
[87]C.P.: 8, 12 Aug., 13 Nov. 1856.
[88]*Journals of the Senate and House of Commons of the General Assembly of the State of North Carolina at its Session of 1856-7* (Raleigh, 1857).
[89]Hamilton, *Ruffin Papers*, 3: 68, Paul Cameron to Thomas Ruffin, 28 Jan. 1860; 2: 605, James H. Ruffin to Thomas Ruffin, 26 July 1858.
[90]Benson J. Lossing, *A Pictorial Field-Book of the Revolution* (New York, 1859), 2: 351.
[91]C.P.: 24 June 1883.

Chapter 7. Working the Land

[1]Cornelius O. Cathey, *Agricultural Developments in North Carolina 1783-1860* (Chapel Hill, 1956), 44, 192-205.

200 / Notes to Pages 65-71

²Cathey, *Agricultural Developments*, 195.
³Ibid., 27.
⁴Ibid., 45-46.
⁵Lefler and Newsome, *North Carolina*, 393-94.
⁶Edmund Ruffin, ed., *The Farmer's Register* (Shellbanks, Va., 1833-1843).
⁷The "Essay on Calcareous Manures" was republished as an appendix in the *Farmer's Register*, 10:; William K. Scarborough, ed., *The Diary of Edmund Ruffin*, (Baton Rouge, 1972).
⁸*Farmer's Register*, 1: 692; C.P.: 23 Apr., 29 Dec. 1842, 25 Feb. 1847, 17 Oct. 1850; Ruffin Papers: 27 Feb. 1847.
⁹C.P.: 1 Dec. 1819.
¹⁰Lefler and Newsom, *North Carolina*, 328-29, 331-32.
¹¹Cathey, *Agricultural Developments*, 78.
¹²C.P.: Undated Papers, Writings of Paul C. Cameron: 27 Oct. 1854; *Arator*, 1 (May 1855): 36-40; ibid., 1 (June 1885): 70-74.
¹³C.P.: 30 Dec. 1851.
¹⁴C.P.: 25 July 1850.
¹⁵C.P.: 14 Dec. 1806; 12 Aug. 1847.
¹⁶C.P.: 12 Aug. 1847.
¹⁷C.P.: 15 Apr. 1846.
¹⁸C.P.: 12 Mar. 1846.
¹⁹C.P.: Nov. 1845.
²⁰B. Cameron: 1973 Additions, 1 Oct. 1854.
²¹C.P.: 30 June 1858.
²²Eighth Census, Products of Industry, 2 (F2. 113P), DAH.
²³Eighth Census, Agriculture Schedule, 45, (F.112P), DAH.
²⁴Tenth Census, Agriculture Schedule, Mangum Township (F.128P), 8, DAH.
²⁵C.P.: 27 Nov. 1844, 24 Mar., 14 July 1857, 13 Mar. 1861.
²⁶C.P.: Undated papers, miscellaneous bills, receipts, etc.
²⁷C.P.: Dec. 1844.
²⁸C.P.: 15 Dec. 1846, 26 Nov. 1850.
²⁹C.P.: 19 Aug. 1847, 4 Mar. 1858, Jan. 1851.
³⁰Hamilton, *Ruffin Papers*, 2: 549, Paul Cameron to Thomas Ruffin, 21 Mar. 1857.
³¹C.P.: 26 Sept. 1846.
³²B. Cameron: Paul Cameron to Joseph Roulhac, May 1854.
³³C.P.: vol. 22, 2 Nov. 1787, 30 Oct. 1789.
³⁴C.P.: 6 Apr. 1826.
³⁵C.P.: 11 Nov. 1831.
³⁶C.P.: 3 Feb. 1836.
³⁷C.P.: 21 Sept. 1863.
³⁸C.P.: Undated papers, Duncan Cameron II, folder 2.
³⁹Seventh Census, Agriculture Schedule, 1183-84 (F2.107P), DAH.
⁴⁰Eighth Census, Agriculture Schedule, 45 (F.112P), DAH.
⁴¹Tenth Census, Products of Agriculture, Mangum Township (F.128), 8, DAH.
⁴²C.P.: 21 Mar. 1857. Probably it should be noted that in the best land available here, Georgeville soil, 80 bushels to the acre is the usual yield at present, and in prime soil, Congeree, 150 bushels to the acre can be expected. Interview with Orange County Agricultural Agent, 29 Aug. 1978.
⁴³Interview with N. E. Gilchrist, 26 Apr. 1978.
⁴⁴Seventh Census, Agriculture Schedule, 1183-1184 (F2.107P), DAH; Eighth Census, Agriculture Schedule, 45 (f.112P), DAH; Tenth Census, Products of Agriculture, Mangum Township (F.128), 8, DAH.

[45]C.P.: Tribute of the Faculty of the University of North Carolina to Paul C. Cameron, 15 Jan. 1891.
[46]C.P.: 1 Feb. 1842.
[47]C.P.: 29 Dec. 1842.
[48]C.P.: 20 Mar. 1845.
[49]C.P.: Oct. 1852, 10 Sept. 1853.
[50]C.P.: 28 May 1868.
[51]C.P.: 1 Nov. 1885.
[52]C.P.: 1–15 Dec. 1806.
[53]C.P.: vol. 104; Dec. 1843.
[54]C.P.: 14 Dec. 1888.
[55]C.P.: vol. 95; Nov. 1845.
[56]Richard Bennehan's tax lists are found in C.P.: Aug. 1791; Aug. 1796; Aug. 1797; Aug. 1798; also Sept. 1802; Mar. 1824.
[57]C.P.: 9 Jan. 1810.
[58]C.P.: 29 Dec. 1842.
[59]C.P.: 28 Aug. 1847.
[60]C.P.: 14 Aug. 1847.
[61]C.P.: 24 Sept. 1847.
[62]C.P.: 19 Aug. 1852; Ruffin Papers: Paul Cameron to Sterling Ruffin, 4 July 1862.
[63]C.P.: 8 Feb. 1889.
[64]Cathey, *Agricultural Developments*, 68–74.
[65]Slave Narratives, Vol. 11, North Carolina, Part 1, p. 296.
[66]C.P.: 22 Nov. 1805, 23 Oct. 1816.
[67]C.P.: 27 Apr. 1842.
[68]C.P.: 9 Apr. 1840.
[69]C.P.: 20 Oct. 1844, 15 Oct. 1866.
[70]C.P.: 11 Sept. 1821.
[71]C.P.: 24 Oct. 1834.
[72]C.P.: 1 July 1841, Dec. 1844, Dec. 1846.
[73]C.P.: 5 Nov. 1853.
[74]C.P.: 8 July 1857.
[75]C.P.: 24 May 1847, 10 Aug. 1852.
[76]C.P.: Jan. 1823, 7 Sept. 1853.
[77]Hillsborough *Recorder*, 20 May 1847.
[78]C.P.: 30 Dec. 1851, 9 Mar. 1852.
[79]C.P.: 29 Aug. 1829.
[80]C.P.: 17 Mar. 1848.
[81]C.P.: 25 May 1871, 24 June 1875, 23 Apr. 1885.

Chapter 8. Overseeing the Work

[1]William K. Scarborough, *The Overseer* (Baton Rouge, 1966), xii.
[2]Scarborough, *Overseer*, 29. Wages for overseers in the Deep South were substantially higher. There the Camerons paid their overseer $600 per year, wages which had risen by 1860 to $1,000.
[3]Ibid., 27.
[4]Ibid., 31.
[5]OCD, Book 10, p. 50; Book 13, p. 218.
[6]C.P.: 27 Aug. 1805.

[7]C.P.: Dec. 1781, 1 Jan. 1786. Ferrell's share was about 12 1/2 percent; the contract merely says one and one-quarter shares.

[8]John L. Bailey Papers: Letter of William Cain to Hugh Woods in Tennessee, 14 Oct. 1816, SHC.

[9]C.P.: 18 Sept. 1804.

[10]C.P.: 17 Sept. 1812.

[11]C.P.: 18 Mar., 23 Nov. 1806.

[12]C.P.: 21 Oct. 1834.

[13]C.P.: Dec. 1836, 1 Jan. 1838.

[14]C.P.: 3 May 1859.

[15]C.P.: 28 Apr. 1878.

[16]C.P.: 27 Dec. 1833.

[17]C.P.: 21 Oct. 1835.

[18]C.P.: 28 Oct. 1835.

[19]C.P.: 18 Oct. 1882.

[20]C.P.: 12 July 1848.

[21]C.P.: 19 Apr. 1884. Traditionally the remark is "It's a long time between drinks," and is attributed to the governor of North Carolina addressing the governor of South Carolina.

[22]Revolutionary War Records, R 6230, National Archives, Washington, D.C.

[23]OCD, Book 17, p. 117.

[24]C.P.: vol. 28, 31 Dec. 1798.

[25]C.P.: 2 Apr. 1836, 20 May 1841.

[26]C.P.: 11 Jan. 1842.

[27]C.P.: 24 Feb. 1844.

[28]OCW, Book F, p. 253. Thomas D. Bennehan's will dated 10 Feb. 1841 (C.P.: 10 Feb. 1841) bequeathed to "my friend and neighbor James Leathers Senr $200." Bennehan made a new will on 28 Apr. 1845 (C.P.: 28 Apr. 1845) after Leathers's death.

[29]OCW, Book E., p. 87.

[30]C.P.: 2 May 1824.

[31]C.P.: 28 Apr. 1845.

[32]C.P.: 31 Dec. 1850, 20 Dec. 1866.

[33]C.P.: Nov. 1866.

[34]B. Cameron: 1973 Additions, 7 Aug. 1878.

[35]C.P.: 19 Feb. 1886.

[36]C.P.: 31 Aug. 1879.

[37]George R. Turrentine, *The Turrentine Family* (1954).

[38]B. Cameron: 27 Sept. 1924.

[39]C.P.: 19 Feb. 1886.

[40]C.P.: 28 Oct. 1887.

[41]C.P.: 16 Jan. 1889.

[42]C.P.: 16 Dec. 1887.

[43]C.P.: vol. 165.

[44]C.P.: vol. 165, 10 July 1887.

[45]C.P.: vol. 113, Dec. 1834.

[46]C.P.: 12 Mar. 1835.

[47]C.P.: 16 Sept. 1835.

[48]C.P.: 27 Apr. 1841.

[49]No deed survives to show John Piper's earliest land purchase, but in another deed (OCD, Book 2, p. 45, 27 Apr. 1769) recording the sale of land from John McVey to John Sheels, the tract conveyed is described as adjoining John Piper's land.

[50]OCD, Book 26, p. 287, shows the relationship of William, Samuel, and John

Notes to Pages 82–88 / 203

Piper, Jr. Orange County Marriage Bonds, DAH, show that Samuel Piper married Ellenor Harris, bond dated 20 June 1831, and William Piper married Melinda Harris, 24 Mar. 1830.

[51]C.P.: 6 Nov. 1839.
[52]Hillsborough *Recorder*, 25 July 1831, 13 Jan. 1837; Shanks, *Mangum Papers*, 4: 403, Willie P. Mangum to his wife, 16 Mar. 1846.
[53]C.P.: 25 June 1840.
[54]Shanks, *Mangum Papers*, 4: 308, William Piper to Willie P. Mangum, 21 Aug. 1845. He had probably taught at the Piper-Cabe schoolhouse on his father's land.
[55]C.P.: 9 Nov. 1848.
[56]C.P.: 8 Dec. 1846.
[57]C.P.: 9 Nov., Dec. 1848.
[58]C.P.: Anne R. Cameron to Paul Cameron, Dec. 1850.
[59]C.P.: 18 Feb. 1867. A number of Samuel Piper's letters may be found in 1865, many of them undated but filed in C.P.: July–Oct., Nov.–Dec. 1865.
[60]C.P.: 12 Aug. 1863.
[61]C.P.: 18 Feb. 1867.
[62]C.P.: 31 Aug. 1879; B. Cameron: 27 Sept. 1924; Durham *Morning Herald*, 20 Sept. 1924.
[63]B. Cameron: 18 Aug. 1894.
[64]B. Cameron: 30 Aug. 1894.

Chapter 9. MILLS, STILLS, AND SHOPS

[1]C.P.: 30 Nov. 1807.
[2]C.P.: 1 Nov. 1818.
[3]C.P.: 1795, undated letter from Richard Bennehan to his son, Thomas, at the university; vol. 75, 5 May 1804.
[4]C.P.: 21 Feb. 1814.
[5]C.P.: Jan. 1820.
[6]OCW, Book E, p. 507, Will of Andrew Williams, 25 Oct. 1837.
[7]C.P.: 25 Sept. 1866.
[8]C.P.: 12 Sept. 1874.
[9]C.P.: 13 Sept. 1874.
[10]B. Cameron: 1973 Additions, Undated papers.
[11]C.P.: vol. 55, 24 Mar. 1807.
[12]C.P.: 2 July 1835.
[13]C.P.: 19 Jan. 1836.
[14]C.P.: 13 Mar. 1829.
[15]C.P.: vol. 34, June 1810.
[16]Eighth Census, Products of Industry, 2, (F2.113P), DAH, lists all active mills in the county in that year and their capital investment.
[17]C.P.: 11 July 1808.
[18]C.P.: 19 Mar. 1805.
[19]C.P.: 30 July 1806.
[20]Orange County Court Minutes, Feb. Term 1816 (C.R. 073.301.17); Feb. Term 1831 (C.R. 073.301.1), DAH.
[21]Petition for a bridge across Eno at Dickson's Mills, Orange County Miscellaneous Records, Bridge Records (C.R. 073.928.9), DAH.
[22]C.P.: 23 Mar. 1807.
[23]C.P.: Dec. 1813, 6 Feb. 1814.

[24] C.P.: 2 Jan. 1813; 15 Mar. 1819.
[25] C.P.: 8 Dec. 1819.
[26] C.P.: vol. 55, 21 July 1821.
[27] C.P.: 2 Oct. 1834; 4 Jan. 1843.
[28] C.P.: 2 Apr. 1836.
[29] C.P.: Nov. 1839.
[30] Orange County Court Minutes, Aug. Term 1836 (C.R. 073.301.22) DAH.
[31] C.P.: 2 Apr. 1836.
[32] C.P.: 1 Dec. 1821.
[33] C.P.: 17 May 1822.
[34] C.P.: Jan. 1824.
[35] C.P.: 4 Apr. 1822.
[36] C.P.: 14 Sept. 1843.
[37] C.P.: 20 May 1841.
[38] C.P.: 2 Aug. 1853.
[39] C.P.: 14 Aug. 1830.
[40] C.P.: 30 Oct. 1830; 18 Aug. 1847.
[41] C.P.: 9 Oct. 1850.
[42] C.P.: 21 June 1848; 13 Sept. 1850.
[43] C.P.: 3 Oct. 1854.
[44] C.P.: 12 Jan. 1835.
[45] C.P.: 1 Dec. 1842.
[46] C.P.: 29 Dec. 1842.
[47] C.P.: 17 Oct. 1810; 10 Aug. 1846.
[48] C.P.: 11, 13 Mar. 1851.
[49] C.P.: 29 Sept. 1854.
[50] C.P.: Nov.–Dec. 1870.
[51] C.P.: 22 Apr. 1872, 8 Apr. 1881.
[52] C.P.: 10 Feb. 1875.
[53] C.P.: 5 Sept. 1875.
[54] C.P.: 28 Feb. 1875.
[55] C.P.: 8 Apr. 1881.
[56] C.P.: 3 Apr. 1886.
[57] B. Cameron: 26 Aug. 1892.
[58] C.P.: Undated papers, folder T-U-V.
[59] B. Cameron: 29 Dec. 1894; 27 Jan. 1895.
[60] C.P.: 16 Dec. 1870.
[61] B. Cameron: 10 Aug. 1889.
[62] B. Cameron: 22 Aug. 1889.
[63] B. Cameron: 29 Aug. 1889.
[64] B. Cameron: 8 Oct. 1895.
[65] B. Cameron: 7 Dec. 1922.

Chapter 10. MASTERS OF SLAVES

[1] This title instead of Masters *and* Slaves is chosen to suggest the one-sided character of the evidence in this chapter. Virtually everything known about the slaves, with the exception of the slave narratives and half a dozen letters, comes through white reports.

[2] Northampton County Wills, North Carolina, Book A, p. 58 (C.R. 071.801.1), Will of Thomas Amis, 28 Sept. 1764, DAH.

[3]C.P.: 5 July 1777.
[4]C.P.: Aug. 1778.
[5]C.P.: May 1771.
[6]C.P.: 7 Oct. 1796.
[7]C.P.: Jan. 1803.
[8]C.P.: June 1804.
[9]C.P.: 2 Apr. 1802.
[10]C.P.: 9 Nov. 1810.
[11]C.P.: 16 Feb. 1816.
[12]C.P.: vol. 117-B, 1 July 1841.
[13]C.P.: 14 Aug. 1847.
[14]Eighth Census, Slave Inhabitants, 33–35, DAH.
[15]Eighth Census 1860, Person County, North Carolina, Slave Inhabitants, 2, DAH.
[16]C.P.: 1 Mar. 1851, 10 Mar. 1853.
[17]Eighth Census, 1860, Greene County, Alabama, Slave Inhabitants, 391 (M 653, no. 30); ibid., Tunica County, Mississippi, Slave Inhabitants, 217 (M 653, no. 603) DAH; C.P. 1 Mar. 1851.
[18]C.P.: 29 Apr. 1859.
[19]C.P.: July 1865.
[20]C.P.: Dec. 1865.
[21]C.P.: Dec. 1865.
[22]C.P.: 4 Dec. 1801. A slave narrative, based on hearsay, collected in the 1930s, says, "Judge Duncan Cameron was a very rich man who lived in Raleigh and owned a plantation in our neighborhood. He used to carry a large cane, and if he met a negro on the road, and he did not raise his hat and bow to him, he would beat him with his cane." The same narrator, James Carry, continued, "I have been told that Paul Cameron, son of Judge Cameron, who owned a plantation out of the town where he lived, used to go out once in two or three weeks, and while there, have one or two slaves tied and whip them unmercifully, for no offence, but merely, as he said, *to let them know he was their master.*" *Slave Testimony: Two Centuries of Letters, Interviews, and Autobiographies,* ed. John W. Blassingame (Baton Rouge, 1977) 135, 139.
[23]Shanks, *Mangum Papers,* 2: 291, undated.
[24]C.P.: 26 Apr. 1835.
[25]C.P.: 20 Oct. 1844.
[26]C.P.: 5 Sept. 1844.
[27]C.P.: 12 Oct. 1844.
[28]C.P.: 1 Oct. 1844.
[29]C.P.: 25 Oct. 1844.
[30]C.P.: ibid.
[31]C.P.: 27 Nov., 7 Dec. 1844.
[32]C.P.: 10 Jan. 1845.
[33]C.P.: 5 Feb. 1847.
[34]C.P.: Undated papers, unclassified notes and fragments..
[35]C.P.: 4 Feb. 1860.
[36]C.P.: Undated papers, Paul C. Cameron, folder 3. Most of the information about this case is contained in a series of undated letters from Paul Cameron to his sisters.
[37]C.P.: 11 Mar. 1853.
[38]C.P.: Nov.–Dec. 1854.
[39]C.P.: 4 Sept. 1859.

[40]Hamilton, *Ruffin Papers*, 3: 127.
[41]C.P.: 28 Mar. 1807, 11 Feb. 1835.
[42]C.P.: 26 Nov. 1819, 18 Dec. 1843; vol. 34, June 1810.
[43]C.P.: 12 Jan. 1835, 1 Feb. 1842, 8 Feb. 1847.
[44]C.P.: 29 Dec. 1842.
[45]C.P.: 10 Aug. 1846, Dec. 1850.
[46]C.P.: 2 July 1835, 4 Mar. 1830.
[47]C.P.: 2 Jan. 1830, 10 June 1854.
[48]C.P.: 17 May 1810, 2 Jan. 1830.
[49]C.P.: 10 Apr. 1838.
[50]C.P.: 25 July 1848.
[51]C.P.: 28 July 1848.
[52]C.P.: Undated papers, Paul C. Cameron, folder 6.
[53]C.P.: Slave Narratives, vol. 11, North Carolina, Part 1, p. 296.
[54]C.P.: 31 Aug. 1848.
[55]C.P.: 15 Sept. 1848.
[56]The fullest discussion of slave naming practices is in Herbert G. Gutman's *The Black Family in Slavery and Freedom, 1750-1925* (New York, 1976), chapter 5.
[57]C.P.: Jan. 1803.
[58]C.P.: 28 Apr. 1845.
[59]C.P.: 2 Dec. 1847.
[60]C.P.: 7 Apr. 1836.
[61]C.P.: 23 Feb. 1854.
[62]C.P.: 7 Oct. 1796.
[63]OCW, Book D, p 94.
[64]C.P.: 13 Mar. 1854.
[65]Wills of Orange County, North Carolina, 1785-1865 (C.R. 073. 801. 17) 49, DAH.
[66]C.P.: 28 Apr. 1845. As executor of Thomas Bennehan's will, Duncan Cameron had to dispose of $1,000 left "for Christian and benevolent purposes." He gave the money to the Wardens of the Poor of Orange County as the beginning of an endowment for the care of the indigent. *Fayetteville Observer*, 4 Apr. 1848, noted by Guion G. Johnson, *Ante-Bellum North Carolina* (Chapel Hill, 1937), 688.
[67]C.P.: 30 June 1848.
[68]C.P.: 5 Mar. 1857.
[69]Lefler and Wager, *Orange County*, 104.
[70]C.P.: 25 Nov. 1839; Duncan Cameron and George W. Mordecai were named executors of the estate of John Rex in his will probated that year.
[71]C.P.: 1 Mar. 1851.
[72]C.P.: 28 Apr. 1845.
[73]C.P.: 5 Apr. 1836.
[74]C.P.: 5 Oct. 1841.
[75]These excerpts are from three different letters quoted in the order cited. C.P.: 25 July and 19 Aug. 1847, 25 Sept. 1846.
[76]C.P.: 25 July 1847.
[77]*African Repository and Colonial Journal*, 24 (1848): 155.
[78]C.P.: 19 Apr. 1848.
[79]C.P.: 29 May 1848.
[80]Seventh Census, 1850, Baltimore County, Maryland, Free Inhabitants, City of Baltimore, Ward 1, Dwelling 667, Family 839 (317.3 U58c7p0) University of North Carolina Library at Chapel Hill.
[81]Virgil's letter is not in the Cameron papers. Its contents were reported by Paul

to his father in an undated letter filed in C.P.: Nov.–Dec. 1851. The liberation of Virgil and his family is probably referred to, somewhat inaccurately, in John H. Wheeler's *Reminiscences and Memoirs of North Carolina* (1984. Reprint. Baltimore, 1966), 356. Paul Cameron is described there as enjoying to tell of a family of slaves devised to him to be liberated who, after having been sent off to Liberia and given provisions for a year and $1,000 in gold, turned up on his doorstep pleading to be taken back.

[82]C.P.: 18 Mar. 1852.
[83]C.P.: 30 Jan. 1835.
[84]C.P.: 1 Apr. 1801.
[85]C.P.: 6 May 1801, 6 Apr. 1802.
[86]C.P.: 1 Apr. 1837.
[87]C.P.: 20 Feb. 1836. Other bad years were 1842 and 1846.
[88]C.P.: 5 Oct. 1814.
[89]C.P.: 5 Mar. 1844, 5 Dec. 1853, etc..
[90]C.P.: 21 Sept. 1843.
[91]C.P.: 15 Mar. 1815, 3 July 1848.
[92]C.P.: 13 Sept. 1855.
[93]B. Cameron: 22 Aug. 1889.
[94]C.P.: 15 Feb. 1826. Thomas N. Cameron seems to have been an excellent physician who kept abreast of the latest knowledge and was ahead of his time in his perception of the importance of record-keeping. As a member of the state legislature in 1850 he introduced a bill that would have required the registration of births, marriages, and deaths. The bill was defeated, and North Carolina did not keep such records until 1913 (Johnson, *Ante-Bellum North Carolina*, 252). He had probably been influenced in his action by a medical convention which met in Philadelphia in 1847 and which had recommended such legislation.
[95]C.P.: 20 Feb. 1836.
[96]C.P.: 28 Dec. 1841.
[97]Eighth Census, Slave Inhabitants, 45, DAH.
[98]C.P.: Dec. 1830, 11 Nov. 1852.
[99]Eighth Census, Greene County, Alabama, Slave Inhabitants, 391 (M 653, no. 30) and Tunica County, Mississippi, 218 (M 653, no. 603), DAH
[100]C.P.: 28 July 1848.
[101]C.P.: Dec. 1850.
[102]C.P.: 23 Dec. 1806.
[103]C.P.: Undated papers, unclassified notes and fragments..
[104]C.P.: 25 Nov. 1841.
[105]C.P.: 14 Aug. 1847.
[106]Slave Narratives, vol. 11, North Carolina, Part 1, 297.
[107]C.P.: 8 Feb. 1844.
[108]*Journal of the Episcopal Church*, 1827, p. 23.
[109]*Journal of the Episcopal Church*, 1828, p. 10.
[110]*Journal of the Episcopal Church*, 1843, p. 25.
[111]Johnson, *Ante-Bellum North Carolina*, 548.
[112]Ibid.
[113]C.P.: 13 Oct. 1880, 5 Aug., 7 Oct. 1884.
[114]C.P.: 1 May 1851.
[115]C.P.: 22 Apr. 1844.
[116]C.P.: Undated papers, Paul C. Cameron, folder 6.
[117]C.P.: 12 Aug. 1856.
[118]C.P.: 21 May 1836.

[119] C.P.: 4 Oct. 1846.
[120] Hamilton, *Ruffin Papers*, 3: 451, Paul C. Cameron to Thomas Ruffin, 11 May 1865.
[121] Ibid., 3: 464, Paul C. Cameron to Thomas Ruffin, 11 Aug. 1865.
[122] C.P.: 2 June 1865.
[123] Ninth Census, Mangum Township, Family 257, DAH.
[124] C.P.: 23 Sept. 1866.
[125] Slave Narratives, vol. 11, North Carolina, Part 2, 35.
[126] C.P.: 29 Nov. 1868.
[127] B. Cameron: Undated papers.
[128] C.P.: 7 Feb. 1858.
[129] C.P.: 12 Feb. 1858.
[130] Cohabitation Certificates, Orange County, North Carolina, 1866–1868, DAH.
[131] C.P.: 17 July 1880.
[132] C.P.: 17 Dec. 1880.
[133] C.P.: 19 Jan. 1875.
[134] Slave Narratives, vol. 11, North Carolina, Part 1, 297.
[135] C.P.: Undated papers, Writings of Paul C. Cameron.
[136] C.P.: 16 Jan. 1891. *See* C.P.: 25 Jan. 1881 for a letter to Serena from her brother William Turner.
[137] B. Cameron: 1973 Additions, 15 Apr. 1914.
[138] B. Cameron: 1973 Additions, 15 May 1914.

Chapter 11. "WHEN ALL WENT DOWN IN NIGHT"

[1] C.P.: 13 Sept. 1855. Although the Camerons were unaware of the connection between their ill health and the prevalence of mosquitoes in summer, they were beginning to find the mosquitoes almost intolerable in the middle 1850s.
[2] C.P.: 22 Feb. 1860, 13 Mar. 1861..
[3] Ruth P. Blackwelder, *The Age of Orange* (Charlotte, 1961), 119–140.
[4] C.P.: 24 Mar. 1865.
[5] North Carolina Historical Commission Papers, R. D. W. Connor to Bennehan Cameron, 17 Dec. 1907, Private Papers, DAH.
[6] C.P.: July 1865.
[7] Hamilton, *Ruffin Papers*, 3: 306, Paul C. Cameron to Thomas Ruffin, 24 Mar. 1863; C.P.: 20 Oct. 1858, 20 July 1859, 16 Nov. 1859, 30 Oct. 1860.
[8] C.P.: 20 Oct. 1858, 20 July, 16 Nov. 1859, 30 Oct. 1860; also Undated Papers, Building and Gardening.
[9] Slave Narratives, vol. 11, North Carolina, Part 1, p. 380.
[10] C.P.: 12 Feb. 1866, Dec. 1865, Paul Cameron's petition to the military authorities; undated letter of R[ebecca] C[ameron] A[nderson] filed in Jan.–June 1865.
[11] C.P.: Dec. 1865, Paul Cameron's petition to the military authorities.
[12] Hamilton, *Ruffin Papers*, 3: 451, Paul Cameron to Thomas Ruffin, 11 May 1865; ibid., p. 464, Paul Cameron to Thomas Ruffin, 11 Aug. 1865; ibid., 4: 35, Paul Cameron to Thomas Ruffin, 4 Oct. 1865.
[13] Hamilton, *Ruffin Papers*, 4, 40, 20 Nov. 1865.
[14] Ibid., 42, 27 Nov. 1865.
[15] Hamilton, *Ruffin Papers*, 3: 449, April 1865.
[16] C.P.: Nov. 1865.

[17]C.P.: 22 Oct. 1866, 1, 23 Oct. 1867, 26 Oct. 1870.
[18]C.P.: Nov. 1866.
[19]C.P.: 5 Dec. 1866.
[20]C.P.: 2 June 1865.
[21]C.P.: Tod Caldwell to Paul Cameron, 1 Jan. 1864; various financial statements of Paul Cameron, 1 Jan. 1864, 29 Apr. 1859, Dec. 1860.
[22]C.P.: 29 Apr. 1859.
[23]C.P.: 1 Jan. 1864.
[24]C.P.: 9 Sept. 1862, 6 Oct. 1863, 18 Nov. 1864, 5 Apr., 19 Aug. 1866, 27 July 1867.
[25]C.P.: 18, 24 Mar. 1865; Hamilton, *Ruffin Papers*, 3: 448, Paul Cameron to Thomas Ruffin, 21 Mar. [1865].
[26]Tombstone in St. Matthews Churchyard, Hillsborough.
[27]C.P.: 2 July 1865, 24 Sept. 1866, 23 Sept. 1867, 30 May 1868.
[28]C.P.: 27 July, 31 Aug., 7 Dec. 1867.
[29]C.P.: 22 Feb. 1866, 1 Feb. 1868.
[30]B. Cameron: 1973 Additions, 4 May 1870; C.P.: 12 June, 1 Nov. 1871, 29 June 1875.
[31]C.P.: 21 Jan. 1873.
[32]Young Duncan Cameron was in Mississippi from Mar. to July in 1866, from Oct. 1866 to June 1867, from May 1868 to July 1870, and from Nov. 1870 to Feb. 1872.
[33]C.P.: 13 Mar. 1872.
[34]C.P.: 19 Dec. 1871, 17 Jan. 1872, 29 June 1874.
[35]C.P.: 25 July 1874; B. Cameron: 29 July 1874.
[36]C.P.: 1 Mar., 8 Aug. 1878, 27 Nov. 1877. *Branson's North Carolina Business Directory for 1884* (ed. Levi Branson, Fayetteville, 1884, pp. XXXII–XXXIII) lists Henry B. Short as president of the Bogue Railroad, a branch line connecting with the Wilmington, Columbus, and Augusta Railroad.
[37]B. Cameron: biographic sketch of Bennehan Cameron written by Robert D. W. Connor for use in the North Carolina Historical Commission's 1919 *Manual of North Carolina*, 29 Nov. 1919.
[38]George Collins's forebears were Josiah I, Jr., and III, whose plantations on Lake Phelps in eastern North Carolina were models of progressive commercial farming and who represented in themselves prosperous planters and leaders in the state. Somerset Place, their home, had a chapel specially built for the slaves, for whom they provided as well a resident missionary. George's father, Josiah III, built the beautiful house standing there today. George and Anne Collins's children were Anne K., Rebecca Anderson, Mary Arthur (died as a child), Henrietta Page, Mary Arthur, Alice Ruffin, and Paul C.
[39]C.P.: 2 Apr. 1867; A. Wright to Paul Cameron, 5 Sept. 1862.
[40]C.P.: George Collins to Paul Cameron, 23 Dec. 1866.
[41]C.P.: 28 May 1867.
[42]C.P.: 6 Nov. 1874, 6 Feb. 1876.
[43]C.P.: 8 Aug. 1878.
[44]C.P.: 27, 28 Nov. 1878, 13 June 1879.
[45]C.P.: 18 Apr. 1885, 14 Mar. 1884..
[46]C.P.: 18 Apr. 1885.
[47]Ruffin Papers: Paul Cameron to Thomas Ruffin, 12 Oct. 1860.
[48]C.P.: 6 Dec. 1860, 20 Apr. 1863; Robert Walker Anderson married Rebecca B. Cameron on 28 Apr. 1863 (Marriages, Bonds, Orange County Court House, Hillsborough).

210 / *Notes to Pages 122-129*

⁴⁹C.P.: 6 Dec. 1860.
⁵⁰C.P.: 16 May 1864; Mary R. Anderson to Mildred Cameron, 12 Feb. 1865.
⁵¹C.P.: 8 Dec. 1864.
⁵²Rebecca B. Anderson married John W. Graham on 9 Oct. 1867 (Marriages, Bonds, Orange County Court House, Hillsborough). Their children were John, Paul C., George M., Isabella D., William A., Joseph, and Anne Cameron.
⁵³C.P.: 2 June 1873, 26 Feb. 1875.
⁵⁴C.P.: 26 Feb. 1875.
⁵⁵C.P.: 13 May 1884.
⁵⁶B. Cameron: 1973 Additions, 17 July 1871.
⁵⁷C.P.: 18 Oct. 1881.

Chapter 12. ONE LONG DARK NIGHT

¹C.P.: 17 Oct. 1867.
²C.P.: 4 Dec. 1875.
³C.P.: A Tribute of the Faculty of the University of North Carolina to Paul C. Cameron, 15 Jan. 1891.
⁴C.P.: The Writings of Paul C. Cameron, Speech to the [Summer] Normal School.
⁵C.P.: 19 Jan. 1854.
⁶C.P.: 27 Sept. 1865.
⁷C.P.: 1 Apr. 1867.
⁸C.P.: B. Cameron: 1973 Additions, 3 July 1872.
⁹B. Cameron: 1973 Additions, 15 Feb. 1875; C.P.: 13 Feb. 1884, also the Will of Paul C. Cameron, C.P.: 17 Jan. 1891.
¹⁰OCD, Book 37, p. 528 (18 Feb. 1868); Book 45, p. 116 (13 Aug. 1856); Book 47, p. 482 (2 Oct. 1882); Book 51, p. 438 (5 July 1887); Book 53, p. 216 (4 Aug. 1874); Book 54, p. 470 (16 Feb. 1872).
¹¹OCD, Book 40, p. 169 (3 May 1870; Book 52, p. 64 (20 Aug. 1888).
¹²C.P.: 28 July 1886, 17 Jan. 1891, Will of Paul C. Cameron.
¹³OCD, Book 54, p. 101 (20 Apr. 1887).
¹⁴C.P.: 4 Feb. 1875; B. Cameron: 29 Nov. 1919; Battle; *History of the University*, 2: 73.
¹⁵C.P.: 15 Mar. 1884; Battle, *History of the University*, 2: 314–15. This building was demolished in 1929.
¹⁶Battle, *History of the University*, 2: 317.
¹⁷C.P.: 3 June 1885, 10 June 1889.
¹⁸OCD, Book 53, p. 216 (4 Aug. 1874); B. Cameron: 1973 Additions, 4 Aug. 1872; C.P.: 11 Dec. 1880.
¹⁹C.P.: 9 Aug. 1872, 5 Aug. 1873; 10 May 1876, 26 Nov. 1874.
²⁰C.P.: 21 Oct., 3 Dec. 1833, *Journal of the Episcopal Church, 1842*, p. 13; B. Cameron: 1 Sept. 1910.
²¹C.P.: 7 Jan., 3 Feb. 1886; B. Cameron: 1 Sept. 1910.
²²C.P.: 21 Feb. 1882.
²³C.P.: 24 Oct. 1873, 22 June 1875 (Paul Cameron's property list).
²⁴*Rocky Mount Mills: A Case History of Industrial Development 1818–1943* (Rocky Mount, 1943), 22.
²⁵C.P.: 2 July 1890.
²⁶Marriage Register, 1873–1880, p. 35, Margaret C. Cameron, 27, married

Notes to Pages 129–134 / 211

Robert Bruce Peeples [sic], 35, of Northampton County on 7 Dec. 1875. Their only child was Anne Ruffin who married Thomas N. Webb.

[27]C.P.: 6 Dec. 1876, 19 Nov. 1877, 27 Aug. 1884, 24 Apr. 1888, 22 Oct. 1889; B. Cameron: C. L. Pettigrew to Bennehan Cameron, 10 Sept. 1896.

[28]C.P.: 17 May 1879.

[29]Marriage Register, 1873–1880, p. 86, Pauline C. Cameron, 26, married William B. Shepard, 35, on 6 Nov. 1879.

[30]C.P.: 20 Feb. 1883, 18, 27 Apr. 1885, 30 Mar. 1888..

[31]C.P.: 6 Feb. 1889.

[32]C.P.: Nov.–Dec. 1885, 25 Feb., 28 Dec. 1886.

[33]C.P.: 25 Feb. 1886.

[34]C.P.: 7 Oct. 1884.

[35]Marriage Register, 1880–1910, 14 Dec. 1896. Mildred's age is there given as 38 although she was actually 40.

[36]By her will (OCW, Book I, p. 240, 12 Sept. 1901) she left $5,000 in trust for the upkeep of the family graveyards at Stagville and Fairntosh and a number of bequests to the servants of her parents: Virgil Thompson, Serena Jeffries, Annie Craig, and Martin Chavis ($100 each) and to Sally Turner ($250), "for her unfaltering kindness" to her mother and herself.

[37]C.P.: 9 Jan. 1885; vol. 161, the accounts of the firm of D. and B. Cameron 1885–1886. Other volumes also contain the accounts of this store: vols. 151, 152 for example. Interview with Goldie Bragan yielded the location of this store.

[38]C.P.: 26 Sept., 13 Nov., 6 Dec. 1882.

[39]C.P.: 29 Jan. 1878, 23 Apr., 31 Oct. 1885.

[40]C.P.: 2 Aug., 12 Sept. 1885, 22 Oct., 26 Nov. 1886.

[41]Tombstone in Saint Matthews Churchyard, Hillsborough.

[42]C.P.: 26 Sept. 1874, 24 June 1878, 2 Sept. 1882, 20 Jan. 1886, 20 Feb., 18 Nov. 1889.

[43]B. Cameron: 1973 Additions, 21 June 1855.

[44]C.P.: 22 Oct. 1889.

[45]C.P.: 6 Feb. 1886.

[46]C.P.: 2 Jan. 1867.

[47]C.P.: 26 Nov. 1878.

[48]Raleigh *News and Observer*, 7 Jan. 1891.

[49]B. Cameron, Diary, 6 Jan. 1891.

[50]Slave Narratives, vol. 11, p. 320.

Chapter 13. BENNEHAN CAMERON AT STAGVILLE AND FAIRNTOSH

[1]C.P.: 17 Jan. 1891.

[2]C.P.: 5 Dec. 1889.

[3]C.P.: Will of Duncan Cameron, 1 Mar. 1851; D. Hillhouse Buel to Mrs. Mordecai, 30 Dec. 1881; Paul Cameron to his wife, 21 Mar. 1886.

[4]Wake County Estates Records, Estate of Margaret B. Mordecai (C. R. 099. 508. 197), DAH.

[5]Raleigh *News and Observer*, 7 Jan. 1891.

[6]Raleigh *News and Observer*, 9 Jan. 1891.

[7]C.P.: 5 Aug. 1884.

[8]C.P.: 24 June 1883.

[9]C.P.: 14 Aug. 1847, 8 Feb. 1889; Robert Kirkland in a letter to Paul Cameron mentions the "stockfarm," 5 Sept. 1887.

10. C.P.: 31 Jan. 1886.
11. C.P.: 8 Sept. 1886.
12. C.P.: 8 Oct. 1879.
13. B. Cameron: 22 Aug. 1889.
14. C.P.: 25 May [1882].
15. C.P.: 19 Feb. 1886, 28 Jan. 1887, vol. 166.
16. C.P.: 2 Mar. 1887, 15 Jan. 1888.
17. C.P.: 16 Jan. 1889.
18. C.P.: 2 Feb. 1889.
19. C.P.: 14 Feb. 1889.
20. C.P.: 24 Feb. 1889.
21. C.P.: 8 Feb. 1889.
22. B. Cameron: 19 May 1889.
23. C.P.: 22 Feb. 1889.
24. B. Cameron: 19 May 1889.
25. C.P.: 27 Apr. 1885.
26. B. Cameron: 10 Aug. 1889.
27. B. Cameron: 22 Aug. 1889.
28. B. Cameron: 22 Aug. 1889.
29. B. Cameron: 1973 Additions, 4 Oct. 1869.
30. B. Cameron: 29 Nov. 1919. This biographic sketch of Bennehan Cameron by R. D. W. Connor, submitted for Cameron's approval before publication in the *North Carolina Manual, 1919,* contains a very full résumé of his life and is the basis for biographical information given here if not noted otherwise.
31. B. Cameron: 7 Dec. 1922.
32. B. Cameron: Oversized papers; also 18 Aug. 1920.
33. Anne Ruffin Cameron's will devised the Raleigh house and ten acres to Bennehan. Since Paul Cameron's will had previously left the house in Raleigh to his wife and then to his granddaughter Anne Graham, a lawsuit had to be brought to settle the matter and Mrs. Cameron's estate. *See* WCD, Book 166, p. 619f, which explains the whole case and its settlement by the July Term of Court, 1901.
34. C.P.: vol. 170, Feb. 1889; B. Cameron: 4, 21, 26 Aug. 1894.
35. C.P.: vols. 165, 166, 167, 170.
36. Raleigh *News and Observer,* 28 Aug. 1897.
37. B. Cameron: 4 Aug. 1894.
38. B. Cameron: 10 Sept. 1894, 5 May 1897, 31 Oct. 1901.
39. B. Cameron: 2 May 1898, 9 Mar. 1901.
40. B. Cameron: Connor's biographic sketch, 29 Nov. 1919.
41. C.P.: 28 Aug. 1891.
42. B. Cameron: 19 Mar. 1893.
43. B. Cameron: Diary, 1891; C.P.: 10 Nov. 1891.
44. B. Cameron: 19 May 1889.
45. B. Cameron: 29 Nov. 1905.
46. C.P.: 15 May, 2 July 1878, 10 Apr., 1 Sept. 1886, 3 Mar. 1887; B. Cameron: William B. Shepard to Bennehan Cameron, 26 Dec. 1908.
47. C.P.: 19 Sept. 1875.
48. B. Cameron: Diary, 8 Sept. 1895; C.P.: 1 Aug., 13 Sept. 1895.
49. B. Cameron: Diary, 28 Oct. 1895. N. H. Busey is meant.
50. B. Cameron: 1 Sept. 1910; Family Data Series, 11 Oct. 1908.
51. B. Cameron: 5 Oct. 1923.
52. Durham *Morning Herald,* 2 June 1925.
53. Durham *Morning Herald,* 4 June 1925.

Bibliography

Manuscript Sources

PRIVATE RECORD COLLECTIONS

Walter Alves Papers. Southern Historical Collection, University of North Carolina Library at Chapel Hill.
Elizabeth Willis Anderson Papers. Southern Historical Collection, University of North Carolina Library at Chapel Hill.
John L. Bailey Papers. Southern Historical Collection, University of North Carolina Library at Chapel Hill.
Richard Bennehan Papers. Private Collections, Archives, Division of Archives and History, Raleigh.
Bennehan Cameron Papers. Southern Historical Collection, University of North Carolina Library at Chapel Hill.
Cameron Papers. Southern Historical Collection, University of North Carolina Library at Chapel Hill.
Sarah R. Cameron Papers. Southern Historical Collection, University of North Carolina Library at Chapel Hill.
Campbell Family Papers. Manuscript Department, Duke University Library, Durham.
Annie Cameron Collins Papers. Southern Historical Collection, University of North Carolina Library at Chapel Hill.
George W. Mordecai Papers. Southern Historical Collection, University of North Carolina Library at Chapel Hill.
North Carolina Historical Commission Papers. Private Collections, Archives, Division of Archives and History, Raleigh.
Thomas Ruffin Papers, Southern Historical Collection, University of North Carolina Library at Chapel Hill.
David L. Swain Papers. Private Collections, Archives, Division of Archives and History, Raleigh.
John Williams Papers. Manuscript Department, Duke University Library, Durham.

PUBLIC RECORD COLLECTIONS

Federal

Eighth Census of the United States of America, 1860, Greene County, Alabama;

214 / Bibliography

Orange County, North Carolina; Tunica County, Mississippi. Archives, Division of Archives and History, Raleigh.
Ninth Census of the United States of America, 1870, Orange County, North Carolina; Wake County, North Carolina. Archives, Division of Archives and History, Raleigh.
Revolutionary War Records, Military Pensions, National Archives, Washington, D.C.
Seventh Census of the United States of America, 1850, Baltimore County, Maryland; Orange County, North Carolina. Archives, Division of Archives and History, Raleigh.
Slave Narratives. Federal Writers' Project, microfiche, Duke University Library, Durham.
Tenth Census of the United States of America, 1880, Orange County, North Carolina. Archives, Division of Archives and History, Raleigh.
United States Post Office Department, "Records of Appointments of Postmasters." Archives, Division of Archives and History, Raleigh.

State

Land Grant Records. Secretary of State's Office, Raleigh.

County

Durham County, North Carolina, Deeds. County Courthouse, Durham.
Granville County, North Carolina, Deeds. Microfilm in Archives, Division of Archives and History, Raleigh.
Northampton County, North Carolina, Wills. Microfilm in Archives, Division of Archives and History, Raleigh.
Orange County, North Carolina, Cohabitation Certificates; Estates Records; Marriage Bonds; Minutes of the Court of Pleas and Quarter Sessions; Miscellaneous Records; Superior Court Minutes; Tax Lists; Wills. Archives, Division of Archives and History, Raleigh.
Orange County, North Carolina, Deeds; Marriage Register 1873-1880, 1880-1910; Marriages, Bonds; Wills. County Courthouse, Hillsborough.
Person County, North Carolina, Deeds. Archives, Division of Archives and History, Raleigh.
Richmond County, Virginia; Wills. County Courthouse, Warsaw.
Wake County, North Carolina, Deeds; Estates Records. Archives, Division of Archives and History, Raleigh.

Newspapers

Durham *Morning Herald*.
Hillsborough *Recorder*.
Raleigh *News and Observer*.

Printed Sources

African Repository and Colonial Journal. 168 vols. Washington, D.C.: American Colonization Society.
Arator. 3 vols. Raleigh, April 1855–August 1857.
Ashe, Samuel P., Louis R. Wilson, and Charles L. Van Noppen. *Biographical History of North Carolina.* 8 vols. Greensboro, 1905–1917.
Battle, Kemp P. *History of the University of North Carolina from Its Beginning to the Death of President Swain,* 2 vols. Raleigh, 1907, 1912.
Bell, Landon C. *Cumberland Parish: Lunenburg, Virginia, 1746–1816.* Richmond, 1930.
Blackwelder, Ruth. *The Age of Orange: Political and Intellectual Leadership in North Carolina, 1752–1861.* Charlotte, 1961.
Blanchard, Elizabeth Amis Cameron and Manly Wade Wellman. *The Life and Times of Sir Archie: The Story of America's Greatest Thoroughbred.* Chapel Hill, 1958.
Blassingame, John W., ed. *Slave Testimony: Two Centuries of Letters, Interviews, and Autobiographies.* Baton Rouge, 1977.
Branson, Eli. *Branson's North Carolina Business Directory for 1884.* Fayetteville, 1884.
Carrington, Wirt Johnson. *A History of Halifax County.* Richmond, 1924.
Cathey, Cornelius O. *Agricultural Developments in North Carolina, 1783–1860.* Chapel Hill, 1956.
Clark, Walter, ed. *The State Records of North Carolina.* 16 vols. Winston and Goldsboro, 1895–1906.
Connor, R. D. W., Louis R. Wilson, and Hugh T. Lefler. *A Documentary History of the University of North Carolina.* 2 vols. Chapel Hill, 1953.
Crittenden, Charles C. *The Commerce of North Carolina 1763–1789.* New Haven, 1936.
Cyclopedia of Eminent and Representative Men of the Carolinas. 2 vols. Madison, Wis., 1892.
Davenport, John S. "Early Settlers in the North Carolina Piedmont, 1749–1763," *North Carolina Genealogical Society Journal* 4, no. 2 (1978): 74–86.
Fogel, R. W. and Stanley L. Engerman. *Time on the Cross: The Economics of American Negro Slavery.* Boston, 1974.
Gutman, Herbert G. *The Black Family in Slavery and Freedom, 1750–1925.* New York, 1976.
Hamilton, J. G. de Roulhac, ed. *The Papers of Thomas Ruffin.* 4 vols. Raleigh, 1918–1920.
Higginbotham, Don, ed. *The Papers of James Iredell.* 4 vols. Raleigh, 1976.
Hoyt, William Henry, ed. *The Papers of Archibald D. Murphey.* 2 vols. Raleigh, 1914.
Johnson, Guion G. *Ante-Bellum North Carolina: A Social History.* Chapel Hill, 1937.
Journals of the Proceedings of the Annual Convention of the Protestant Episcopal Church in the State of North Carolina. Selected vols.
Journals of the Senate and House of Commons of the General Assembly of the State of North Carolina. Selected vols.
King, George H. S., ed. *The Register of North Farnham Parish 1663–1814 and Lun-*

enburg Parish 1783–1800, Richmond County, Virginia. Fredericksburg, 1966.
Kirby, Robert M. *Soil Survey of Durham County, North Carolina.* Washington, D.C., 1976.
Knorr, Catherine L., comp. *Marriage Bonds and Ministers' Returns of Charlotte County, Virginia, 1764–1815.* 1951.
Lefler, Hugh T. and Albert R. Newsome. *North Carolina: The History of a Southern State.* Chapel Hill, 1954.
Lefler, Hugh T. and Paul Wager. *Orange County 1752–1952.* Chapel Hill, 1953.
Lossing, Benson J. *A Pictorial Field-Book of the Revolution.* 2 vols. New York, 1850, 1859.
Main, Jackson Turner. *The Social Structure of Revolutionary America.* Princeton, 1965.
Meade, Bishop. *Old Churches, Ministers and Families of Virginia.* 2 vols. Philadelphia, 1857.
Merrens, Harry R. *Colonial North Carolina in the Eighteenth Century: A Study in Historical Geography.* Chapel Hill, 1964.
Rouse, Alice R. R. *The Reads and Their Relatives.* Cincinnati, 1930.
Ruffin, Edmund, ed. *The Farmer's Register.* 11 vols. Shellbanks and Petersburg, 1833–1843.
Sanders, Charles Richard. *The Cameron Plantation in Central North Carolina (1776–1973) and Its Founder Richard Bennehan.* 1974.
Saunders, William L., ed. *The Colonial Records of North Carolina.* 10 vols. Raleigh, 1886–1890.
Scarborough, William K., ed. *The Diary of Edmund Ruffin.* 2 vols. Baton Rouge, 1972.
―――. *The Overseer: Plantation Management in the Old South.* Baton Rouge, 1966.
Scott, James G. and Edward A. Wyatt IV. *Petersburg's Story: A History.* Petersburg, 1960.
Shanks, Henry Thomas, ed. *The Papers of Willie Person Mangum.* 5 vols. Raleigh, 1950–1956.
Turrentine, George R. *The Turrentine Family.* 1954.
Wheeler, John H. *Reminiscences and Memoirs of North Carolina and Eminent North Carolinians.* 1844. Reprint. Baltimore, 1966.
Wilson, William F. and P. Albert Carpenter III. *Region J. Geology: A Guide for North Carolina Mineral Resources Development and Land Use Planning.* Raleigh, 1975.

Index

Adams, John (cabinet maker), 19
Adshusheer Indians, 2
African Repository, 104
Alabama plantation, 70, 97, 108, 127, appendixes A, F
Alamance County, N.C., 89, 97
Alves (slave surname), 101
Alves, Amelia Johnston, 9, 18, 21, 52, 188 n.1
Alves, Walter, 18, 20, 36
American Colonization Society, 102, 104
Amis, Amey (slave surname), 101
Amis, John, 72
Amis, Mary. *See* Bennehan, Mary Amis
Amis, Thomas, Jr., 14, 22, 94, 101
Amis, Thomas, Sr., 5, 25, 94
Amis, Thomas Gale, 14, 15
Amis, William, 12-13, 72
Amis family, 72
Amy (slave), 60, 102
Anderson, Daniel, 18, 21, 29, 38, 192 n.49
Anderson, George, 19, 23, 97, 192 n.49
Anderson, George, and Company, 23
Anderson, Mary Cameron, 20, 22, 85, 122; and Duncan Cameron, 25, 38-39; and Lochiel, 29
Anderson, Robert Walker (Wm. Ed. Anderson's son), 122, 209 n.48
Anderson, Walker (Mary Cameron Anderson's son), 192 n.48, 193 n.21
Anderson, William Edward, 41, 42
Ann (slave), 60
Arator, 67
Armistead, Col. William, 97
Ashe, Thomas S., 192 n.48

Badger, George E., 98
Bahama, N.C., 194 n.42

Ball, James (mason), 89
Baltimore, Md., 74, 104
Bankhead National Highway, 138
Bank of the State of North Carolina, 39
Barnum's Hotel, N.Y., 142
Battle, Kemp P., x
Battle family, 128
Bauer, Dr. Louis, 45
Bell (slave surname), 101
Bell, Anna (slave), 104
Ben (slave), 60
Ben (slave shoemaker), 109
Bennehan, Dominick, 3
Bennehan, Dominick, II, 14
Bennehan, Dudly (Dudley), 3, 25
Bennehan, Fereby (Phebe) (slave), 103-4
Bennehan, Margaret (Peggy) (slave), 103-4
Bennehan, Rachel, 3
Bennehan, Mary Amis: death of, 12, 16, 29; described, 7; letters of, xvi; marriage, 5; mentioned, xiv, 26, 30; slaves of, 5, 94, 103
Bennehan, Rebecca. *See* Cameron, Rebecca Bennehan
Bennehan, Richard: and agriculture, 65, 69, 70; and Duncan Cameron, 21-22, 23-24, 27; and slaves, xvi-xvii, 94, 102, 103, 106, appendix B; and Raleigh, 14; and small pox, 105; and the American Revolution, 4-5; and the university, 13-14; apprenticeship, 3-4; as businessman, 4, 9, 23, 24, 85; birthdate of, 187 n.1; described, 197 n.76; family of, 2-3; friends of, 14, 21; gifts of, 13, 27; land purchases of, 5, 9, 13, 23, 24, 35, 80, appendix A; limitations of birthplace for, 188 n.8; marriage of, 5; mentioned, vii, ix, 1, 2, 12, 61,

72–73; overseers of, 5, 78, 80; status of, 5–7, 12
Bennehan, Thomas D.: and Duncan Cameron, 15, 25; and nephews, 15, 43–44, 55; and slaves, xvi–xvii, 101–3; and Stagville Plantation, 15–16, 74, 75, 77, 80, 85; bachelorhood of, 14–15, 132; birthdate of, 11, 189n.13; career of, 15–16, 77; death of, 55; gifts of, 16, 52, 80, 103, 202n.28, 206n.66; mentioned, xiv, 25, 27, 60, 61, 73, 105, 112; partnerships of, 13, 85; quoted, 15, 36, 50; schooling, 13
Bennehan, Virgil (slave), 16, 96, 103–4, 206n.81
Bennehan, William (Rich. Bennehan's nephew), 13
Bennehan, William ("Toast") (slave), 103–4
Bennehan-Cameron plantation complex, ix, x, 36
Bennehan house, 10, 11, 12, 16
Bennehan mill, 13, 69, 87–89, 90, 91–92, 99
Bennehan Square, 14, 57, 133
Bennehans and Cameron, firm of, 24, 25, 35, 36
Bennett Place, Durham, 142
Bentonville, battle of, 120
Bingham School, Oaks, N.C., 120
Black, W. F. (overseer), 139
Blacknall family, x
Blakely, ? (tanner), 100
Blandford, Va., 17
Blandford Church, Petersburg, Va., 143
Bob (slave), 60
Bobbitt, Arthur (overseer), 60, 78–79, 82, 97
Bobbitt, Lucy, 79
Bobbitt, Mrs. ? Woods, 79
Bobbitt's plantation, 68, 70, appendix F
Boge, Jim (slave), 59
Boggan, Patrick, 9
Boggan, William, 9
Bogue Railroad, 209n.36
Bonney, Mary L., 62
Boone, Daniel, x
Borum and McClean, firm of, 75
Borglum, Gutzon, 142

Boyce's Mill, 91
Brandon (slave surname), 101
Brick House Plantation: deeded to Duncan Cameron, 94, 195n.8; furnishings of, 5–6, 12; livestock and tools at, 72, appendix F; mentioned, 68; purchase of, 5; renovated, 30
Briggs, John J. (cabinet maker), 30
Bristol Parish, Va., 17
Brooklyn [N.Y.] Orthopedic Institute, 45
Brooks, Andrew (carpenter), 19
Brown, A. G., 61
Brown, Miss ? (governess), 61–62
Browne, William Garl, 55
Bryant, Mary McClean (governess), 40, 61
Buck Shoals, Eno River, 88
Bullock field, Brick house Plantation, 68
Burke, Mary (Polly), 42
Burke, Gov. Thomas, x, 7, 78
Burnside: and Cameron Park, 116; building of, 49; life at, 115; mentioned, 62, 112, 113, 122; repurchased and enlarged, 60–61, 127, 128; sold, 50
Busey, N. H., 142
Butler, Samuel (carpenter), 30

Cain, James, 78
Cain (slave surname), 101
Cain, William, 10, 20, 49, 90, 193n.13
Cain family, 2, 29, 35
Cain place (quarry), 33
Cameron, Anne Owen, 35, 45, 47
Cameron, Anne Owen Nash, 17, 32
Cameron, Anne Ruffin. See Collins, Anne R. Cameron
Cameron, Anne Ruffin: and Duncan Cameron, 49, 54; and gardening, 52–53; and her children, 51, 52, 110–11, 122, 131; and Paul Cameron, 49–52, 115–16, 131–32, 155n.1; and slaves, 99, 108, 112–13, 117; mentioned, 33, 43, 47, 56, 86, 116
Cameron, Bennehan: and former slaves, 112, 114; and horses, 58, 73,

Index / 219

74, 139–40; and Paul Cameron, 58, 91–92, 107, 120, 127–28, 132–36; and Salem Chapel, 194n.42; at Fairntosh, 139–40, 141, 142; at Stagville, 134–40; career of, 137–43; character of, xiii, xiv, 141–43; children of, 142; education of, 120, 121; mentioned, vii, 53, 62, 115, 130; overseers of, 80, 81, 83
Cameron, Bennehan, Papers, vii
Cameron, Col. Donald W., 143
Cameron, Duncan: and daughters, xvi, 45, 61, 105; and Fairntosh, 27–47, 52, 54, 55, 109, 194n.42; and Hillsborough, 23, 51; and Paul Cameron, xi, 41–42, 44, 49–59, 82–83, 86; and politics, 20–21, 25, 37, 191n.35; and slaves, xvii, 47, 57, 94, 102–9, 112, appendix B, 205n.22; and son Thomas, 42–43; as brother, 37–38, 39; as planter, 23, 24, 35, 65, 70–78, 88, 90, 97, 195n.8; banker, 37–40, 47; birth of, 17; career of, xi, 18, 20–21, 192n.48; characterized, xi, xiii, 23, 25; charity of, 128, 206n.66; death of, 58–59; duel of, 22; education of, 18; illness of, 46–47; marriage of, 14–15, 21, 22; mentioned, vii
Cameron, Duncan, II, 55, 59
Cameron, Duncan, III: and former slaves, 113; at Fairntosh, 69, 71, 75, 80, 81, 83, 134; birth of, 55, career of, 130–31; death of, 131; described by father, 56, 123, 131; education of, 120–21; illness of, 60; marriage of, 121; mentioned, 53, 62, 116, 189n.13, 209n.32
Cameron, Sir Ewen, of Lochiel, 17
Cameron, Francis, 140
Cameron, George (slave wagoner), 112–13, 114
Cameron, Jean, 15, 29, 31, 40
Cameron, Jean Syme (Duncan Cameron's daughter), 35, 45
Cameron, Jean Syme (Paul Cameron's daughter), 59, 110
Cameron, Rev. John: and Duncan Cameron, 18, 20–21, 25; birthplace of, 29; career of, 17–18, 39; death of, 30; mentioned, xi, 99, 143, 191n.11

Cameron, John A., 23, 37, 41, 54, 192n.48, 193n.21
Cameron, Margaret Bain. See Mordecai, Margaret Cameron
Cameron, Margaret M. See Peebles, Margaret Cameron
Cameron, Mary Amis, 33, 56, 60, 111
Cameron, Mary Anne, 25, 32, 40, 45, 61
Cameron, Mary B. Short, 121, 130
Cameron, Mary Warren, 130
Cameron, Mildred Coles (Duncan Cameron's daughter): and governess, 40; and slaves, 95, 99, 108, 111; birth of, 35; estate of, 133; gift to Salem Chapel of, 32; illness of, 45; mentioned, 18, 40, 62, 70, 120
Cameron, Mildred Coles (Paul Cameron's daughter), 52, 62, 130, 211n.36
Cameron, Paul C.: and Anne Ruffin Cameron, 49–52, 115–16, 131–32, 155n.1; and children, xi–xiii, 41, 51, 55–56, 59–62, 110–11, 120–21, 123, 126, 129–32, 134–38, 141; and Civil War, 115–18; and gardening, 52–53, 116, 128; and mills, 89–92; and music, 33, 54, 61, 86; and overseers, 78–81; and slaves and slavery, xvii–xviii, 93–114, 205n.22; and Thomas D. Bennehan, 15, 44, 52, 55, 103; and the university, 42, 125, 127; as planter, 27, 52, 59–60, 62, 65–76, 97, 115, appendix E; as son, xi–xii, 33–34, 44, 47, 49–50, 52, 58, 59, 136; at Fairntosh, 50–63; birth of, 26; characterized, xi–xiii, 58, 122–23, 125–26, 133–34; construction work of, 31, 32, 49, 57–58, 61, 128; death of, 132; education of, 41–42, 44; in the legislature, 62–63; name of, 191n.11; wealth of, 36, 119, 128, 133, 134, 142
Cameron, Pauline, II, 130
Cameron, Pauline C. See Shepard, Pauline Cameron
Cameron, Rebecca (daughter of Duncan Cameron III), 130
Cameron, Rebecca Bennehan: and children, 41, 47, 52, 109; and Fairntosh, 28, 29, 30, 47, 52; and husband, 25, 38; and slaves, 94, 100,

101, 106, 109; birth of, 11, 189n.13; characterized, xvi, 22, 196–97n.76; death of, 45, 109; marriage of, 14, 22; mentioned, vii, 87; suitors of, 14
Cameron, Rebecca Bennehan, Jr. (Duncan Cameron's daughter), 32, 35, 45
Cameron, Rebecca Bennehan, III (Paul Cameron's daughter). *See* Graham, Rebecca Cameron
Cameron, Sally Mayo, 141
Cameron, Thomas A. D: and slaves, 95, 108; birth of, 25; education of, 41–43; inheritance of, 90; mentioned, 70, 79, 120, 133; shooting of, 43–44
Cameron, Dr. Thomas Nash, 41, 107, 207n.94
Cameron, William, 23, 25, 32, 37, 197n.76
Cameron, Winney (slave), 113
Cameron-Collins children, 209n.38
Cameron family, 17, 45, 50, 95, 99, 189n.13
Cameron Family Papers, vii
Cameron-Graham children, 210n.52
Cameron Mills, Person County, 35–36, 81
Cameron Park, Hillsborough, 116
Cameron's New Mill, 69, 88–92, 99
Campbell, Catlett, 102
Cane Creek, 89
Caldwell, Joseph, x, 12
Carr, Gov. Elias, 140
Carr, Gen. Julian S., 143
Carrington, Mildred Coles, 18
Carrington, Paul, Jr., 18
Carrington, Paul, Sr., 18
Carrington family, 2
Carrol, Alexander (distiller), 86
Carry, James (slave), 205n.22
Catawba Indians, 1
Caulk, Leavin (wagon maker), 74
Chapel Hill, N.C., ix, 13, 32, 42, 127
Charles (slave), 70
Chatham Railroad, 129
Chavis, Martin, 211n.36
Cherokee Indians, 1
Choctaw (horse), 139
Christina (slave nurse), 111
Cincinnati, Society of the, 142
Civil War, xiii, 93, 115–23

Clarendon Coal Field Company, 128
Clark, J. M. (miller), 90
Cocke, ? (silversmith), 6
Coles, Mildred, 18
Collier, William (brickmaker), 28, 30
Collins, Anne R. Cameron, 53, 62, 114, 130; described, 56, 122; in Hillsborough, 122, 128; in Mississippi, 120, 121; marriage of, 110, 121
Collins, Anne R. (George Collins's daughter), 135
Collins, George P., 90, 92, 110, 121–22, 129, 139
Collins, Josiah, Jr., 110, 209n.38
Collins, Josiah, III, 121, 209n.38
Collins, Laban (mason), 89
Connor, R. D. W., 115
Cook, Col. ?, 31
Cotheran, James, 78
Cothran, Margaret (midwife), 106
Cothran, William, 106
Courtis, James (painter), 30
Coxe (slave cooper), 99
Craig, Annie (servant), 211n.36
Creedmoor, N.C., 138
Cross Roads Church, Alamance County, 97
Cumberland Parish, Lunenburg County, Va., 18
Cyrus (slave miller), 90, 99

Dandridge (slave artisan), 99
Daniel (slave miller), 90, 99
Davie, Gen. William R., x, 7, 13, 14, 21
Davis, Annie (servant), 112
Delaware City, Del., 73
Demps[ey] (slave), 53
Dicey (Umstead slave), 102
Dickenson, Esther (slave), 100
Dickenson, Jim (slave), 100
Dickerson branch railroad line, 137
Dillaye, Harriet A., 62
Di Martino, Capt. Antonio (music master), 33, 61
Dixon, Caleb (millwright), 89
Dixon, Solomon (millwright), 75
Dockary, John (miller), 90
Dollar, William G. (millwright), 89

Index / 221

Dortch, Young (carpenter), 19, 86
Duffy, William, 22
Duke family, x, 2
Dunn, Thomas and Robert, firm of, 54
Dunnagan (slave surname), 101
Durham, N.C., 122, 137, 138
Durham County, N.C., ix
Durham, W. P., 81, 139
Durham and Northern Railroad, 137
Durham Triassic Basin, 1, 27, 87

Easter (slave), 60
Eastman National Business College, Poughkeepsie, N.Y., 120
Edenton, N.C., 128, 129
Edmund (slave), 98
Edwards, Doc (slave), 74, 100, 109, 113, 114
Ellerbee Creek, 80, 88
Ellis, D. J. (millwright), 91
Emiline (Umstead slave), 102
Eno Indians, 2
Eno Plantation, 60, 92, 108; livestock and tools at, appendix F
Eno Quarter, 108
Eno River, ix, 1, 60–61, 68, 81; mills on, 87–92
Epperson, Francis (mason), 88
Esther (slave), 103

Faddis's tavern, Hillsborough, 19
Fairntosh Plantation: agriculture, 53, 65–76, 200n.42; cemetery, 32–33, 85, 211n.36; construction and renovation of, 27–47, 56, 139, 193n.8; furnishings of, 54–55; livestock and tools at, 74, 75, appendix F; location of, ix; mentioned, vii, 62, 86; overseers of, 77, 81–83; railroad station at, 92; slaves at, 105, 108, 116–17; under Bennehan Cameron, 121, 133–43; under Duncan Cameron, 27–47; under Duncan Cameron III, 134; under Paul Cameron, 50–76
Farmers' National Congress, 138
Farmers' Register, 66, 71
Fayetteville, N.C., 37, 41, 69, 100
Ferintosh, Ross-shire, Scotland, 29
Ferrell, Hezekiah (overseer), 5, 78
Few's mill, 81–82

First National Bank, Durham, N.C., 137
Fish Dam Ford, 23
Fish Dam Plantation, 13, 24, 68, 79, 85, 86
Fish Dam Sam (slave), 101
Fish Dam Store, 13, 23, 24, 192n.52
Flat River, 1, 69, 88, 100
Flat River area, ix–x
Flat River Plantation, 78
Fort, Elias (carpenter), 29, 86, 193n.26
Fort, Frederick, 193n.26
Fort, John (carpenter), 28, 29, 30, 31, 86, 88, 193n.26
Fort, William K. (carpenter), 28, 193nn.8, 26
Fowle, Gov. Daniel, 134
Fred (Anderson slave), 85

Gilchrist, N. E., 71
Gilpins Mills, 38
Glascock, William, Jr., 3
Gooch, John (carpenter), 30
Goodloe, David S. (carpenter), 193n.8
Goodwin, Frances, 14, 15
Gorman, Henry (plasterer), 28, 30
Grace (Amis slave), 101
Gracie, Archibald, 192n.49
Gracie, Anderson and Company, 192n.49
Graham, Anne (Rebecca Cameron Graham's daughter), 212n.33
Graham, Anne Shepard, 130
Graham, John W., 122
Graham, Rebecca Cameron: marriages of, 122, 209n.48, 210n.52; mentioned, 56, 62, 119, 121
Graham, William A. (son of Rebecca Cameron Graham), 130
Graham, Gov. William A., 122
Granville, John Carteret, Earl, 2
Granville County, N.C., ix, 35
Granville District, 2
Graves, R. H., 127
Great Falls Manufacturing Company, 128
Green, J. R., 90
Green, John (blacksmith), 13, 85, 189n.26
Green, Major, 90, 91

Green, Bp. William M., x, 32, 46, 59, 110
Greene County, Ala., 97
Guilford County, N.C., 18, 23, 74
Guilford Courthouse, battle of, 18
Guilford Courthouse Battleground, 142

Hale County, Ala., 97
Halifax, N.C., xiv, 73
Hamilton, D. H., 127
Hammond, Leroy, 3
Hannah, Aunt (slave), 101
Hardscrabble (Cain plantation), 29, 193 n.13
Hargis, Lawrence, 35, 36
Harrall, Costen J., 194 n.42
Harriet (Umstead slave), 102
Harris, Ellenor, 79, 202–3 n.50
Harris, Melinda, 79, 202–3 n.50
Harris, Nathaniel, 79
Harris, Col. Robert, 79
Harris, Tyree, 5
Harris, Williams (overseer), 79
Harris family, 2, 35, 82
Harris Hill cemetery, 91, 107, appendix D
Harris plantation, 71
Harry (Amis slave), 101
Hart (slave surname), 101
Hart, Cy[rus] (slave), 117, 132
Hart, Thomas, 7, 14
Haskins (slave surname), 101
Haskins, Norwood (cabinet maker), 19
Haw River, 49
Hawkins, John D., 46
Haywood, William H., Jr., 42, 192 n.48
Heartt, the Misses, 119
Henderson, N.C., 69, 112
Henderson, Richard, x
Henry (slave weaver), 60
Hermitage, the (Murphey and Ruffin plantation), 49, 197 n.1
Hicks's mill, 87
Hill, H. G., 120
Hillsborough, N.C: and Duncan Cameron, 18–20, 23; and Paul Cameron, xiv, 49, 51, 60–61, 62, 115–32; and the Collinses, 122; and slaves, 106; description of, ix, 1, 19, 49, 51; mentioned, 12, 58, 62, 73, 83, 87
Hillsborough Academy, 42
Hillsborough Military and Polytechnic Academy, 120, 127
Hillsborough Savings Institution, 63
Hogg, Gavin, 192 n.48
Holmes, John (wagon maker), 74
Holt, Gov. Thomas M., 134, 140
Hooper, William, 7
Hopkins family, 2
Horner, James Hunter, 126, 127
Horner, Thomas, 81
Horner, William, 81
Horner Classical Academy, Oxford, 120
Horton, William (carpenter), 9, 19
Horton Grove: barn, 57–58; slave houses, 30, 57, 86, 107–8
Hughes Academy, Cedar Grove, 120

Indian Trading Path, Old, 1, 3, 9
Indians, 1, 2
Iredell, James, x, 7, 14

Jarvis, Gov. Thomas J., 140
Jeffries, Serena Turner (servant), 113, 114, 139, 208 n.136, 211 n.36
Jem (slave), 53
Jenny (slave), 98
Jerry (slave wagonner), 100
Jim (slave), 19, 29, 94, 97
Jim (slave cooper), 99
Jim (slave distiller), 87
Jim's Place (Jim Ray's), 111, appendix F
Jinney (slave), 60
Johnson, Frank (roving musician), 86
Johnston, Amelia. *See* Alves, Amelia Johnston
Johnston, Gen. Joseph E., 142
Johnston, Gov. Samuel, xiv, 7, 14
Johnston, William, x, 1, 2, 4; death of, 9; mill of, 87, 89
Jones, Cadwallader, Jr., 50
Jones, Jasper (slave), 118
Jordan (Jurdon), Abner (slave), 112
Jordan (Jurdon), Dicey (slave), 112
Jordan (Jurdon), Ellen (slave, 112
Jordon (Jurdon), Ovid (slave blacksmith), 112
Justis (slave surname), 101

Index / 223

Kay, Richard, 14
Kennon, Charles, 87
Kenyon, Malbon (teacher), 42
Kevan, Andrew, and Brother, firm of, 74
Kinchey, Ezekiel, 5
Kingsbury, Miss ? (governess), 61
Kingsbury, Theodore, 61
Kirkland, William, 18, 49
Knap of Reeds Creek, 88

Labouisse, Sally Cameron, 194n.42
Lamb, William (overseer), 98
Latta (slave surname), 101
Laws (slave surname), 101
Laws, George, 97
Laws, Leonard, 79
Leathers, Fielding, 80
Leathers, James, 16, 80, 88, 89, 202n.28
Leathers, Moses, 80
Leathers, William, 80
Leathers, William, Jr. (overseer), 80
Ledge of Rocks Creek, 88
Lee, Gen. Fitzhugh, 140
Len (Alabama slave), 98
Lewellin, Charles (overseer), 98
Lewis (slave artisan), 99, 100, 102
Lewis Toe (slave shoemaker), 109
Liberia, 102, 103, 104
Liberia Packet, 104
Lindley, Joshua, 53
Little River, ix, 1; mill on, 87, 89, 91
Little River cemetery, 91, 101, 107, appendix D
Little River Plantation, 52, 68, 103
Little River store, ix, 1, 4, 9, 94
Lochiel, 29, 193n.21
Lochiel, Scotland, 17
Lochiel, Laird of, 143
Lockhart and Thompson, firm of, 28
Lossing, Benson J., 63, 126
Lougee, William (tinsmith), 33, 56
Low, Daniel (Alabama slave), 98
Luke (slave), 34, 60, 101
Lynchburg and Durham Railroad, 137

McCay, James (artisan), 19
McCulloh, Henry, 2, 9

McCulloh family, 7
McDuffie, D. G. (surveyor), 9, 36, 133
McGwire, Dr. Hunter, 129, 131
McMannen, John A., 75
McNair house, 122, 128
McPheeters, Rev. William, 42
McSweaney and Hennessey, firm of, 31
Malone, Isham (miller), 89, 90
Mangum, Sen. Willie P., x, 41, 82, 98, 192n.48
Mangum family, x, 2
Mangum Street Methodist Church (Calvary Methodist Church), Durham, 194n.42
Martin, James, 4, 5
Martin, John, 27
Martinsville, N.C., 18, 23
Mary (Amis slave), 103
Mason (slave), 60
Matthew (slave miller), 90, 99
Mayo, Col. Peter, 141
Mayo, Sally Taliaferro, 141
Meaks (slave surname), 101
Means, James, 88
Mecklenburg County, Va., 17
Memorial Hall, University of North Carolina, 127, 210n.15
Meredith, ? (blacksmith), 86
Micklejohn, Rev. George, 22
Mima (servant), 112
Minerva (slave nurse), 110
Mississippi plantation, 70, 71, 98, 108, 120, 121
Mitchell, Dr. Lueco, 46–47, 132
Moore's Creek Bridge, battle of, 5
Mordecai, George W., 46, 95, 120
Mordecai, Jacob, 40
Mordecai, Margaret Cameron: birth of, 29; gifts of, 32, 129; mentioned, 40, 59, 120, 130, 131, 136; property of, 57, 95, 128, 133; responsibilities of, 43, 45–46, 90
Mordecai Family Papers, vii
Morehead Banking Company, 37
Moore, Robert, 58
Moriah (slave nurse), 111
Morson, Hugh, Jr., 127
Mount Bethel United Methodist Church, Bahama, 194n.42
Munro, James, 27
Murphey, Archibald D., x, 37, 49, 58,

66, 192 n.48
Murray, Eli, 74, 97

Nancy (slave), 60
Nash, Gov. Abner, 17, 18
Nash, Anne Owen, 17, 32
Nash, Gen. Francis, 7, 17, 18, 142
Nash, Frederick, 20, 25
Nash, Mary Read, 17
Nash, Col. Thomas, 17
Nash and Kollock School, Hillsborough, 119, 120
Nat (Alabama slave), 98
Ned (slave), 60, 101
Nelly (slave), 60
Nelson (slave), 60
Neuse River, ix, x, 35, 91
Nichols, Joe (slave carpenter), 113, 114
Nichols, William (overseer), 82, 97
Norfolk, Va., 69, 102
Northampton County, N.C., 5, 12, 94, 101, 129
North Carolina Manumission Society, xvii
North Carolina Railroad, 58, 62, 67, 129, 130
North Carolina State Agriculture Society, 138
North Carolina State Fair, 68
Norvel (slave wagoner), 100
Norwich University, Northfield, Vt., 42
Norwood, John W., 118
Nottaway Parish, Va., 18
Nutt, Elkanan (cabinet maker), 29

Occaneechee Indians, 2
Orange County, N.C.: Bennehan and Cameron plantations in, 35, 52, 88; gift to poor of, 206 n.66; landowners in, ix; mentioned, viii, 74, 100, 116; overseers' wages in, 77–78, 80, 83, 98; settlers in, 1, 2
Orange County Agricultural Society, 67
Orange County Board of Agriculture, 66–67
Orange County Society for the Promotion of Agriculture, the Mechanic Arts, and Manufactures, 67

Orange Guards, 140
Overby, William, 56
Oxford, N.C., 61, 100, 112, 120, 138
Oxford and Clarksville Railroad, 137
Oxford Female Seminary, 83

Palmer, Martin (carpenter), 9–11, 193 n.13
Palmer, William (cabinet maker), 19
Panther Creek, 87
Parks (slave surname), 101
Parrish family, x
Parsons Nursery, Flushing, N.Y., 116
Partridge, Capt. Alden, 42–43
Partridge's Academy, Norwich, Vt., 42, 44
Patterson, Rev. George, 110
Peaks (slave surname), 101
Peaks (Peeks) plantation, 79.
Peebles, Anne, 129, 210–11 n.26
Peebles, Margaret Cameron: illness of, 129, 130, 131; marriage of, 129, 210 n.26; mentioned, 56, 62, 110
Peebles, Robert Bruce, 129, 210 n.26
Pee Dee Manufacturing Company, 128
Peeksville Plantation, 87
Peggy (slave), 102
Penny Bend, Eno River, 195 n.6
Person County, N.C., ix, 35, 52, 81, 99
Person County plantations, 86, 195 n.1; and mills, 69, 81, 88, 90, 99; farm equipment on, 74, appendix F; overseers on, 78, 95, 111; slaves on, 95, 97, 106
Petersburg, Va.: as market, 1, 3–4, 12, 69; goods ordered from, 54, 88, 97, 109; mentioned, 73, 100, 105, 112, 119
Petersburg Academy, 17
Petersilia, Karl (music master), 61
Phil (slave), 103
Philadelphia, Pa., 38, 74, 98, 104, 111; medical treatment in, 45, 46, 62
Phillips, Mary, 14
Pictorial Field-Book of the Revolution, The, 63, 126
Pike, John (music master), 54
Piper, Annie Turrentine, 79
Piper, Ellenor Harris, 79, 202–203 n.50

Piper, John, 81
Piper, Joseph G. (overseer), 79, 118
Piper, Melinda Harris, 79, 202–203 n.50
Piper, Samuel (overseer): as overseer, 82, 83, 116; daughters of, 61, 83; house of, 33; letters of, 203 n.59; marriage of, 79, 202–3 n.50; mentioned, 53, 57, 86, 118
Piper, William (overseer), 79, 82, 202–3 nn.50, 54
Piper family, 81, 120
Pompey (slave wagoner), 100
Prince (slave), 60
Pulaski (steamship), 37

Quebec-Miami International Highway, 138

Ragsdale, Nimrod (mason), 89
Raleigh, N.C.: and Bennehan Square, 14, 57; and Camerons, xiv, xv; mentioned, ix, 50, 52, 102, 122; runaway slaves from, 98
Raleigh Academy, 42
Raleigh and Augusta Air Line Railroad, 137
Raleigh and Gaston Railroad, 112, 129
Randolph, V. M., 196–97 n.76
Ravenscroft, Bp. John, x, 32
Ray (slave surname), 101
Ray, Jim (slave overseer), 111
Ray, Leonard (blacksmith), 86
Read, Col. Clement, 17
Red Mill, 87
Red Sulphur Springs, Va., 32, 45
Rex, John, 102
Reynolds, Mr. ? (Delaware farmer), 73
Rice, Charlotte (Lotty), 16, 103, 190 n.58
Rice, Thomas, 16
Richards, William L., 61
Richmond, Va., 105, 129, 141
Richmond County, Va., 2–3
Robbin (slave shoemaker), 109
Rochester, Nathaniel, 7, 14
Rocky Mount Mills, 128
Rogers, John, 42
Rosshire (Ross-shire), Scotland, 29, 39
Roulhac, W. S., 121
Rowland & Brothers, firm of, 69

Rudd, Rev. John C., 42, 43
Ruffin, Edmund, 66
Ruffin, Thomas: and gardening, 53–54, 116; and P. C. Cameron, xii, 49, 57, 58, 60, 66, 71; and slave attack, 99; bank president, 38; estimate of D. Cameron of, 59; mentioned, x, xi, 40, 111
Ruffin, William K., 81, 121
Ruffin, Thomas, Papers, vii

Saint Mary's School, Raleigh, 61, 120, 126, 128
Saint Matthews Church, Hillsborough, 32, 143, 194 n.42
Saint Philips Church, Durham, 152 n.42
Salem Chapel, xvi, 128, 189 n.13, 194 n.42; and slaves, 109–110; building of, 31–32; consecrated, 32, 194 n.43
Sarah (Fairntosh slave), 60
Savage, John G., 54
Scottish Society of America, 143
Scrub (slave), 4, 94
Sears, Ben (slave tanner and mechanic), 75, 100
Sears, John (slave), 111
Seawall, J., 88
Seay, Robert, 13
Sharp, Elizabeth, 19
Shepard, Anne, 130
Shepard, Mildred Coles Cameron, 52, 62, 130, 211 n.36
Shepard, Pauline C. Cameron, 32, 62, 72, 128–30, 211 n.29
Shepard, William B., 72, 129, 130, 211 n.29
Shepard's Point Land Company, 63
Sherman, Gen. William T., 142
Shocco Indians, 2
Shop Hill, 30, 86, 107, 108
Shore, Dr. John, 105
Short, Col. Henry B., 121, 209 n.36
Short, Mary B., 121, 130
Sibley Manufacturing Company, 128
Siller (slave), 98
Sinclair, Robert, firm of, 74
Sioux Indians, 2
Sir Archie (race horse), 12, 72, 73
Slaves, 93–114, appendix B; after

226 / Index

emancipation, xviii, 103–104, 111–14, 127; and emancipation, 101–4; and illness, xv, 47, 55, 59–60, 104– 7; and P. C. Cameron, 100, 111– 13, 132; cemeteries of, 91, 107, appendix D; clothing of, 109; housing of, 107–8; letters of, xvi, 104, 111; mentioned, 58, 70; numbers of, 7, 27, 63, 93–95; skilled, 87, 90, 99–100; surnames of, 100–101
Smedes, Rev. Aldert, 61, 128
Smith, James (overseer), 80–81, 135, 139
Snow, Samuel, 37
Snow Hill Plantation: and Wm. Johnston, ix, x, 1, 2; inherited by Thos. Cameron, 90; livestock and tools at, appendix F; mentioned, 9, 18, 53, 68, 70, 118; purchased by Bennehans and Cameron, 36; saw mill at, 68–69
Solomon (slave cooper), 99, 106
Somerset Place (Collins plantation), 209 n.38
Sons of the American Revolution, 142
Southerland, Fendal (overseer), 16, 79, 80
Southerland, Lucy Bobbitt, 79
Southerland, Orpah, 79
Southerland, Philip (overseer), 79, 86, 98, 116, 118, 134
Southerland, Samuel, 88–89
Southerland, W. A., 86
Southern Cotton Growers Protective Association, 138
Southern National Highway, 138
South Lowell, N.C., 75
Spanish-American War, 140
Spencer, Abraham (plasterer), 31
Spencer, Cornelia Phillips, 127
Sowell (slave surname), 101
Squire (slave), 97
Stabler, Edward, 4
Stagg, Judith, 9
Stagg, Thomas, 9
Stagville Plantation: and agriculture, 68–71; and Bennehans, 9–16; and Paul C. Cameron, 16, 52, 103; and slaves, 102, 105, 113, 114; barn at, 57–58; blacksmith shop, 85–86; building of, 10–11; cemetery, 81, 136, appendix D., 211 n.36; described, 63, 126; location of, ix, 36; mentioned, vii, 31, 73, 117; overseers at, 77–84, appendix C; Red Mill at, 92; renters of, 81; under Bennehan Cameron, 133–40
Stagville Post Office, 10, 43
Stagville store, xviii, 13, 23, 43, 51; building of, 9, 10; decline of, 51, 101; reestablished, 130
Staley, Abraham (millwright), 88
Staley, Conrad (millwright), 88, 89
Staples, Jack (slave), 54
State Bank of North Carolina, 38
State Dairyman's Association, 138
Stephens, M. C., 38
Stith, Henry, 198 n.15
Stone Mountain Monument, Georgia, 142
Stott, Ebenezer, 105
Stott, Mrs. Ebenezer, 21–22
Stott, Watson and Ebenezer, firm of, 12
Strayhorn, William, 9
Streton (slave shoemaker), 109
Stronach, William (stonemason), 33, 194 n.60
Strudwick, Dr. Edmund, x
Strudwick, Dr. William, 132
Struthers, John, and Son, firm of, 32
Swain, Gov. David L., x
Sykes, ? (overseer), 28
Syme, Rev. Andrew, 40
Syme, Jean Cameron, 15, 29, 31, 40

Tate, Mark A., 13
Tatum, Absalom, 102
Taylor, Alexander, 11
Terry, Joseph (millwright), 88
Tharpe, William, 13
Thompson, Virgil (servant), 211 n.36
Tilley's mill, 90
Tom (slave), 60
Transylvania Company, x
Triassic Basin, Durham, 1, 27, 87
Turner, Gov. James, 18
Turner, Josiah, Jr., 63
Turner, Sally (servant), 211 n.36
Turner, William (servant), 208 n.36
Turrentine, Alexander, 81
Turrentine, Annie, 79
Turrentine, Orpah Southerland, 79

Turrentine, Samuel (pioneer), 81
Turrentine, Samuel, 28, 79, 81
Turrentine, William D. (overseer), 79, 81, 83, 130, 139, 194 n.42

Umstead, Ben (slave), 101, 102, 103
Umstead, Dr. John, 96, 102-3
Umstead, Mary (slave), 102, 103
Umstead, Gov. William B., x
Umstead family, 2
University of Aberdeen, Scotland, 39
University of North Carolina, Chapel Hill, ix, 23, 27; and P. C. Cameron, 42, 63, 113, 125, 127; and Thos. D. Bennehan, 15; Bennehan gifts to, 13; practical courses at, 68; preparatory school of, 11, 13

Vance, Gov. Zebulon B., 140
Van Pelt, ? (wagon maker), 74
Veasey (slave surname), 101
Vestal, William F., 57, 86, 91
Vick, John T., 121
Virginia Military Institute, Lexington, 120, 140

Wake County, N.C., ix, 35, 91, 119
Walker (slave surname), 101
Walker (slave shoemaker), 109
Walker, Agnes (slave), 98, 99
Walker, Bryant (slave), 98, 99
Walker, Mary (slave), 96, 98, 99
Walker, Francis (Frank) (slave), 98-99
Walker, Nathaniel (overseer), 95
Walker, Robert, 192 n.49
War of 1812, 36, 37
Warren mansion (Edenton), 128

Washington College (now Trinity), Hartford, Conn., 44
Watson (slave surname), 101
Watson, Bennett (carpenter), 19
Watson, Lotan G. (teacher), 42
Webb, Anne R. Peebles, 129, 210-11 n.26
Webb, Dr. James: as doctor, 46, 60, 97, 106; mentioned, x, 19, 22, 102, 132
Webb, James, Jr., 121
Webb, Thomas N., 210-11 n.26
Wheeler, Gen. Joseph, 112, 117
Wilbourne, Temperance, 14
Wilderness, Battle of the, 122
Wilfong, Elizabeth, 19
Wilkins, John (blacksmith), 13, 85
William (slave), 102
William and Mary, College of, Williamsburg, Va., 39
Williams, Andrew (blacksmith), 13, 32, 85
Williams, Samuel (slave), 114
Williams, Victoria (slave), 114
Willie (slave), 60
Wilson's School, Dr. Alexander, Melville, 120
Witherspoon, Rev. John, 42
Woodbridge, John, 3
Woods, Hugh (overseer), 78, 79
Woods, Joseph, 98, 109, 118
Woods, Mrs., 79
Woods, Wilson (miller), 75, 90
Woodville Plantation (Fairntosh), 28, 36

Yarbrough (slave surname), 101
Yarbrough, Samuel, 13, 80
Yellow Daniel (slave), 101

www.ingramcontent.com/pod-product-compliance
Lightning Source LLC
Chambersburg PA
CBHW022110150426
43195CB00008B/347